ISLANDERS DEPORTED

ROGER E HARRIS

PART 2

The development and censorship of the Internment Camp Mail Services associated with British subjects deported from the Channel Islands during the German Occupation of 1940–1945.

C.I.S.S. PUBLISHING
63 Ravensbourne Gardens, Clayhall, Ilford, Essex

Copyright 1983 Roger E. Harris
First published by Channel Islands Specialists Society 1983
ISBN 0 946806 03 9

All rights reserved.
No part of this publication may be reproduced, stored
in a retrieval system, or transmitted, in any form or by any means, electronic,
mechanical, photocopying, recording or otherwise, without the prior
permission of the copyright owners.

Produced by Prima Graphics, Camberley, Surrey

Preface–Part 1

While on a visit to Guernsey ten years ago, I was taken to meet an old lady who had some World War II Occupation ephemera and postal history that she wanted to sell. Amongst the hoard were some unusual prisoner of war letters from Germany and a document that the old lady had 'repaired' with miles of sellotape the night before I visited her. After several hours of careful restoration work, I found that what I had in my hands was a deportation order from 1942 and a collection of Channel Islands internees' letters from Germany, not prisoner of war letters as I had first believed.

I tried to find out the history of the letters and the deportation order but the handbooks published by the Channel Islands Specialists' Society at the time only devoted three lines to internee mail, while in the Channel Islands there were as many different stories of the deportations as there were internees. Few authentic books were to be found on the subject except for Frank Stroobant's *One Man's War*; most of the others merely repeated unfounded myths and legends in even more fanciful ways.

Shortly after, I had to go abroad for three years, but during that time I was able to develop my collection of internee letters and start a more serious study of their contents and the markings on them. When I returned to England, the Channel Islands Specialists' Society asked me to write a book about my postal history study and so *Islanders Deported Part II* was born. As the postal history got more and more complex I began to realise that a proper history of the subject was also called for to give the background, and so *Islanders Deported Part I* also came into being. Hence *Part II* actually preceded *Part I*.

Initially the research for *Part I* was very slow, already many of the internees had died of old age and I began to wonder if I would be able to complete the work. Then thirty years after the war the official secret documents from the war years became available for study and suddenly I found that I had a wealth of research material that was going to take me years to sort out. Later visits to the Islands filled in some of the missing parts and gradually the true history of the deportations appeared through the legends.

I am glad that I have been able to complete the story while there are still people living who can remember it and who lived through it. I am aware that some people, especially some internees, will not be happy with some of the 'truths' told in the following pages, but I hope that the majority of people will be interested by the story and that some will be encouraged to continue the study more seriously. For the Channel Islands specialist, there is a very fascinating collection of postal history to be developed, every day brings forth more exciting finds. For the non-specialist, there is an interesting aspect of World

War II history to learn about, these Channel Islanders were the largest group of British people to be interned in Europe by Hitler. From whatever standpoint you the reader have come to this book, I hope you will enjoy it; it has given me many years of enjoyable self-indulgent research.

                                              Roger E Harris
                                              Carpenders Park
                                              Hertfordshire

                                              April 1980

Preface–Part II

At long last and with much relief and pleasure, I am able to write that *Islanders Deported Part II* is finished and I hope complete. Although this part of the combined volumes of *Islanders Deported* was started before *Part I*, it has met with several set backs over the years which, coupled with the continued discovery of new items, have delayed the publication of the finished work until this date.

Islanders Deported Part I was well received by a wide spectrum of interested persons and I must apologise to them, and especially to the numerous well-wishers who wrote to me, for the considerable delay in the publication of this *Part II*. I understand the disappointment and frustration felt by some people, but I hope the long wait will prove worthwhile and will be compensated in some measure by the completeness of the finished work.

I hope the two volumes will stimulate more interest and research in the topic of Internee mail, and that this new *Part II* will aid the collector and researcher in understanding the importance of material that they may see or be fortunate to own. Although I have tried to make the book as complete as possible, new material still comes to light and so *Islanders Deported Part II* should be regarded more as a guide to the various items to be found rather than a record of every item that can exist. I hope that in this role at least it achieves its goal and that the reader will find it a useful addition to his reference library.

> Roger E Harris
> Gibbs Couch
> Carpenders Park
> Hertfordshire
>
> October 1983

Contents

Preface PART I iii
Preface PART II v

SECTION I
The Development of the Mail Service for
   the Channel Islands Internees 3
Mail to the Internment Camps from the United Kingdom
Mail to the Internment Camps from the Channel Islands
Mail returned to the camps 23
Mail from within Europe to the Internment Camps 35
Inter-Camp Mail 36
Mail through the Red Cross 38
Official Mail from the International Red Cross
   and the Y.M.C.A. 39
Mail from parts of the British Empire 41
Undelivered Channel Islands Mail addressed to a
   deportee 43
Map: Mail Routes for Channel Islands Internees 45
APPENDIX I. Origin of the Internee Mail Service 47
APPENDIX II. The Internee Parcel Post Services 51

SECTION II
The 'Universal' Stationery used in the Internment Camps 60
The 'Universal' Interniertenpost Postcard 61
The 'Universal' Interniertenpost Lettersheet 62
'Exceptional' Stationery used in the Internment Camps 62
Map: Location of German Internment Camps 63
Dorsten Transit Camp Mail 64
Biberach Internment Camp Mail 67
Wurzach Internment Camp Mail 87
Laufen Internment Camp Mail 97
Kreuzburg Internment Camp Mail 131
Liebenau Internment Camp Mail 135
Compiègne and St. Denis Frontstalag Camps Mail 137
Tittmoning Camp 145
Other Camps 147

SECTION III
Censorship, Postal Markings, The Red Cross and Miscellaneous
   Documents and Ephemera associated with the Internees
German Censorship..151
Map: Location of German Censor Offices 153
Channel Islands Censor Cachet....................................165
The 'Mysterious' Four Digit Cachet...............................168
German Prisoner of War Camps (and Civilian
   Internee Camps)..171
Italian Prisoner of War Camps 184
British Censorship 185
British Post Office Markings 195
French Post Office Markings.......................................201
Swiss Postmarks, Cachets and Censor Labels.......................202
Cachets and Postmarks from the Rest of the World 205
Unidentified Cachets 206
The Red Cross 207
Miscellaneous Objects, Documents and Ephemera 213
Sources 223
Selected Bibliography 227
Acknowledgements 229

SECTION IV
Catalogue of all items in SECTION I, SECTION II
   and SECTION III 235

Section I

The development of the Mail Service for the Channel Islands Internees.

Mail to the Internment Camps from the United Kingdom.

Mail to the Internment Camps from the Channel Islands.

Mail from within Europe to the Internment Camps.

Inter-Camp Mail.

Mail through the Red Cross.

Official Mail from the International Red Cross and the Y.M.C.A.

Mail returned to the camps.

Mail from parts of the British Empire.

Undelivered Channel Islands Mail addressed to a deportee.

MAP: Mail Routes for Channel Islands Internees.

APPENDIX I. Origin of the Internee Mail Service.

APPENDIX II. The Internee Parcel Post Services.

The Development of the Mail Service for the Channel Islands Internees

Today there is considerably more mail in existence for a researcher to study that has come from the Internment Camps to the United Kingdom or the Channel Islands than has gone from these places to the Internment Camps. This chapter deals with the development in general of the Internee-Post as it applied to the Channel Island Internees and more specifically with mail to the Internment Camps. Mail from the Internment Camps, which is reasonably prolific, is dealt with in greater detail elsewhere in the chapters on the individual Internment Camps.

It is easy to understand why mail received at the Internee Camps is very difficult to find today, especially if one considers that an Internee keeping such correspondence would have to pack and take it to England with him when he was repatriated and then keep it with him, often for several months, until he returned to the Islands. It is therefore almost incredible that after the tribulations of a further thirty-plus years, there is such mail still in existence. Most of the mail found today tends to come from only a few correspondences and the researcher owes a debt of gratitude to those families, such as the Trevorrow family, who not only saved all their letters but had the foresight to write on each the date when it was written and the date when it was received at the camp.

Mail to the Internment Camps originated from two main sources:

(a) The United Kingdom
(b) The Channel Islands

Other sources of mail are known, but items recorded from these are obviously even more scarce:

(c) Mail from Europe – primarily Germany, and usually from an Internee on an outside work party or in a hospital.
(d) Inter-camp Mail from another Internee camp or Prisoner of War Camp.
(e) Mail through the Red Cross – usually messages from the U.K.
(f) Official Mail from the International Red Cross in Geneva, or Y.M.C.A. – usually to the British Camp Commandant.
(g) Mail returned to the camp following the disruptions to communications caused by D day and the Allied advance into Europe.
(h) Mail from parts of the British Empire – from friends or relatives in Canada, Australia etc.

Mails to the Internment Camps from the United Kingdom and mails from the Channel Islands followed entirely different routes and were handled in completely different ways. Long before the deportations of September 1942, a Prisoner of War mail service between England and Germany was in existence (see Appendix I 'Origin of the Internee Mail Service'), while mail to and from the Channel Islands to Prisoners of War was sent through the German Feldpost. In the 'Guernsey Evening Press' of Wednesday February 25, 1942 there appears a half column which instructs readers not to endorse mail 'Via Red Cross'. It is entitled:

'MAIL FROM PRISONERS OF WAR – HOW MESSAGES MAY BE SPEEDED' and states:

'All relatives of Prisoners of War in Germany and other European countries occupied by the German Forces may have a chance of receiving the mail from their Prisoner of War very much quicker than heretofore if in their next letters to their Prisoner of War they ask him (and provided he will exactly comply with this request) to add on the address:

>   Guernsey (or Sark as the case may be),
>   Kanalinsel,
>   Besetztes Gebiet,
>   Durch Deutsche Feldpost ueber
>   Frankreich

and *not* to mark his letters 'Via Red Cross.'

All letter envelopes to and from Prisoners of War must be marked on top in German 'Kriegsgefangenensendung' which also helps to speed up the delivery of Mail to and from Prisoners of War.

SPECIMEN ENVELOPES

To Prisoner of War:

```
          Kriegsgefangenensendung

          Pte. John Du Marchi
          Kriegsgefangenen-Nr. 1234
               Stalag XX1D
               Deutschland.
```

From Prisoner of War:

> **Kriegsgefangenensendung**
> Mrs. John Du Marchi,
> "Le Repose", Vale,
> Guernsey, Kanalinsel,
> Besetztes Gebiet.
> Durch Deutsche Feldpost ueber Frankreich

Please cut this out for future reference'.

Prior to this directive many letters from the Prisoner of War Camps had been delayed by being mis-routed by the International Red Cross via England. These letters would be endorsed with the 'NO SERVICE/RETURN TO SENDER' boxed cachet and would then have to return to Geneva from where hopefully they eventually reached their correct destinations in the Islands.

By the time the deportations of the Channel Island Internees first took place in September 1942 the routes for the transmission of mail were already firmly established. Mail from the United Kingdom was first censored by the British and then handed over to the Protecting Power. It followed a similar route to that of Red Cross Messages, via Lisbon, Portugal, Switzerland, Munich or Frankfurt and thence to the camps in Germany where it was censored again. Mail from the Channel Islands was handled by the German Feldpost and either went by sea and then overland through France to Germany or sometimes straight by air into Germany. It was not censored in the Islands and only received censorship at the camp. Mail from the Prisoner of War Camps to the United Kingdom or to the Channel Islands would first be censored at the Camps and then follow the same routes as mail to the camps, but of course in reverse. Some of this mail would acquire additional censoring at various German Transit Censor Offices (see Chapter 'German Censorship'); mail to the United Kingdom might be dealt with at Berlin, Munich or Frankfurt while mail to the Channel Islands often received the additional censoring at Cologne, or Paris. Mail arriving in the United Kingdom would again be processed by the British Censor, but mail for the Channel Islands would be delivered without any further delay.

Some Internees were first taken to a Reception Camp in North Germany – Dorsten – Stalag VIF, and for a while nothing was heard of them. On 3 October the Germans issued an announcement in the Islands that they hoped to be able to make a definite statement shortly about the question of communications with the persons recently deported, meanwhile at Dorsten the

Internees were being issued with cards to send to their relatives. When these cards started to arrive in the Islands on 9 November and in England on 6 November, the Internees had already been moved on to Laufen, Biberach and Wurzach Camps because at a meeting on 23 October 1942 the Oberkommando der Wehrmacht had decided that Dorsten was unsuitable for women and children. Relatives and friends receiving the cards from Dorsten, and ignorant of the Internees' move to Southern Germany, began to enquire how they should reply to them. In Guernsey 'The Star' of Thursday 19 November, 1942 printed the following statement:

'HOW TO REPLY.

Many islanders who have received post-cards from relatives and friends in the Channel Islands Internment Camp in Germany have inquired how to reply.
They should write their letters in the ordinary way and address the envelope exactly according to the particulars given in the bottom left-hand corner of the postcard they received. The envelope should be sealed and the sender's own name and address written on the back.
It should then be handed in at the German Field Post Office in Stanley Road. Needless to add, letters should be confined to matters of family and personal nature, and nothing of any military significance should be referred to. Instructions will be issued later regarding parcels'.

The following evening the 'Evening Press' printed:

'HOW TO REPLY TO EVACUEE'S CARDS.

With regard to communication with evacuees now in Germany the Guernsey sender must know the complete address of the recipient's camp. Only when this is known can the letters be addressed and handed in at the Field Post Office, Stanley Road'.

In a news broadcast in England on 19 November 1942 the B.B.C. stated that 800 cards had been received in the United Kingdom from the Internees, and the Channel Islands Monthly Review for December 1942 published extracts from some of these cards, all of which originated from Stalag VIF. The Channel Islands Monthly Review stated:

'Friends may write to:
   Larger-Bezeichnung Stalag VIF. Germany'

(i.e. Dorsten) and it went on to say that the International Red Cross was issuing food parcels and that other parcels could not yet be sent: 'Instructions for next of kin parcels will be issued'.

It is almost certain that no mail reached the Internees while they were at Dorsten as after six or seven weeks they had already moved on before their first postcards had reached their destinations. Of the mail left in existence today I have only been able to record one cover addressed to Dorsten and it is from the Channel Islands, it bears no cachets of Dorsten camp and was redirected to Wurzach where it did receive a single circle cachet of the Officer Prisoner of War Camp at Wurzach-Oflag 55 VD. This cachet is the only one recorded on Internee mail and is described below.

The letter addressed to Dorsten and redirected to Wurzach and Biberach.

The Internees to whom the letter is addressed were actually interned close by Wurzach at Biberach and as the letter carries no directions or manuscript markings, it seems likely that all the Channel Island Internee mail addressed to Dorsten was either intercepted at some point or collected at Dorsten and forwarded en-masse to Biberach and Wurzach. This may account for the 'BRITANNIQUE' cachet which the cover also bears and which is not recorded on any other Internee mail, but is known on some Prisoner of War mail from the Channel Islands.

main are pathetic to read, for all appeal for food and warm clothing; the trunks that were supposed to have been sent have not yet been received'.

but on 22 January 1943 he writes more happily:

'Large numbers of Red Cross letters arrive; those from deportees are much more cheerful'.

It is interesting to note that he refers to the letters from the Internees as 'Red Cross letters'; this is a mistake as the Red Cross did not handle letters until well after D Day in 1944. The mistake probably arose with the mail from the camps arriving in the Islands along with a batch of Red Cross messages from England, both being transported by the German Feldpost from France.

In Guernsey at about the same time, the 'Evening Press' of Wednesday 20 January 1943 published two columns entitled 'Evacuees Write to Guernsey'. This was on the whole a cheerful account and reproduced several letters received in the Islands during the previous few days, including two from Mr. Garfield Garland who had been elected Camp President at Dorsten and again Camp Leader at Biberach. One of Mr. Garfield Garland's letters was addressed to the Bailiff of Guernsey, sending him wishes from all the Guernsey people at the camp, thanking the Islanders for their magnificent 'send-off' when deported and then mentioning the good physical state of the Internees.

By the end of January the transmission of mail from the Islands to the Camps seems to have settled down and in Guernsey 'The Star' of Saturday 30 January 1943 printed:

'POSTAL RULES FOR C.I. CAMP

New regulations, announced by the Bailiff on Thursday, for the transmission of letters, parcels and money to the C.I. Camps in Germany are now in operation.

Points particularly to be noted are:—

Letters may be posted in any pillar box in the island, as also may they be for prisoners of war.

Parcels for individuals must be taken to the General Post Office, where delcaration forms have to be filled in, and pre-payment made. Attention is directed to the list of articles which must not be sent, including perishable foodstuffs.

Money may only be transferred through the States Supervisor, with whom contact should be made at the States Office, South Esplanade.'

It will be noted from the above that the mail no longer had to be handed in at the German Feldpost but could 'be posted in any pillar box in the island.'

In both the Islands of Jersey and Guernsey concern had been aroused about the physical conditions of the Internees in the Camps by some of their early letters. Each Island under the administration of the Bailiff set up its own system for organising relief parcels for the Camps. It is interesting to note that conditions for the Internees under the watchful eye of the International Red Cross and the Protecting Power improved so rapidly that by August 1943 the Internees were sending money back to the Islands and six months later they were sending their own relief parcels for the people left behind in the Islands.

In Jersey the parcels had been organised by the 'Jersey Internees Aid Committee' and on 23 January 1943 this organisation issued a public statement:

'... parcels up to 15 kilos may be sent at fixed postal rates, declaration forms to be obtained at the British Post Office .... they must be handed in at the German Field Post Office.'

Contemporary to this, I have in my collection an interesting card sent out by the Secretary of the St. John Ambulance Association to an official which reads:

```
                                    5th Feb. 1943.


            You are invited to attend an important
      Meeting of the St. John Ambulance
      Association Emergency Committee to be
      held at the Bailiff's Chambers on Tues.
      Feb.9th at 2:30pm.

            Business:-   Parcels for Internees.


                                  [signature]
                                    Hon. Sec.
```

St. John Ambulance Association Card.

The card is of further interest because it was posted in Jersey during a shortage of local 1d. stamps and so has received the single circle 2d. PAID handstamp for 5 FE 43, JERSEY, CHANNEL ISLANDS.

On 13 February 1943 the Internees Aid Committee modified their instructions for private parcels for internees, these now had 'to undergo inspection at a depot before being taken to the German Field Post Office', and on 6 March 1943 the German Authorities reduced the weight restrictions to 10 lbs. or 5 kilos.

In Guernsey there was an 'Island Fund' to finance the parcel scheme and 'The Star' of Saturday 30 January 1943, along with the 'Postal Rules for C.I. Camp' already quoted, printed the following:

'How New Island Fund will Operate
TO THOSE IN NEED

An organisation has been created for distributing money and commodities among needy internees. Donations for this purpose should be sent to the Bailiff, Royal Court House, or the National Provincial Bank, High Street.

Gifts in kind can be handed in at any post-office in town or country, suitably packed. No perishable foodstuffs will be accepted.'

In the United Kingdom strict regulations were already laid down concerning parcels for Prisoner of War camps and Internment Camps. (see Appendix II 'The Internee Parcel Post Service'). The Channel Island Evacuees in England along with other friends and relatives of the Internees were as concerned as their fellows in the Islands about the Internees' circumstances. The 'Channel Island Refugees Committee' published on 4 January 1943 in the 'Channel Islands Monthly Review' a report which contained the following details of the kinds of parcels which could be received by the Internees:

'Deported persons receive three kinds of parcels. The first, food parcels, are sent in bulk by the British Red Cross to the camps. This means that persons arriving in the camps get the parcels immediately. Nobody but the British Red Cross can send food parcels. The second class is that of parcels containing cigarettes, tobacco, books, certain periodicals, music, gramophone records, packs of cards and sports equipment, which can be sent by anybody, provided the articles are bought and despatched through a firm having a Government licence to export. Refugees can find out what local firms have this licence by asking at their local Citizens' Advice Bureau. The third kind of parcels is called 'next-of-kin' parcels. These are despatched four times a year, and are sent by the person or body who has been approved by the British Red Cross as 'parcels next-of-kin'. The parcels next-of-kin receive special coupons and special labels from the British Red Cross, without which the parcel cannot be sent. There are, of course, many cases in which those who have been or desire to be nominated as parcels next-of-kin cannot afford to send parcels, which cost on an average over £2.10s.0d. each. My

Committee are happy to say that through the support of the Canadian Red Cross and the British War Relief Society in the United States of America, they are able to undertake the sending of next-of-kin parcels for all refugee parcels next-of-kin who are unable to do so themselves. We have been trying to get in touch with all the parcels next-of-kin to find out whether they wish us to be registed in their stead, but should some not have heard from us we hope they will write to us and tell us their wishes.'

In the Channel Islands the various regulations about letters and parcels addressed to the Internment Camps were finally crystallised by Feldkommandantur 515 in a directive to the respective Island Authorities on 10 March 1943. 'The Evening Press' of Friday 12 March 1943 in Guernsey reproduced a letter from John Leale, the President of 'The Controlling Committee of the States of Guernsey' to the Editor of the paper stating these new and final regulations:

'INTERNEE POSTAL REGULATIONS'

(Letter to the Editor)

Sir – I have received the following letter from the Feldkommandantur 515: 'Re: Mail for the British subjects evacuated from the Channel Isles.'

I am giving you below an extract from the regulations concerning the sending of mail to prisoners of war and civilian internees, for your information:—

PERMITTTED

Ordinary letter mail up to 2 Kg; ordinary Post Cards; also, addressed to the Camp in Germany, Parcels up to 5 Kg., or, if contents cannot be divided, up to 10 Kg.

All the above mail will be carried free of charge.

No parcel cards or customs declarations are to be sent with parcels addressed from foreign countries to enemy prisoners of war and civilian internees in Germany.

NOT PERMITTED

'The sending of registered letters, remittances, postal orders, printed matters, business papers and samples, as well as parcels to be paid for on

13

delivery, as well as the claiming for receipt or receipt advice.'
I would be glad if you would give this matter publicity.

JOHN LEALE
President
The Controlling Committee
of the States of Guernsey.

Hirzel House,
  Guernsey
10th March 1943.

Letters to the Internment Camps from the Islands are therefore found without any postage stamps on but with the Channel Island address of the sender on the reverse. They do not usually bear any postal markings or transit markings and were not censored until they reached their final destination at the Internment Camp where they then received an inward censor cachet.

A typical example of mail from Guernsey to the Internment Camp of Biberach. The cover has been endorsed by the sender 'INTERNIERTENPOST', and has received a Biberach Censor cachet Type Bb.C.5. in blue black.

Some mail to the Internment Camp did carry local Channel Island stamps, but these had no function as the service was post-free and the stamps were not valid during the war years outside the Islands. This was obviously just a method of showing the Internees examples of their 'new' stamps issued in the Islands and also indicates how examples then eventually reached England before the end of the war.

A newspaper wrapper from Guernsey to the Internment Camp at Biberach. The Guernsey 1d. Arms stamp affixed to the wrapper was totally superfluous as although this was the local printed paper rate, all mail to the camps travelled post-free.

In March 1943 in the United Kingdom the 'War Organisation of the British Red Cross Society and Order of St. John of Jerusalem, Prisoners of War Department' at St. James's Palace in London S.W.1., issued a leaflet 'PW/73C/43', dealing with 'Letters to Civilian Internees by Prisoners of War Post'. As this leaflet was often sent in response to an inquiry about an Internee, it also gave the correct address for that particular Internee as well as detailing the three methods of sending a letter to the Internee:

1. Sealed letter sent by surface mail (post-free).
2. Sealed letter sent 'Air Mail' and charged 5d.
3. Special unsealed Air Letter-cards, price 3d.
   (Including an Air Mail fee of $2\frac{1}{2}$d.)

Reproduced below is the full information printed in leaflet PW/73C/43 for an Internee at Biberach Internment Camp.

WAR ORGANISATION
of the
BRITISH RED CROSS SOCIETY and ORDER OF ST. JOHN OF JERUSALEM
PRISONERS OF WAR DEPARTMENT

Telephone No:　　　　　　　　　　　　　　　　St. James's Palace.
ABBey 5841.　　　　　　　　　　　　　　　　　London S.W.1.
　　　　　　　　　　　　　　　　　　　　　　　March, 1943.

LETTERS TO CIVILIAN INTERNEES BY PRISONERS OF WAR POST

Letters should be clearly written; should deal with personal matters only, and should not exceed both sides of one sheet of notepaper.

The sender's name and address must be written on the back of the envelope; but if the writer is serving in His Majesty's Forces, the name and address of the Unit must not be given, but a private address should be substituted.

Letters should be posted in the ordinary way, and should not be sent to the Prisoners of War Department to be forwarded. They should be addressed as follows:

PRISONERS OF WAR POST
Kriegsgefangenenpost
Mrs. Irene C. Hayward.
British Civilian Internee No. **10013**.
Ilag Biberach Riss,
Germany.

No stamp is required if letters are sent by ordinary mail; but if they are sent by air-mail, they must have a 5d. stamp and be marked 'BY AIR MAIL'.

Special Air letter-cards for use in communication with British Prisoners of War and Interned Civilians in enemy-occupied territories are now obtainable at the principal Post Offices, at a cost of 3d. each

Enclosures:

Unmounted photographs or snapshots of a purely personal nature may be enclosed in letters to civilian internees, but no other pictures or printed matter of any kind. Any enclosure may cause the letter to be delayed for special examination. The name and address of the addressee and of the sender should be written on the back of photographs, etc.

No enclosures may be sent in Air Mail Letter Cards.

The information about 'Enclosures' was of particular interest and significance to the Channel Island Internees as it presented a method and opportunity of getting photographs of people in England through to the Islands via the Camps. This opportunity was not afforded by the normal Red Cross Messages sent between England and the Channel Islands and one can imagine the immense pleasure it gave to people in the Islands who were suddenly able to receive photographs of their children evacuated to the United Kingdom almost three years before in 1940 and whom they had since never seen. Photographs sent via the Camps between the Channel Islands and England are easily identified as they usually bear on the reverse a censor cachet of the Internment Camp via which they had been forwarded. Sadly this concession did not last as messages I have read from Biberach in November 1943 say 'no longer allowed to receive or send photographs' and again in April 1944 'Unable to forward photos, these get returned'. Also a Red Cross Message sent from Jersey to the United Kingdom on 4 March 1944 requesting that the recipient should forward some photographs of children via an Internee at Wurzach, received the displeasure of the British Censor who attached to the Red Cross Message, 'British Postal Censorship Label P.C.223' dealing with Prisoner of War Mail. The relevant part of the label states:

'1. Letters addressed to Prisoners of War or Internees may not contain letter or other enclosure intended for transmission to a third person, unless that person is also a Prisoner of War or Internee in a recognised Internment Camp.'

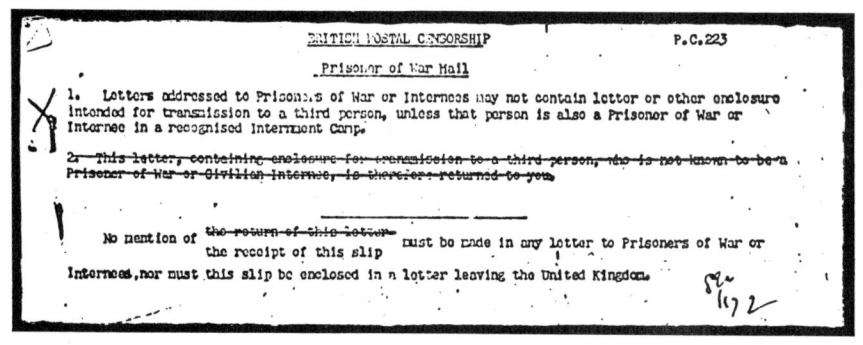

British Postal Censorship Label P.C.223.

I doubt if the concession was ever reinstated, I have not been able to find any later reference to it and the whole routing and transmission of Internee Mail was to be drastically curtailed after the D-Day landings.

Letters from the United Kingdom were censored by the British before leaving England and again by the Germans on arrival at the Internment Camp. Very

17

occasionally if a letter was censored in Germany at a transit office (see chapter on 'German Censorship') it would not again be censored at the Camp and so does not carry a Camp Censor cachet.

As stated in the leaflet PW/73C/43 there were three methods of sending a letter to the Internment Camp from the United Kingdom.

1. Sealed letter sent by surface mail (post-free)

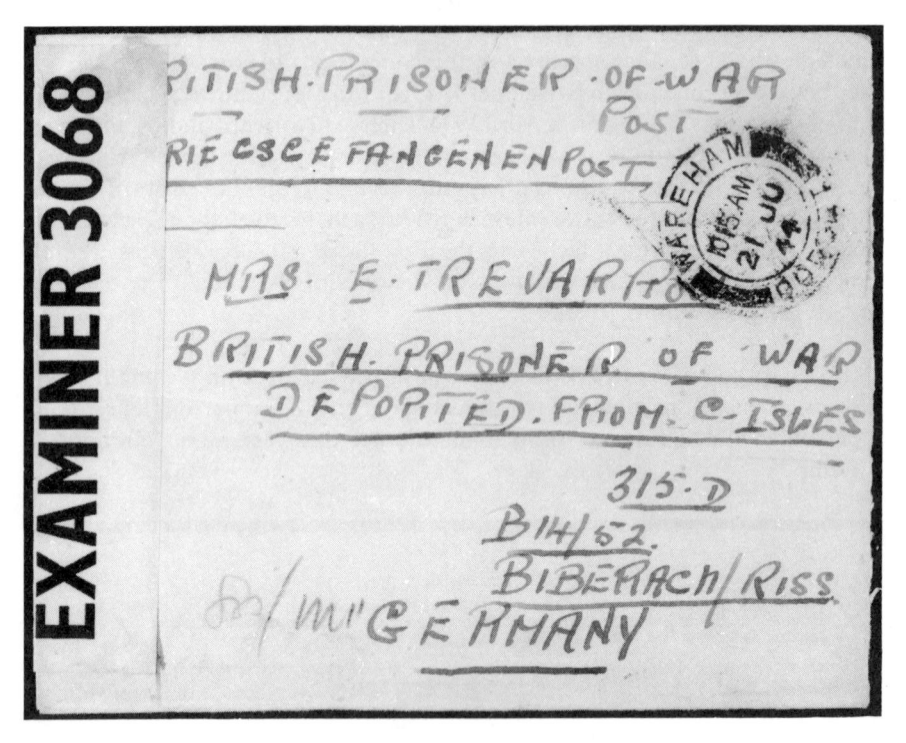

An ordinary unstamped envelope endorsed by the sender in manuscript 'British Prisoner of War Post-Kriegsgegangenenpost', has received a Wareham Dorset postmark of 21 JU.44 and has been opened and resealed by British Examiner 3068, tape P.C.90. Normally the letter would also receive an Internment Camp Censor cachet on arrival. This letter was written on 17 June 1944 and received at Biberach on 17 August 1944.

2. Sealed letter sent 'Air-Mail and charged 5d

Very few examples of this method of sending mail to the camps are recorded, probably because the Airmail routes were intended more for Sweden, Africa, and the Far East rather than into Europe where there were no direct flights until 1944. I have in my own collection two covers addressed to Laufen in 1943, but in both examples the stamps and the airmail stickers have been removed before the covers reached Germany.

An example of a letter sent to Laufen in 1943 by 'Air-Mail'. The stamp and airmail sticker have been removed after posting but before the cover has reached Laufen. The Laufen censor cachet Type Lf.C.1. number 4 has been struck where the postage stamp was once affixed.

The only example that I can record of a cover with the 5d. stamp remaining intact on it was sent to Biberach on 21 May 1944. It carries an air-mail label and British Censor Tape No. 7819 and must have travelled on one of the first direct flights into Europe following the D-Day advance in 1944.

19

2a. Sealed letter sent with a 2½d. Postage Stamp

This method is a hybrid of Methods 1 and 2 described above. I can record several examples where a 2½d. stamp (not 5d.) has been used on an ordinary letter to the Internment Camp and one would suppose that it was intended for the payment of Air-Mail postage to Europe. However, the letter has not been endorsed 'By Air-Mail' as demanded by the Red Cross leaflet PW/73C/43. Whatever the reason for using the 2½d. stamp on a 'post-free' service, nothing was gained by the sender as such letters took the same time to reach their destination as those sent by Method 1.

An ordinary envelope with a 2½d. George VI definitive cancelled with a 'CORFE CASTLE – WAREHAM' postmark of 6.15 p.m. 15 NOV. 43. The letter has been opened and resealed by British Examiner 8967 with a tape P.C.90 and has also received a Biberach Censor Cachet Type Bb.C.5. in blue-black. The letter was written on 12 November 1943 and received at Biberach on 8 January 1944.

3. Special unsealed Air Letter-cards

These Air Letter-cards became available in England for 'Prisoner of War Post' on 21 July 1941 and were included in the Internee Post scheme. The Air-letters were of a single sheet which folded three times and had an imprinted value of 2½d. (the European rate). The Airmail fee could only pay for Air-Mail to Lisbon from where the card went overland until the liberation of France in 1944 permitted flights to be made to Switzerland. However, there is no evidence to show that these letter-cards travelled any faster than unpaid letters as all the documented times of transit that I have seen are the same as for the ordinary unstamped letter. Because the letter was unsealed it tended to receive a British 'Crown over Passed' Censor cachet rather than an Examiner Tape P.C.90.

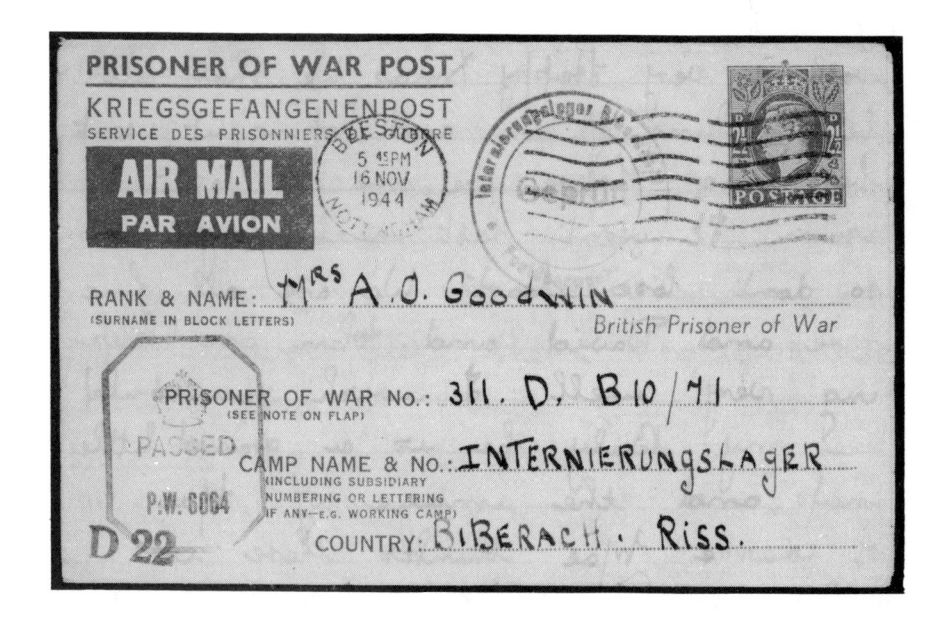

A 'Prisoner of War Post' Air Letter-card which has received a 'BEESTON NOTTINGHAM' machine cancel of 5.45 p.m. on 16 NOV. 1944 and has been censored with the British 'Crown over Passed' Censor cachet 'P.W.6064' in crimson. The Air Letter-card is addressed to Biberach and has received the Biberach Censor Cachets Types Bb.C.4. and Bb.C.6. struck in violet.

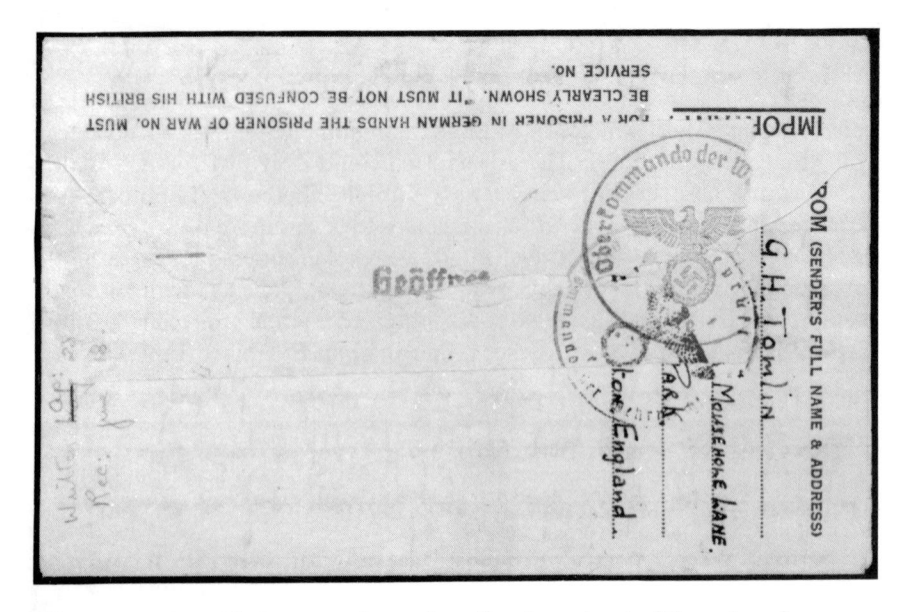

The reverse of an Air Letter-card sent from Southampton to Biberach and Censored in England with the British 'Crown over Passed' censor cachet P.W.3142 struck in crimson. This Air Letter-card was not censored on arrival at the camp because it has been censored at the Frankfurt transit censor office where it received an 'Oberkommando der Wehrmacht' Censor tape and Eagle and Swastika Censor Cachet of the 'Oberkommando der Wehrmacht' with the identifying letter 'e' of the Frankfurt office struck in scarlet. The letter was written on 28 April 1943 and arrived at the Camp on 18 June 1943.

The Mail Service to the Internment Camps settled down and became quite regular with letters from England taking on average about six weeks to reach their destination while letters from the Islands took as little as ten days to reach the Camps. Some Islanders in the Camps became quite complacent as they recorded receiving their Newspapers regularly from the Islands and complained of a delay in late 1943 of mail from England and the Islands. A greater delay was to follow six months later!

News of the Invasion of Europe on D-Day 6 June 1944 was met with great jubilation in the Channel Islands and the Internment Camps. If either could have forseen the ensuing eleven months their jubilation would probaly have been tempered. D-Day heralded for the people left in the Channel Islands a final year of even greater deprivation, and for the Camps a complete dislocation of the Mail services with, for some months, a severance of all news and contact with the Islands. As it was, some of the Camps had not heard from England for eight weeks prior to the Invasion of Europe although some mail did eventually arrive at the Camps ten days after D-Day.

22

A. J. Sherwill (Sir Ambrose Sherwill, K.B.E. M.C.) the then Camp Captain of Laufen Internment Camp, writing one day after D-Day, on 7 June 1944 to England said:

> 'Now that the invasion has started we here are presumably cut off from the Channel Islands till the invasion fails, which I do not anticipate for a moment, or until the C.I. are retaken by England, when correspondence destined for there will go via England. I hope the latter solution will occur and that quickly and without too much loss among the population.'

Later in the letter he went on to say:

> 'Will you try to arrange to send me as soon as possible, if you can get permission, a large Union Jack, say 12 ft. in length. I want to have it available...'.

He may have been more pessimistic if he had known that the Channel Islands would be by-passed and not retaken by England until almost a year later, and that the Camp would not need his Union Jack until 4 May 1945, almost the same date that the Islands were retaken. Incidentally, the Union Jack was never sent from England, but Padre Gerhold made one in the Camp from a linen sheet.

The Camps were indeed cut off from the Channel Islands. L. P. Sinel records in his diary on 13 June 1944:

> 'The German Post Office is accepting no more letters for delivery to deportees in German Internment Camps'.

And a message from Biberach Camp to England on the same date starts:

> 'As we cannot write to Guernsey now, have an extra P.C. to spare to write to you.'

In England the Channel Islands Monthly Review for August 1944 printed on its front page:

> 'Communication between the islands and Internment camps in Germany has been severed since D-Day and is unlikely to be restored.'

This act not only stopped the mails from being sent between the Islands and the Camps, but also caught some in transit through France where their progress was halted and a 'Return to Sender' Instructional mark applied. Few examples of this disruption to the service survive today especially as many were lost with the destruction of the German Feldpost system in France.

23

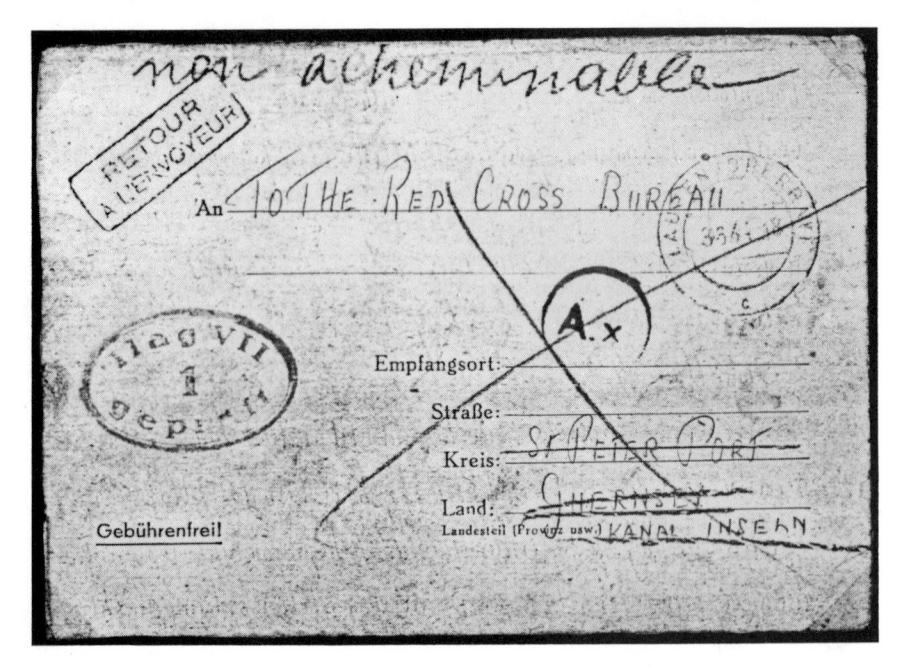

A letter which left Laufen three days before D-Day on 3 June 1944, addressed to Guernsey managed to reach Paris where it received a Crimson A.x. in circle, transit censor cachet (Type Ps.C.1. Durchlaufstempel of Paris, used only between March and August 1944 – see chapter on 'German Censorship'). It was undelivered because of no service and received a French boxed 'RETOUR A L'ENVOYEUR' instructional mark.

Some other Internees also had Sherwill's idea that 'correspondence destined for there (the Channel Islands) will go via England', and so instead of following the old instructions to use the German name for the Channel Islands 'KANAL INSELN' they reverted to calling them 'Channel Islands' in the address and also endorsed them 'via England'. Such letters did indeed go to England but they were never delivered in the Islands until after the war as throughout the war there was never a service to the Islands via England.

The German Feldpost did still manage to get a very limited amount of mail through to the Islands from the Camps as L. P. Sinel records on 5 July 1944 in his diary:

> 'German hospital ship arrived yesterday with mail for troops and from Islanders at Biberach, Laufen and Wurzach.'

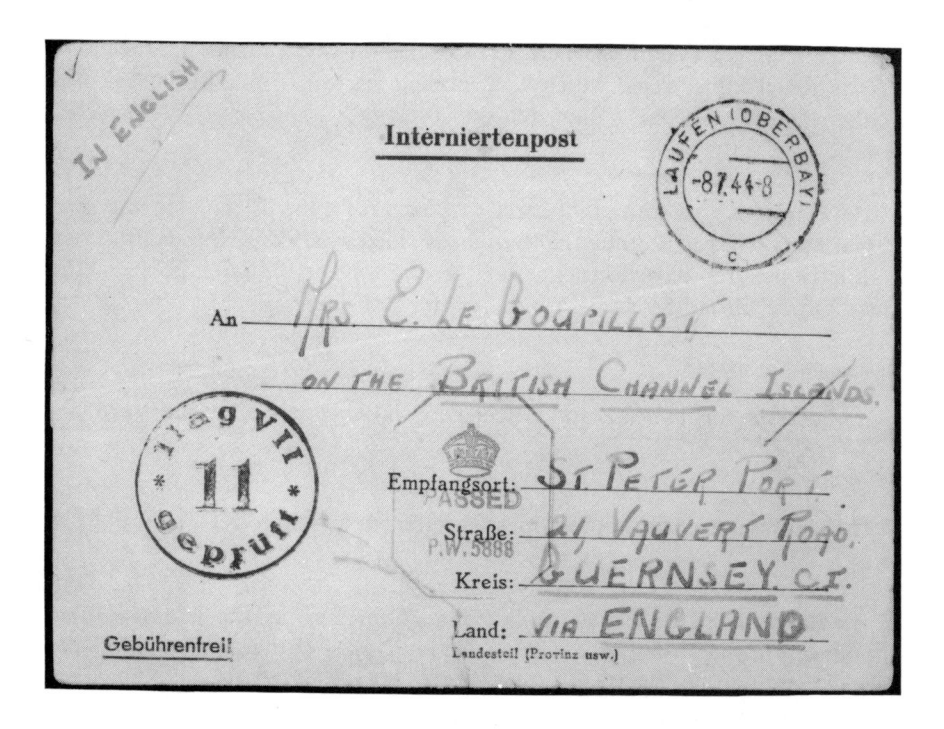

A very patriotic letter from Laufen dated 8 July 1944 which has received a Laufen Censor Cachet, number 11, Type Lf.C.2. The writer has endorsed the letter 'In English', 'on the **BRITISH CHANNEL ISLANDS**' and '**GUERNSEY C.I. VIA ENGLAND**'. It has received a British 'Crown over Passed' Censor Cachet P.W.5888 on arrival in England, but that is as far as it would have travelled until after the war. This letter is a little sad as the writer – Henry J. Le Goupillot was one of the ten men from the Channel Islands who died and were buried at Laufen.

As the Allied advance through Europe slowed down and the Islands remained cut off, the International Red Cross stepped in and took over from the German Feldpost the transmission of the Internees mail between the Islands and the Camps. (They also did it between the Camps and England). On a postcard from Wurzach to Jersey on 19 November 1944, the writer says, 'At last I am able to write a few lines to Jersey . . . do hope you will be able to reply,' and a day later a letter from Laufen says 'After long interval, I am once more enabled to write to you, this time by the kindness of the Red Cross . . . No news from England or the Islands'. It is interesting to note that many of the letters at this time from all the Camps were endorsed in the top left hand corner with the word 'English' by their authors.

In the Islands a system was being established for transporting Internee Mail on the Relief Ship 'Vega' which was soon to set sail from Lisbon. Selected extracts from L. P. Sinel's diary tell the story:

'8 December 1944

The Germans give notice that Red Cross Letters for the C.I. civilian internees in Germany will be taken by the Red Cross ships which are expected to arrive within the next few days; four pages may be written and the letters posted at the Head Office, Broad Street by 6 p.m. on the 11th Dec.

31 December 1944

.... Mail from the internees and prisoners of war have arrived on the 'Vega' ...

15 January 1945

The Germans are to grant facilities for letters to be sent to P.O.W.'s, one per month'.

In England the Earl of Munster, Under-Secretary at the Home Office announced in the House of Lords on 30 January 1945 that a relief ship – the 'Vega', would sail for the Channel Islands from Lisbon on 1 February and that Mails from internees and prisoners in Germany had been delivered and mail for Germany collected. He hoped that ultimately it would be possible to send messages from England. However, what the Earl of Munster failed to mention was that the mail from the internees had been carried to Lisbon by Air Mail. A note on a Prisoner of War List originating from the Red Cross in Lisbon in January 1945 and now residing in the Public Records Office at Kew states:

'Red Cross Channel Islands Section say that internees can now write direct to relatives in the Channel Islands by *AIR MAIL* which is carried by the 'VEGA' from Lisbon. G.P.O. Confirms.'

Back in Jersey L. P. Sinel recorded on 10 February 1945 that accommodation would be available on the 'Vega' for mail for civilian internees in Germany and that instructions were given concerning 'special forms' obtainable at the Bailiff's Enquiry and News Office. The last part of Sinel's statement, 'special forms available at the Bailiff's Enquiry and News Office' was for me one of the most frustrating mysteries of the whole history of the Internee Mail Service as a used example of one of these forms had until 1978 never been found and it was one of the few certain examples of Internee mail carried on the 'Vega'. Some years ago O. W. Newport showed me an unusual Letter Form which originated in the Islands and which is now in the collection of Don McKenzie; this form is a mint example of the 'special form' referred to by Sinel.

```
                    FOLD HERE
          INTERNIERTENPOST,
                  Gebührenfrei!



   An
   Vor und Zuname: ........................................................

   Internierten Nr.: ........................................................

   Lager-Bezeichnung: ....................................................

               DEUTSCHLAND (ALLEMAGNE).

   ..............................    FOLD HERE   ..............................




                              Absender:
                              Name: ........................................
                              Adresse: ....................................
                              ..................................................
                              KANAL INSELN
```

The Interniertenpost Letter Sheet from the Channel Islands

This letter sheet when opened out is $10^1/_2''$ wide and $8^1/_4''$ high. When folded in half it gives three blank pages for writing, the two inside ones have 'Write clearly here' printed on them. The fourth side has 'INTERNIERTENPOST' in bold capitals above a space for the address and a space for the sender's name and address. When folded twice more the letter tucks into its own flap and leaves the address on one side and the sender's name and address on the reverse.

The printing is as follows:

.... FOLD HERE ....

<u>INTERNIERTENPOST</u>
<u>Gebührenfrei !</u>
An
Vor und Zuname: ....
Internierten Nr: ....
Larger-Bezeichnung: ....
DEUTSCHLAND (ALLEMAGNE).

.... FOLD HERE ....

Absender:...................
Name:.....................
Adresse: ....
....
KANAL INSELN.

On a visit to Jersey in 1978 I at last managed to locate two used examples of this form in the private collections of members of the 'Channel Islands Specialist's Society'. One of these forms had travelled from Jersey via the International Red Cross in Geneva and had reached Laufen Internment Camp before its liberation. The form in itself is obviously very interesting as it bears the double circle cachet of the Red Cross in Geneva and the censor cachet Type Lf.C.3. of Laufen Camp, but it is even more unusual in that it is one of the few items of mail to be censored in the Channel Islands by the Germans before being forwarded to the Continent. A full description of this German Censor cachet used in the Channel Islands appears at the end of the chapter 'German Censorship' as Type Ch.Is.C.1.

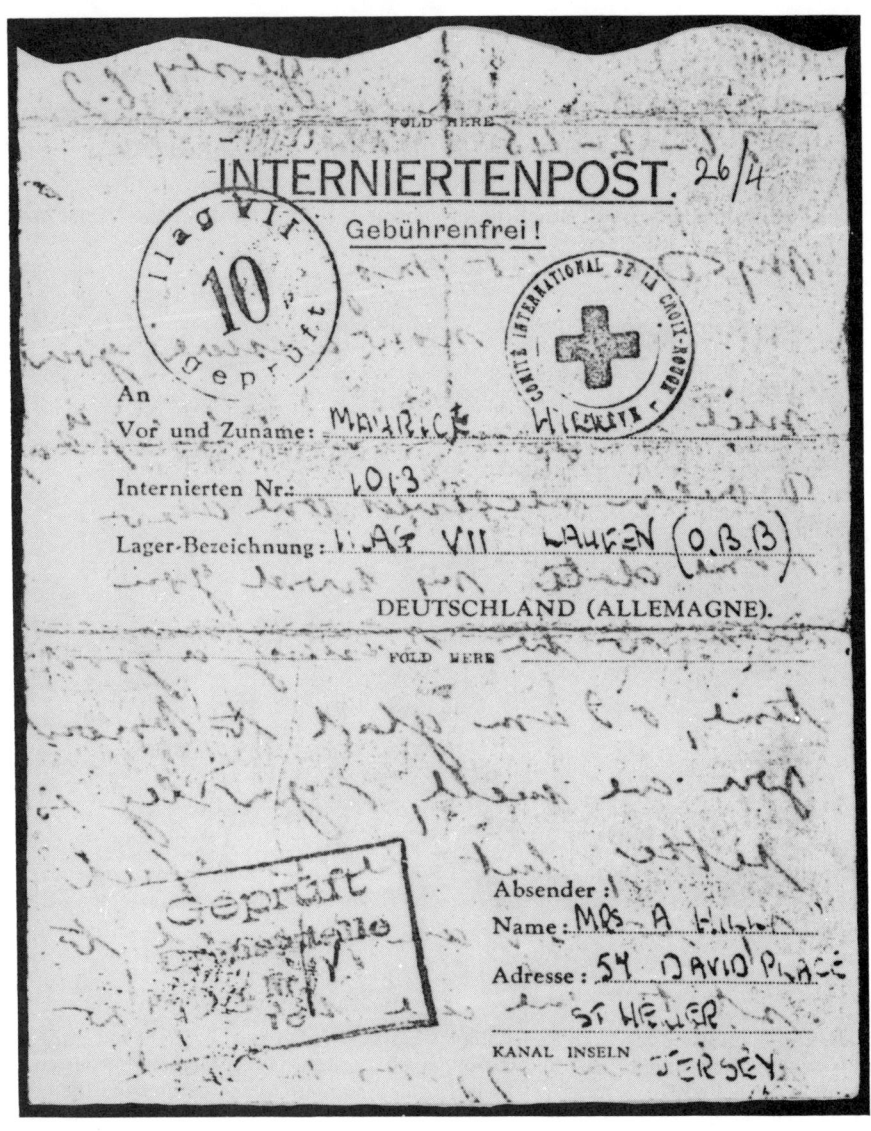

A used example of the special Channel Islands Interniertenpost Lettersheet sent from Jersey to Laufen.

On Valentine's Day, 14 February 1945, A. J. Sherwill writing again from Laufen says:

'A very few letters dated early in January have reached this camp and speak of the joy in Guernsey at the receipt of a consignment of Red Cross parcels.'

The last comments L. P. Sinel makes about Internee mail on the 'Vega' are:

'20 February 1945:

Mail from internees and P.O.W.'s on "Vega".

24 February 1945:

Mail may be sent to the civilian internees in Germany this to be taken by the "Vega" on her next journey.'

The International Red Cross Relief ship 'VEGA'. The 'VEGA' brought not only life-saving food supplies and Red Cross parcels to the Channel Islands, but also long awaited Red Cross messages from England and letters and cards from the Channel Islands prisoners of war and internees. When the 'VEGA' left the Islands and returned to Lisbon, she carried a precious cargo of Red Cross messages destined for England, and letters for the Prisoner of War and Internee camps in Germany. Examples of such letters are now very rare.

Although the 'Vega' made more visits to the Islands L. P. Sinel no longer mentions Internee mail, only Red Cross Messages, as having been delivered, and even these were several months old.

It is very difficult to identify for certain Internee mail that travelled between the Camps and the Channel Islands via Lisbon and the 'Vega'. Throughout the period that mail was handled by the International Red Cross there was no one uniform marking or cachet applied to letters that can help identification. As already stated, many letters from the Camps at this time were endorsed in the top left hand corner with the one word 'English', but by no means did all letters carry this endorsement. Many more letters addressed to the Islands received a British 'Crown over Passed' Censor Cachet with a number following the letters 'P.W.' in it. This cachet should have been applied in England and so by implication letters bearing it never went to their correct destination until after the war. A very small number of letters from the Camps have received the double circle (Type R.C.C.I. McKenzie Type 1) Red Cross Cachet of the 'COMITE INTERNATIONAL DE LA CROIX ROUGE' at 'GENEVE'. These obviously were handled by the Red Cross, but as even some of these with Channel Island addresses on have also received British 'Crown over Passed' Censor cachets, one cannot be certain that they also travelled on the 'Vega'. If the Post Offices in the Islands had date-stamped the Internee Letters on arrival then the answer would have been simple, but without any conclusive indication of this nature, if one is to identify a letter with a very high probability of being carried to the Islands on the 'Vega', then it must satisfy certain qualifications. These are:—

1. Endorsed in top left hand corner with the word 'English'.

2. Have a despatch date which fits the period the Red Cross were known to have handled Island-bound mail i.e. late November 1944 through to April 1945.

3. Bear an Internment Camp Censor cachet – which means the letter was not handled after the Camp was liberated by the Allies.

4. Preferably also bear the single circle Red Cross cachet of the International Red Cross Committee at Geneva.

5. Definitely must *not* bear a British 'Crown over Passed' Censor cachet or British Censor Tape 'P.C.90.'

6. Be addressed to the Islands – obviously – but not 'via England'.

If a letter can satisfy all these qualifications it is probable that it reached the Islands via the 'Vega'.

Interniertenpost

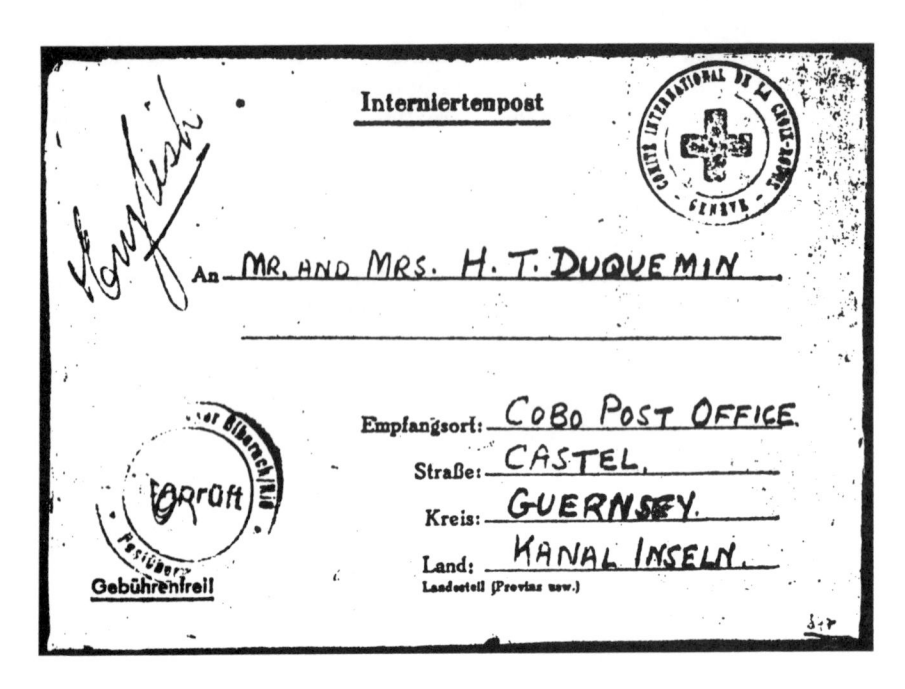

An MR. AND MRS. H. T. DUQUEMIN

Empfangsort: COBO POST OFFICE
Straße: CASTEL,
Kreis: GUERNSEY.
Land: KANAL INSELN.

A letter which probably reached the Islands via the Relief ship 'Vega'.

The letter satisfies all the qualifications listed. It was sent from Biberach on 19 March 1945, over a month before that Camp's liberation, and was censored at the Camp. It is endorsed with the word 'English' and bears the Geneva Red Cross cachet. Also its address is given in German as 'Kanal Inseln' and it does not mention going 'via England' nor has it received any British Censoring.

It is much easier to be certain that a letter leaving the Islands was carried on the 'Vega' as although one does not have any despatch date on the envelope to help one, if the letter carries any form of Red Cross cachet then it must have been carried on the ship since, before the 'Vega' carried letters, they would be sent through the German Feldpost and never reach Geneva or the International Red Cross. Having said that, it must be stated that 'Vega' letters existing today are very rare. I have already stated that a used example of the 'Special Form' issued by the Bailiff's Enquiry and News Office in Jersey for transmission on the 'Vega' was not discovered until 1978, and I can only record a few examples of ordinary letters carried on the 'Vega', these usually being from Guernsey as that Island, to my knowledge, never printed or issued any of the 'Special Forms'.

Letters leaving England in April and May 1945 never reached the Camps as they arrived in Switzerland when communications with Germany were breaking

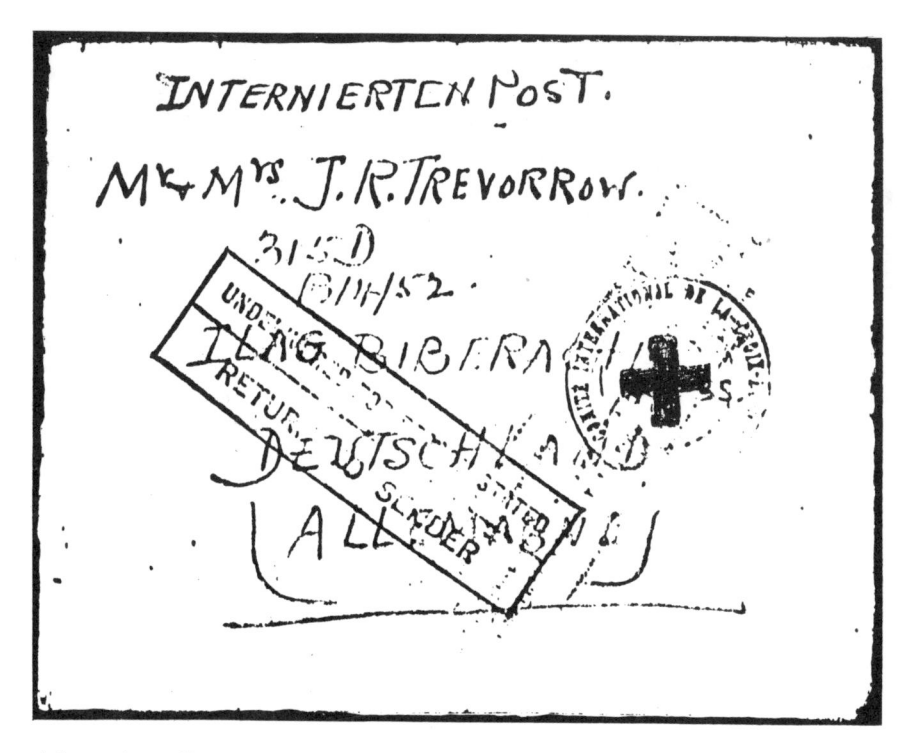

A letter from Guernsey to Biberach carried on the Relief ship 'Vega'.
The letter bears the double circle Red Cross Cachet of Geneva and also a boxed cachet in purple on the reverse reading 'This letter/postcard has been returned by the Swiss Post Office who were unable to re-forward it to Germany because of the interruption of communications'. The front also carries a double boxed cachet in crimson 'UNDELIVERED FOR REASON STATED/RETURN TO SENDER'.

down and the camps were being liberated. Such letters were returned to England where they received an instructional marking similar to the one above on the Guernsey cover and stating that 'This letter has been returned by the Swiss Post Office who were unable of re-forward it to Germany because of the interruption of communications'.

Other letters from England which had already left Swiss hands were captured by the advancing Allied armies before they could be delivered to the camps. These letters were also returned to England and received a boxed cachet in purple reading 'This letter formed part of undelivered mails which fell into the hands of the Allied forces in Germany. It is undeliverable as addressed and therefore returned to you.'

These and other instructional markings are explained and illustrated in the chapter 'British Censorship; British Post Office Markings.'

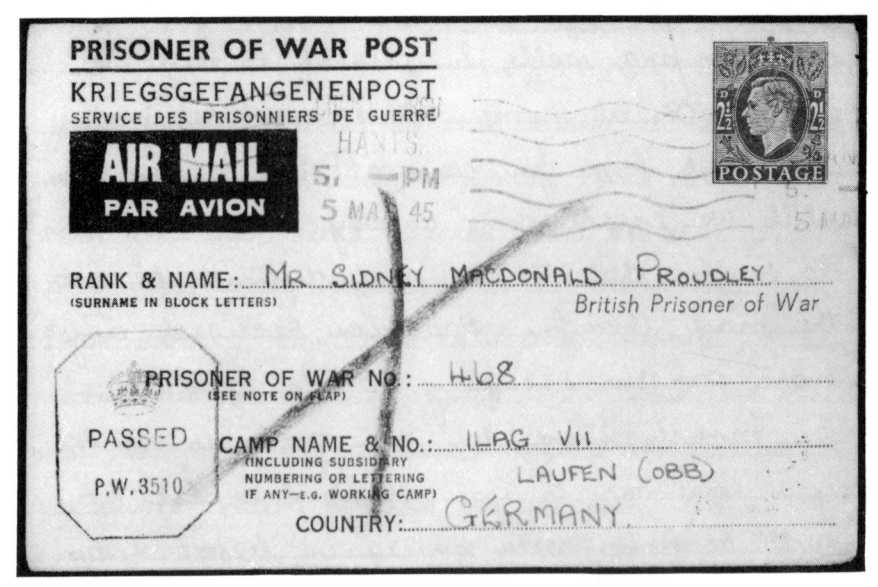

Air Letter Form to Laufen returned by the Swiss Post Office.
  This Air Letter Form was posted to Laufen from England on 5 May 1945, one day after the camp was liberated. It received a British 'Crown over Passed' P.W.3510 censor cachet but has not received any German censor cachets. The address has been crossed out with a blue crayon and the letter was then returned to England where it was endorsed on the reverse with an Instructional marking in purple explaining its reason for return.

A limited amount of mail was sent from the Internment Camps following their liberation, but examples are extremely difficult to find today. The few covers (and their cachets) that are recorded are described in detail in the respective chapters following dealing with each camp, as every letter is different and individual to a camp. As the mail, after liberation, was no longer subject to censoring by the Germans, the only cachets the letters tended to receive were those of the liberating army and any Red Cross Group associated with it. Some were now endorsed 'Prisoner of War Post' (Note: not Internee Post) but this endorsement was not applied by the sender as it tends to be in the same handwriting on different letters. It is interesting to note that some of the immediate post Camp-liberation mail addressed to the Channel Islands may still not have been routed via England as it reached the Islands without receiving a British 'Crown over Passed' censor cachet, whereas letters addressed to England at this time did still receive this British censor cachet.

  At the beginning of this chapter I listed eight sources of mail to the Internment Camps. I have dealt above fairly exhaustively with (a) *mail from the United Kingdom* and (b) *mail from the Channel Islands* and I have mentioned (g) *mail returned to the camp following the disruptions to communication caused by*

D-Day and the allied advance into France. This however still leaves five other important categories of mail to the camps to be dealt with, albeit that these are very scarce.

They are:

(c) *Mail from Europe*

Most mail in this category was sent from within Germany or Austria. If an Internee was seriously ill and could not be dealt with in the camp hospital, he might be taken to another hospital outside the camp. At Laufen there are records of Internees being taken to Salzburg and at Biberach to Ochsenhausen. The 'Interniertenpost' did not operate from these places and consequently Internee patients had to use the domestic German postal service at the 12 pf. letter rate if they wanted to communicate with relatives and friends in the Camps. These letters on arrival at the camp were censored in the normal way.

A letter from Ochsenhausen to Biberach.

This letter was sent from an Internee in Ochsenhausen hospital on 8 May 1944 to his wife in Biberach Camp. It is stamped at the 12 pf. rate and has received an Ochsenhausen postmark and a Biberach Camp Censor Cachet Type Bb.C.4. on arrival.

35

(d) *Inter-Camp Mail*
One of the reasons why this category of mail is so scarce is that at various times, for security reasons, the Germans banned communications between the different Prisoner of War Camps and between the Internment Camps. The most likely source of Inter-Camp mail between Internees, is from Compiègne in France to Laufen and Kreuzburg when married couples on the 1943 deportations were separated, the wives and children staying at Compiègne and their husbands going on to Laufen and Kreuzburg. The only recorded example of this Inter-Internment Camp mail is a letter sent by a woman Internee at Compiègne to her husband whom she thought was in Kreuzburg. He was actually in Laufen and so the letter was endorsed with the cachet 'Nicht im Ilag VIII' (i.e. Kreuzburg) and then forwarded to Laufen. Eventually the sender and her husband were reunited at Biberach Camp.

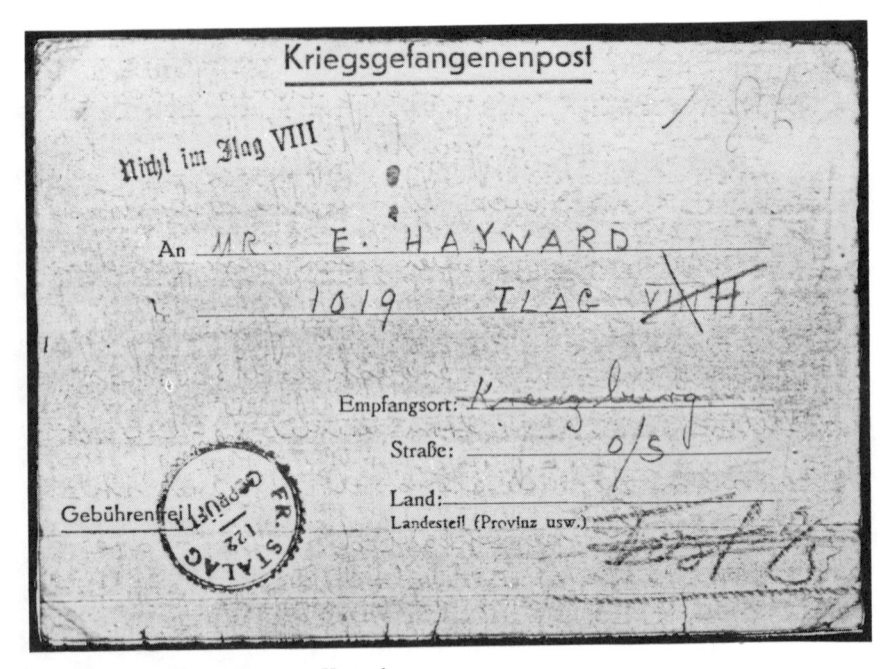

A letter from Compiègne to Kreuzburg.
  The letter bears a cog-wheel censor cachet of Compiègne 'FR. STALAG 122 GEPRUFT' and the scarce cachet of Kreuzburg 'Nicht im Ilag VIII'.

A few examples of inter-camp mail between other camps do exist; I have a card sent from Laufen to Biberach in February 1944, but I have yet to see an example of a very regular service that ran between Wurzach and Biberach. This was the unofficial, secret service when letters were carried between the two camps by internees driving the weekly provisions lorry. The service continued to function until one day when the internees were searched on arrival at Biberach and the unofficial mail was discovered. (see **PART I** Chapter 'Wurzach Internment Camp').

Throughout the Occupation of the Channel Islands by the Germans, people were arrested and sentenced to various terms of imprisonment in France or Germany for crimes committed against German Military Law. These crimes could include, possessing a radio, harbouring escaped slave workers, making 'V' signs, making defamatory remarks against the Germans or spreading the B.B.C. news. People convicted of these crimes were usually very badly treated and often ended up in Concentration Camps where many died. (See **PART I** Chapter 'Prisons and Concentration Camps'). A very interesting example of Inter-Camp mail that I have in my collection is a card from an Internee at Laufen Camp – Leslie Green – to his father in a Prison near Paris. The father, Stanley Green, was sentenced for a radio offence in 1943 but he was one of the few lucky ones to survive Fresnes and Belsen before eventually being transferred to Laufen to be reunited with his son. The card was sent from Laufen on 27 May 1944 and is addressed to Mr. S. G. Green No. 4877 at Villeneuf, St. Georges, Seine-et-Oise, France, before his transfer to Belsen.

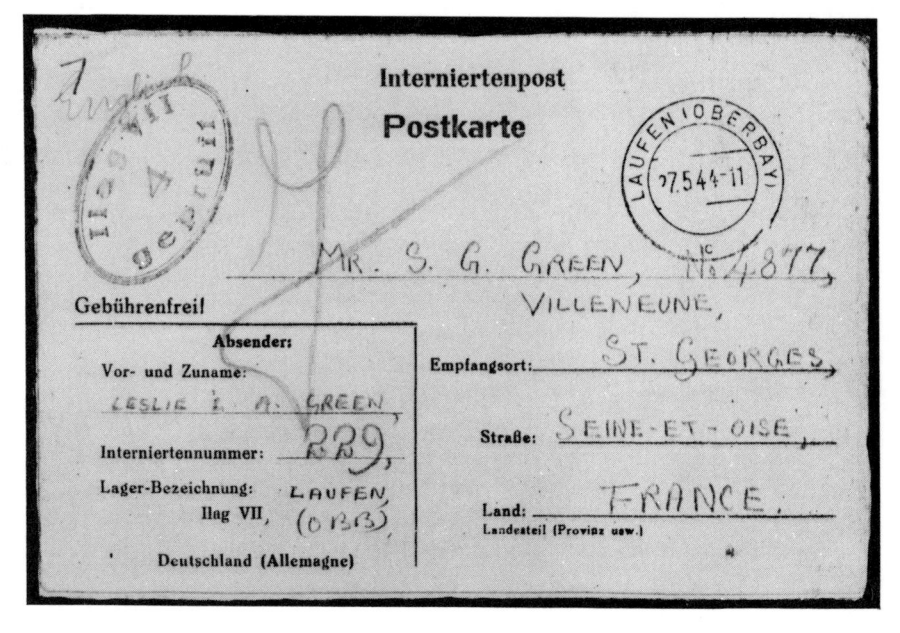

The Internment Card from a son at Laufen to his father at Villeneuf, St. Georges near Paris.

The card has received the Laufen double oval censor cachet No. 4 Type Lf.C.1 as well as an initial on the front in blue crayon. On the reverse is a small cachet 'Le Vaguemesure' in purple with a pencil initial beside it.

37

(e) *Red Cross Messages*

When the Islanders were suddenly deported in September 1942 and others in February 1943 there were many Red Cross Messages en route to the Islands from England addressed to these deportees. Some of these were re-routed and forwarded to the Camps where they were censored on arrival by the Germans and received a camp censor cachet. Don McKenzie in his book 'The Red Cross Mail Service for Channel Island Civilians 1940–45' records one of these messages forwarded to Biberach, another forwarded to Laufen is illustrated below.

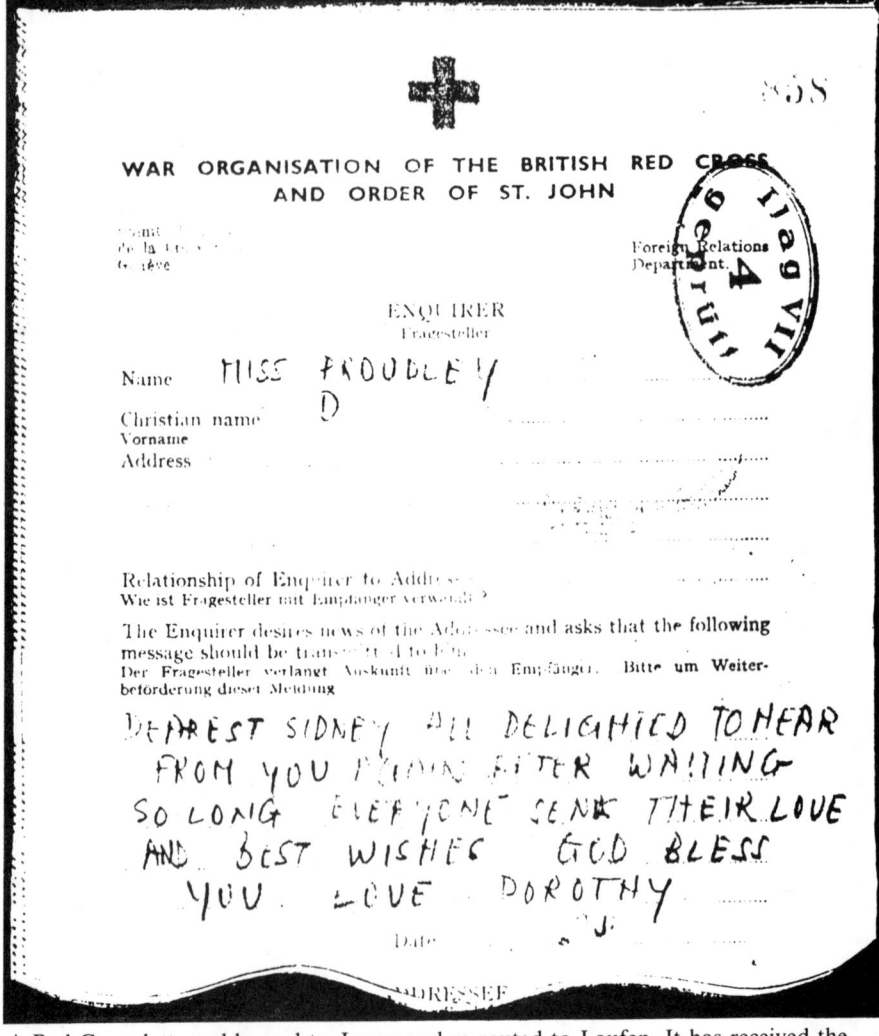

A Red Cross letter addressed to Jersey and re-routed to Laufen. It has received the Laufen double oval censor cachet No. 4, Type Lf.C.1.

(f) *Official Mail from the International Red Cross in Geneva*
The British Camp Captains were able to communicate with, and receive replies from three 'benefactors' in Switzerland. These were 'The Protecting Power' itself (Switzerland) which defended the rights of the Internees, 'The Red Cross' that looked after their physical well-being, i.e. food and clothing, and 'The Y.M.C.A.' that saw to their educational, spiritual and recreational comforts. In my own collection, I have one letter from the British Camp Captain at Wulzburg to Switzerland (see illustration in **PART I** chapter on 'WULZBURG: WEISSENBURG/BY') and I can record one postcard from the Y.M.C.A. in Geneva to the British Camp Captain of Wurzach Camp.

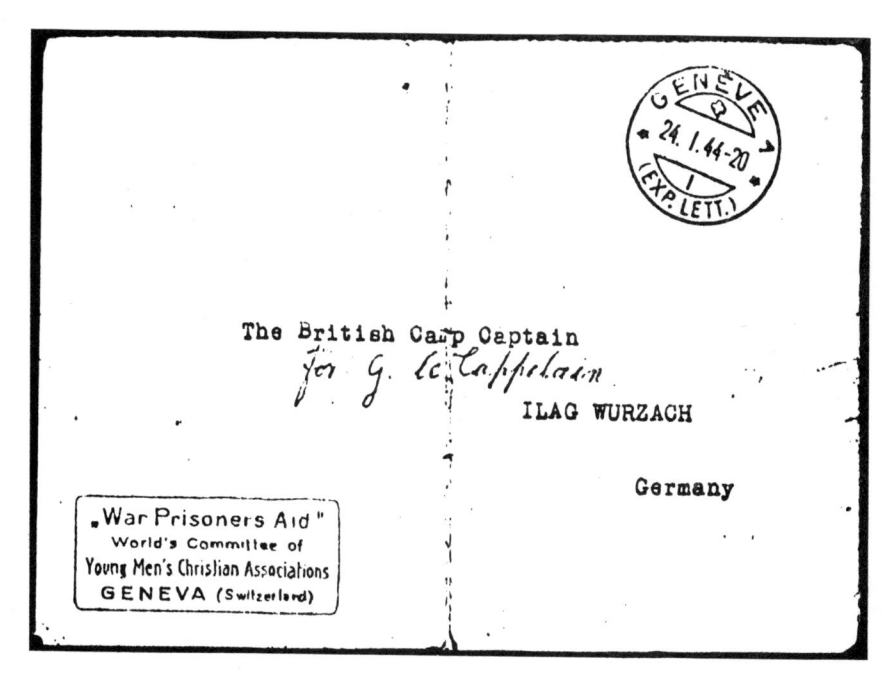

A postcard from the Y.M.C.A. in Geneva to Ilag Wurzach.
 Note the Geneva Postmark with the Cross, and the cachet struck in purple of the ",,War Prisoners Aid"/World's Committee of/Young Men's Christian Associations/GENEVA (Switzerland).'

The message side of this postcard reads:

> 'War Prisoner's Aid of the Y.M.C.A.
> 37, Quai Wilsen, GENEVA.
> Switzerland.
>
> Dear Sir,
>   *Ref. YMCA Shipment No. 56813 despatched* 2.12.43.
>   The Junior Branch of the Canadian Red Cross recently made a substantial gift of musical instruments to the British Red Cross, for the benefit of British prisoners of war. We are writing to let you know that the instruments you received in the above-mentioned shipment are a part of this gift, the Y.M.C.A. being only the distribution agent. We are sure that you will greatly appreciate the action of the Junior Branch of the Canadian Red Cross in making these instruments available.
>
>   Yours sincerely
>   Signature.
>   J. H. Jungkunst.'

24.1.44.

(h) *Mail from parts of the British Empire*

Naturally this is a very scarce category of mail, but at least one correspondence from Canada to Biberach is well documented. A strong contingent of Channel Islanders live in Canada. During and shortly after the war, these people had their own 'Aid Society' for the Channel Islands and so it is not surprising that out of the whole of the British Empire, any surviving correspondence should come from Canada. The letters that have been recorded are Prisoner of War lettersheets sent by Mrs Mary Lawson in Ontario to Mr. and Mrs. G. Hornby in Biberach. Both were Jersey families.

The letters usually took about two months to travel to their destination and were always censored in Canada and at the Camp. Some of the letters from Canada bear a 10c stamp while others were sent without one, but even when a postage due marking was applied the time taken for the letter to reach the camp was not affected and there is no record of the tax being collected in the camp.

A Canadian Prisoner of War Post Lettersheet from the Lawson-Hornby correspondence.

The letter was posted in Fort Erie, Ontario on 1 June 1944 and received the boxed 'TAXE PERCUE 10 CENTS' mark in crimson because it was posted without a stamp. It was examined in Canada by censor D B/656 and bears his cachet in black. It was then forwarded to Biberach where it received the Biberach Censor cachet Bb.C.5 struck in blue/black and was then delivered to Mr. and Mrs. Hornby on 3 August 1944.

Two other types of postal stationery exist for the transmission of messages to the camps, but authentically used examples have yet to be recorded.

1. *Wurzach Prisoner-of-War Reply Postcard*

In June and July of 1943 Wurzach Internment Camp used a supply of postcards from Wurzach Officer Prisoner of War Camp Offizierlarger 55 (VD). These cards were double the size of the normal postcard and when folded across the centre one half could be detached and used to send a reply back to the camp. The postcards were bi-lingual, printed in French and German, and the reply half had the Wurzach Officer Camp address preprinted in full on it. (The card is illustrated and described in full in the chapter 'Wurzach Camp' dealing with the printings of the camp stationery). Examples of these cards are known used from Wurzach to Jersey and England but no example has so far been recorded of the reply half of the card used back to Wurzach.

2. *Preprinted envelope for use to Mr. Roy N. Machon interned at Laufen Camp*

The pre-printed envelope addressed to Laufen but used on 26 April 1948 in Guernsey as a First Day Cover.

This envelope seems to have no official status and was obviously a private printing possibly executed by a relative of Mr. R. N. Machon. The pre-printing reads:

INTERNIERTENPOST
An Mr. ROY N. MACHON
INTERNIERTEN Nr. 1130
LAUFEN/OBB,
LAGER-BEZEICHNUNG,
ILAG VII
DEUTSCHLAND (Allemagne)

Quite why this was produced I do not know but it is interesting to record that it does not have the senders' name preprinted on the reverse as was demanded by the German Feldpost. I have yet to see an example used during the war; the only one I have, was used in Guernsey as a first day cover for the Royal Silver Wedding issue of 26 April 1948 when a Guernsey address has been added to the front by the use of a rubber stamp.

Undelivered Channel Islands Mail addressed to a deportee

When the Channel Islanders were deported in 1942 and 1943, letters were often posted to them at their old home address in the Islands, but if their house had been taken over by the Germans, or the camp to which they were taken was not known, then these letters would be returned to the sender. Even some years after the Internees had been deported, examples of these undeliverable letters would still emanate from Firms or Official Agencies in the Islands who were unaware that the person had been deported. A letter which could not be delivered would receive a boxed cachet in violet reading:

UNDELIVERED FOR REASON STATED
RETURN TO SENDER

(see later Chapter 'British Post Office Markings' – Type U.K.P.O.C.6). The Postman would also endorse the letter stating why it could not be delivered. As the Germans never permitted the use of the word 'deported' in relation to the Internees, the Postman was obliged to write 'Evacuated' as the reason for non delivery, but in order to indicate that the letter had not been addressed to one of the true Evacuees who left the Islands for England in 1940, he would usually add some criptic comment such as 'now in Germany' to his endorsement.

Examples of undelivered letters addressed to the deportees are relatively scarce and attract a high premium, but they should not be confused with other letters that have received the 'undelivered' cachets. Deportees' letters are easy to identify as the postmark must be dated after the first deportations in September 1942, the name of the addressee must obviously be that of a recorded Internee and the endorsement by the Postman will usually indicate

43

that the person has been taken to Germany. I have never seen one of these letters that has subsequently been redirected to an Internee Camp and so one must assume that they were always returned to the sender.

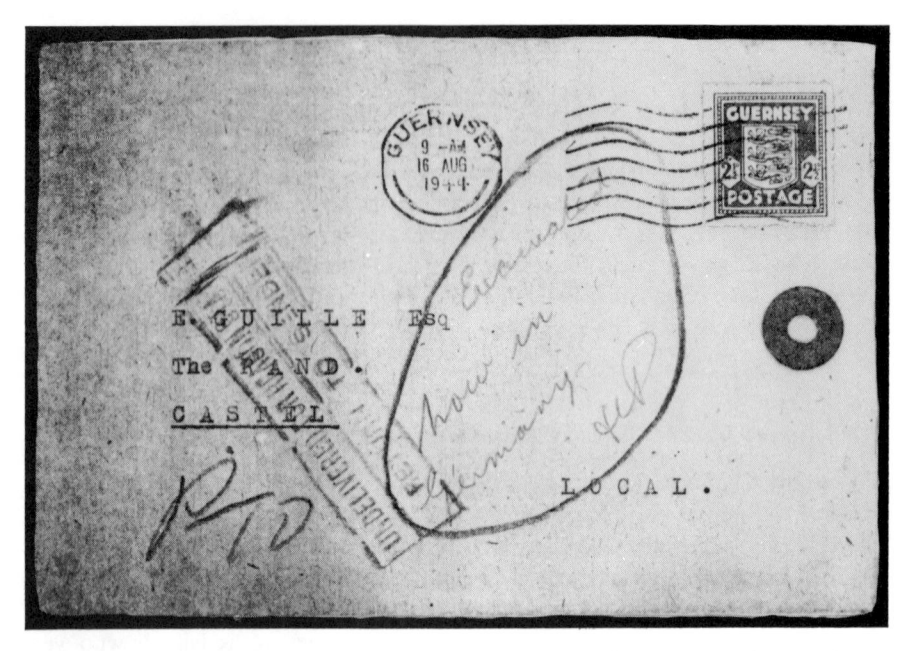

An example of a letter addressed to a Guernsey deportee from W. A. Nicholls & Sons Ltd. in St. Peter Port.

As the letter was undeliverable, it has received the violet boxed cachet 'UNDELIVERED FOR REASON STATED/RETURN TO SENDER', and an endorsement by the Postman in an indelible pencil reading 'Evacuated/Now in Germany' and his initialled signature.

Mail Routes for
Channel Island Internees

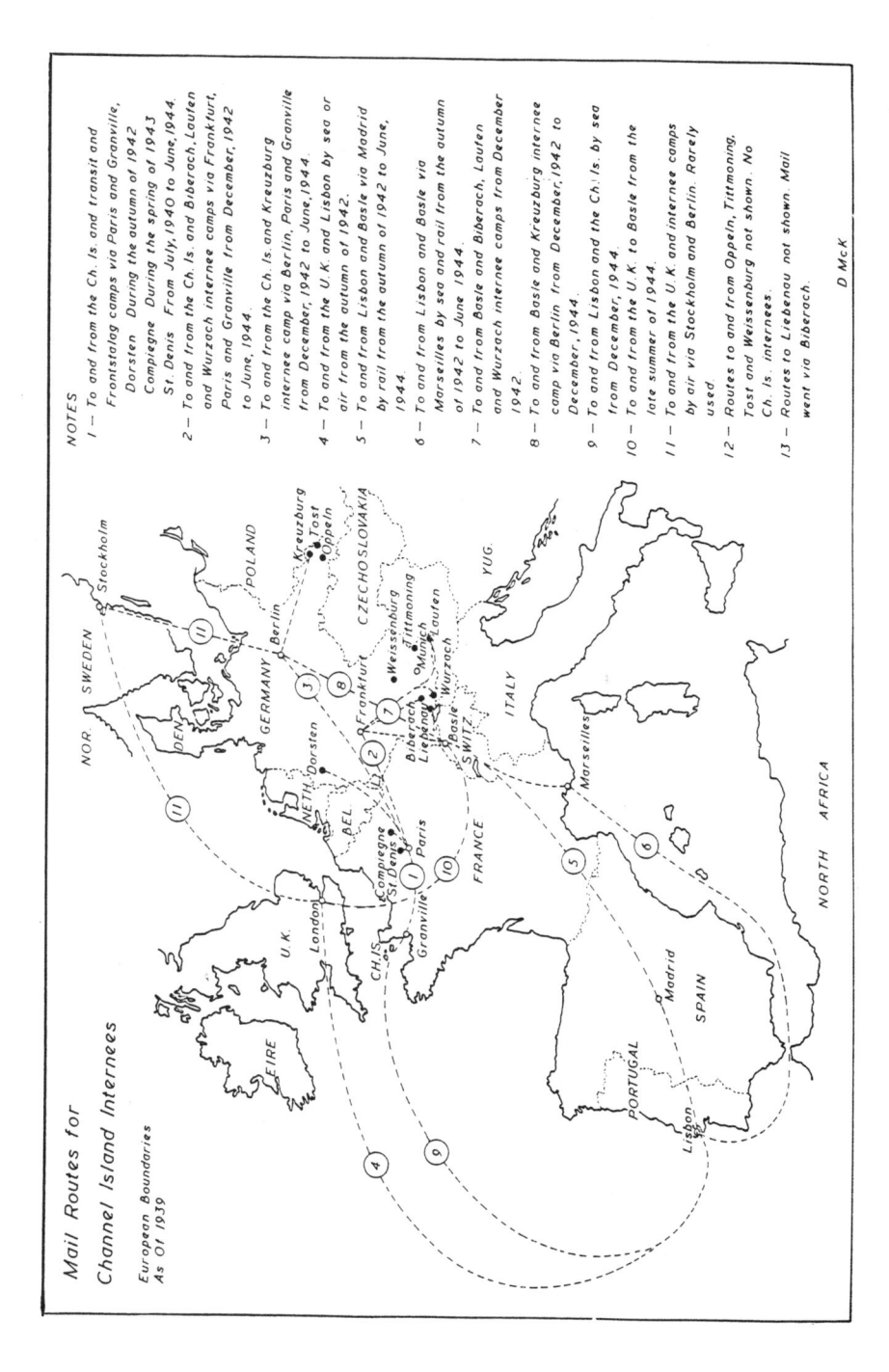

European Boundaries
As Of 1939

NOTES

1 – To and from the Ch. Is. and transit and Frontstalag camps via Paris and Granville, Dorsten During the autumn of 1942 Compiegne During the spring of 1943 St. Denis From July, 1940 to June, 1944.

2 – To and from the Ch. Is. and Biberach, Laufen and Wurzach internee camps via Frankfurt, Paris and Granville from December, 1942 to June, 1944.

3 – To and from the Ch. Is. and Kreuzburg internee camp via Berlin, Paris and Granville from December, 1942 to June, 1944.

4 – To and from the U.K. and Lisbon by sea or air from the autumn of 1942.

5 – To and from Lisbon and Basle via Madrid by rail from the autumn of 1942 to June, 1944.

6 – To and from Lisbon and Basle via Marseilles by sea and rail from the autumn of 1942 to June 1944.

7 – To and from Basle and Biberach, Laufen and Wurzach internee camps from December, 1942

8 – To and from Basle and Kreuzburg internee camp via Berlin from December, 1942 to December, 1944.

9 – To and from Lisbon and the Ch. Is. by sea from December, 1944.

10 – To and from the U.K. to Basle from the late summer of 1944.

11 – To and from the U.K. and internee camps by air via Stockholm and Berlin. Rarely used.

12 – Routes to and from Oppeln, Tittmoning, Tost and Weissenburg not shown. No Ch. Is. internees.

13 – Routes to Liebenau not shown. Mail went via Biberach.

D McK

Appendix 1.
Origin of the Internee Mail Service

Clauses relating to the treatment of Prisoners of War in the Hague Convention of 1907 were enlarged by the Geneva Convention of 1929 into a document of 97 articles. Article 36 governs the transmission of Prisoner of War mail.

Enemy aliens in a belligerent country were not covered by international convention. For many years the International Red Cross Committee (I.C.R.C.) had endeavoured to rectify this situation. Its efforts had made so much progress that a draft Convention had been approved by an International Red Cross Conference held in Tokyo during 1934. This Convention was to have been submitted to a Diplomatic Conference, convened by the Swiss Federal Council for the beginning of 1940, but it was not held owing to the outbreak of war in September 1939. Being unwilling to leave this unhappy class in so indeterminate a position, the I.C.R.C. sought from the belligerent countries, an agreement that interned civilians should be granted a status on the basis of the draft Tokyo Convention. It obtained the consent of the belligerents to their being treated MUTATIS MUTANDIS, as prisoners of war. It must be emphasised that this consent only covered the treatment of interned civilians and was not applicable to 'free' civilians such as the Channel Islanders resident on the islands, or the some 3,500 British citizens living at liberty in occupied France during July 1941, or the British citizens living at liberty in Greece, or the 'isolati' resident in Italy. These 'isolati' were a group of civilians who did not 'enjoy' the status of internment, and therefore failed to benefit from the services for interned civilians. The Italian authorities prescribed their places of residence – often in isolated mountain villages. One family of Channel Islanders, caught in Italy, were subjected to this form of restriction but they were later transferred to Biberach by the Germans prior to the surrender of Italy.

Responsibility for observing the provisions of the Convention rested with the Governments of those States which had ratified it. Amongst them were the major belligerents, Germany, Italy, France, Great Britain and the United States. In the House of Lords on 24 October 1939, Lord Cobham, Under-Secretary of State for War, said:

'The treatment of interned civilians in the United Kingdom will not be less favourable than that accorded to prisoners of war'.

The representatives of Japan at Geneva had agreed and signed the Convention but Japan did not ratify it and was not bound by its provisions. However, through the Argentine Government (the Protecting Power), it informed the British Government in February, 1942, that it would nevertheless observe its terms, MUTATIS MUTANDIS, in respect of the British, Canadian, Australian, New Zealand and Indian prisoners whom it had taken. This agreement to observe the Convention covered civilian internees as well as military prisoners of war. The manner in which Japan gave effect to this undertaking did, to say the least, leave something to be desired. Soviet Russia had not signed the 1929 Convention, consequently its Government had not ratified it. As a result, the Soviet Union forwarded no information on prisoners of war in their hands, nor did it permit the use of mail facilities to either prisoners of war or internees.

The net result of the mutual consent given by the belligerents was that interned civilians of enemy nationality obtained amenities which they would not otherwise have enjoyed. Their names were communicated to the adverse party via the I.C.R.C. and to the Central Prisoners of War Agency. They were allowed to correspond with their next-of-kin. Their camps were visited by representatives of the Protecting Power and of the I.C.R.C. and they could receive food parcels and other forms of relief as well as next-of-kin parcels four times a year.

The Transmission of Mail

Although the I.C.R.C. was instrumental in obtaining the agreement of the signatories to the 1929 Convention, it was not vested with the responsibility of ensuring that a mail service was operated.

Article 36 of the 1929 Convention, which governs the transmission of prisoner of war mail and by agreement the mail of internees, provides for the exchange of mail by post and by the shortest route. The part of intermediary played by the I.C.R.C. was therefore not a matter of obligation. In practice, however, the I.C.R.C. was always ready to act as intermediary when asked to do so.

The belligerent countries arranged amongst themselves, generally by the channel of the Protecting Powers, for the exchange of mail. In respect of Europe, throughout the greater part of the war, the exchange took place through the Swiss postal service, in particular via Basle. The major portion of all mail went straight through by way of the Basle office, from the country of the sender to that of the addressee.

Occasionally private persons or postal administrations had reason to believe that the I.C.R.C. would be better placed for forwarding mail, as it might have had more complete or up-to-date addresses and that its help would ensure a more reliable delivery. Such mail was delivered to the I.C.R.C., either because the sender clearly specified on the envelope 'c/o The International Red Cross Committee', or because the postal administration in the country of origin, or the Swiss postal services themselves passed on whole bags of mail. Bags of mail were sometimes sent in error to the I.C.R.C. by transit offices of neutral countries.

Mail destined for the Channel Islands from the Internment Camps was not handled by the I.C.R.C. until November 1944. Prior to this, Island bound mail was transmitted by the German Feldpost and any that was sent to the I.C.R.C. was subject to delay and often ended up being mis-routed to England.

Appendix II.

The Internee Parcel Post Services

Four primary parcel post services operated on behalf of the Channel Islands internees, these were:

(a) From the United Kingdom to the camps via the British and International Red Cross.
(b) Official Red Cross Parcels from other parts of the British Empire.
(c) From the Channel Islands to the camps via the German Feldpost.
(d) From the camps to the Channel Islands via the German Feldpost.

(a) From the United Kingdom to the camps.

The first service was an extension of that already in existence for Prisoners of War. In 'Appendix I, Origin of the Internee Mail Service', it is stated that the International Red Cross (the I.C.R.C.) was not responsible for the operation of the mail service, however the British Red Cross was specifically charged with operating the parcel post service from the U.K. In the House of Commons on 5 December 1939, the then Secretary of State for War said that the British Red Cross Society and Order of St. John of Jerusalem, in consultation with the Government Departments concerned, had to set up a Prisoners of War, Wounded and Missing Department. He added,

> 'This organisation is the accredited authority for packing and despatching parcels to British Prisoners of War'.

A few days later on 12 December 1939, the 'London Times' carried a statement describing the types of parcels then being planned, they were:

1. The 'Initial Parcel' to the newly captured prisoners, these were later discontinued.
2. A food parcel to each prisoner three times a fortnight, weighing approximately 11 lbs or 5 kilogrammes.
3. A medical comforts parcel.
4. Bread parcels – sent experimentally and later replaced by flour and biscuit parcels.
5. A personal parcel sent quarterly, providing a medium whereby relatives might send articles to individuals in whom they were especially interested. These later became generally known as 'Next-of-Kin' parcels.

The first parcels were despatched in October 1939, by air through the Swiss Legation bag, a second batch was sent on 10 November 1939, and from that date further supplies were regularly despatched. The first acknowledgement of receipt was received in London on 15 November 1939.

With the changing fortunes of the war, the service to Europe was altered, so that by 1942, when the Channel Islanders were interned, the route was via Lisbon, Spain, France, Switzerland and thence to Germany. That is, it was the same route as that traversed by the letters of 25 words sent via the Red Cross Message scheme.

Essentially all parcels other than the 'Next-of-Kin' personal parcels can be classed as non-postal and considered merely as a logistical transportation problem in the movement of supplies. However, the personal parcel service may be classed as postal, in the sense that the relative of the prisoner or internee paid, not only for the contents, but also a fee to cover the transportation of the parcel. The fee was, of course, variable and dependent upon the weight of the contents.

The method of handling personal parcels was somewhat similar to that used for registered parcels. The sender would go to a Red Cross Bureau, state the intended contents, from those on the permitted list, then pay both the cost of the contents and the transportation cost. The list of contents was then entered and carbon copied onto a triple copy document known as a British Red Cross Contents List, Form P4. The original list together with the first carbon was packed inside the parcel while the second carbon was retained by the Bureau. On receipt of the parcel, the Prisoner of War or Internee, signed the first carbon to acknowledge receipt, and this was returned to the originating Bureau. This, together with receipts for all other parcels signed for by a camp representative, enabled the losses from all causes and to all parcels to be kept as low as 0.152%.

The individual personal parcel was packed, wrapped, addressed and shipped by the Red Cross, not by the next-of-kin who only paid for it. Sometimes the persons in England could not afford to send a next-of-kin parcel, four times a year, to their Channel Island internee relative. This was often the case where the Channel Island family that had been deported was a large one. In such cases the relatives in England could 'nominate' the Channel Islands Refugee's Committee as next-of-kin, and this organisation would send a parcel on their behalf. (See examples illustrated below.)

A 'PERSONAL PARCELS CENTRE' type of Form P4 of the British Red Cross Society and Order of St. John parcel post service to Prisoners of War and Internees. The example illustrated relates to a parcel sent on 22 March 1943 by the Channel Islands Refugee's Committee in London to Elsie Northey, a Channel Island internee in Biberach. The parcel was received in the camp on 27 July 1943.

3. Received Tues July 27th 2 2 MAR 1943   P/4

BRITISH RED CROSS SOCIETY AND ORDER OF ST. JOHN

PERSONAL PARCELS CENTRE.

Sent to: NORTHEY. Elsie

Service No. _____ Rank _____

Name NORTHEY Elsie

Prisoner of War No. 1080 Red Cross Ref. No. C/11845 A

Camp Address Ilag Biberach Riss Germany

CONTENTS ½ lb. Gift Chocolate added

No.	Item	No.	Item
1	shoes	—	Towel
2	stockings	—	Face
1	housewife	—	Comb
2	vests	—	Tooth Brush
2	knickers	1	Powder
1	nightgown	—	Body Powder
1	dress	—	S Towel
1	scarf	—	2 Bags
1	jacket	—	Soap
			4

10

[P.T.O.

Two distinct types of British Red Cross Contents List, Form P4, are recorded. They are easily identified as one has the contents listed on the front and the details of the Internee entered on the back of the form, while the other has the contents list and Internee's details all on the front. They are further easily differentiated, because although both are designated 'P4' in the top right corner, one is titled 'NEXT OF KIN PARCELS CENTRE', while the other is titled 'PERSONAL PARCELS CENTRE'.

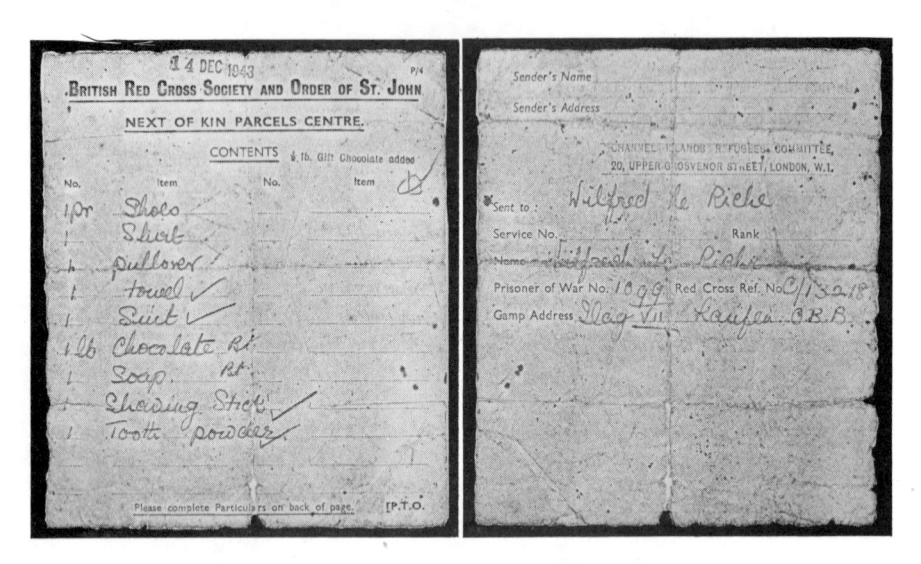

The front and reverse of the 'NEXT OF KIN PARCELS CENTRE' type of Form P4 of the British Red Cross Society and Order of St. John. The parcel was sent by the Channel Islands Refugee's Committee to Wilfred Le Riche, an Internee in Laufen.

Collectors are advised to beware of Red Cross parcel box tops or wrappers that are found in the Channel Islands. These sometimes purport to have come from personal parcels addressed and sent to either an Internee or P.o.W. camp, but they are more likely to have come from the bulk food parcels shipped directly to the Channel Islands via the S.S. VEGA from December 1944. They are an interesting souvenir for a Red Cross collection, but they are not examples of the personal parcel postal service to the Internment Camps. I have only seen one example of a genuine parcel wrapper sent to an Internment Camp. It was correctly addressed to Biberach Camp and had received a Camp Censor cachet on arrival at the camp. As very few Red Cross parcel wrappers addressed to the Internment Camps can have survived, then the only readily available record of the existence of the parcel service is a British Red Cross Contents List, Form P4, saved by an internee. Even these are very difficult to locate.

(b) **Official Red Cross Parcels from the British Empire.**

Certain countries in the British Empire, notably Canada, Australia and New Zealand, assisted with the British Red Cross Parcels schemes, and some batches of parcels from these countries were received by the Channel Islands Internees in their camps. It is unlikely that any person in these countries was nominated as 'Next of Kin' for the personal parcel scheme even though several Channel Islanders did have relatives in Canada and at least one family had relations in Australia. The parcels received by the Channel Islands Internees were the regular food parcels and some occasional 'special sending' such as clothing for babies or musical instruments. In the preceding pages under (f) *Official Mail from the International Red Cross in Geneva*, I have recorded and illustrated a postcard which relates to a shipment of musical instruments bound for Wurzach Camp from the Junior Branch of the Canadian Red Cross. It is probable that this is the only remaining postal record of the parcel services from the British Empire to a camp that held Channel Islands Internees.

(c) **Parcels from the Channel Islands to the camps via the German Feldpost.**

In the preceding chapter on the development of the mail services for the Channel Islands Internees, I have already charted the foundation and development of the parcel service from the Channel Islands to the camps. Although a service for prisoners of war had existed in the Islands for two years, the sudden exit of some 2,000 deportees in 1942 and the resulting increase in demand for a service did cause the German Postal Authorities some initial problems.

At the outset people were permitted to send any articles from a prescribed list, the weight restrictions were fairly generous, but the sender did have to pay postage when handing the parcel in to the German Feldpost. Shortly after this the weight limits were reduced and the sender had to fill in a declaration form at the British Post Office in the Islands. Eventually in March 1943 the weight restrictions were further reduced to only 5 Kilos but the parcel was sent post free and the main restrictions on contents were no money or perishable goods.

Relatives and friends in the Islands could send as many personal parcels as they wished while 'Aid Committees' were set up in both Islands to send parcels of a more general nature. The service declined, firstly when it was realised that the Internees were fairly comfortable in the camps, and then as the situation for the people in the Islands became more desperate than for their relatives in the camps. The demand for the service virtually stopped in the summer of 1944.

It is possible that parcel wrappers from this service exist, but I have never seen any. As with letters from the Channel Islands to the camps, it is unlikely that the wrappers will bear any postal markings although they should have received a cachet from the censor on entering the camp. It would be interesting for the collector to see one of the first parcel wrappers from the period when postage had to be pre-paid at the German Feldpost, but unfortunately it is very unlikely that such a wrapper will have survived until this day.

(d) **Parcels from the camps to the Channel Islands via the German Feldpost.**

There is very little record of the parcel service from the camps to the Channel Islands and I have never seen any wrapper from such a service. It is recorded that the Internees did send gifts back the Islands, these included presents that they had made, photographs (often originating in England), and food, chocolate and cigarettes saved from their Red Cross Food Parcels. It is on record that in the Christmas of 1943 some Internees were able to send a complete Red Cross Food Parcel back to their relatives in the Islands, but the International Red Cross Committee took a dim view of this and forbade it happening again, especially when some Internees had the audacity to ask for a replacement for the parcel that they had sent to the Islands.

I have not been able to discover if the parcel service from the camps was post free or what the rates were if indeed the Internees did have to pre-pay the postage. The service would have been unable to function after the summer of 1944 when the Channel Islands were isolated by the advance through Europe of the Allies.

Section II

Mail from the Channel Islands Internment Camps.

The 'Universal' Stationery used in the Internment Camps.

The 'Universal' Interniertenpost Postcard.

The 'Universal' Interniertenpost Lettersheet.

'Exceptional' Stationery used in the Internment Camps.

MAP: Location of German Internment Camps.

Dorsten Transit Camp Mail.

Biberach Internment Camp Mail.

Wurzach Internment Camp Mail.

Laufen Internment Camp Mail.

Kreuzburg Internment Camp Mail.

Liebenau Internment Camp Mail.

Compiègne and St. Denis Frontstalag Camps Mail.

Tittmoning Camp.

Other Camps.

Mail from the Channel Islands Internment Camps

Every Internee over the age of sixteen years received from the German Authorities in the Internment camps, three lettersheets and four postcards each month on which they could communicate with their relatives and friends in any part of the world. (Doctors and Priests normally received double this quota.) These lettersheets and postcards were pre-printed to a standard format similar to such stationery used in Prisoner of War camps, but with the camps' own name or number printed in a sender ('Absender') panel on each postcard or lettersheet. The service was post-free and to indicate this the stationery was headed on the address side with the printed word 'Interniertenpost'.

After the Internee had written his or her message on the card or lettersheet, it would be subject to censorship in the camp where it would receive one of the camps' own censorship cachets. Preferential treatment was afforded to the Channel Islanders and very little real censorship took place at this point, indeed the Islanders were permitted to write as many words or lines of writing as they could cram on the page, something that was strictly forbidden in the Prisoner of War camps. When the letter left the camp it might pass through a German Transit Censor Office where it would receive more German Censor cachets and perhaps stricter censoring before being forwarded to its destination. If that destination was the Channel Islands then usually nothing more happened to the communication, but if it was intended for England then it would have to pass through the British Censor before being released for delivery by the British Post Office.

Identification of the various types and printings of the 'Interniertenpost' stationery is made by reference to the layout of the heading 'Interniertenpost', the lines for the address and the 'Absender' panel found on each lettersheet or postcard. These various printings, along with the Censor Cachets peculiar to each camp are described in full detail in the following chapters dedicated to each of the individual Internment camps. British and German Censorship cachets as well as other markings found on the letters and cards are described in Section III of this book.

Prisoner of War 'Kriegsgefangenenpost' stationery was also used in the Internment camps at odd times, and this, as well as 'universal' and the various types of 'exceptional' stationery that have been found are all described in the following pages.

59

The 'Universal' Stationery used in the Internment Camps

Kriegsgefangenenpost Postcards *Type Un.Kg.P/C.1.*
Kriegsgefangenenpost Lettersheets *Type Un.Kg.L/S.1.*

Every major Prisoner of War Camp and Internee Camp run by the Germans had its own individual Post-Free Postcards and Lettersheets with the camp's own name, or number, and address preprinted in the 'Absender' panel on these cards and lettersheets. Smaller camps, temporary camps and major camps that had exhausted their own supply of stationery, would resort to the use of the 'universal' Kriegsgefangenenpost postcard or lettersheet.

I have used the term 'universal' because this stationery could be used in any of the camps throughout Germany or the Occupied countries as it did not carry a camp name in the 'Absender' panel. The Prisoner of War or the Internee would write his camp name and number in the 'Absender' panel, or it would be inserted by the Germans via the use of an Identification cachet of the camp. These 'universal' cards and lettersheets are easily identified as they bear the word 'Kriegsgefangenenpost' on the address side and have nothing pre-printed on the 'Lager-Bezeichnung' line for the camp name in the 'Absender' panel.

Numerous printings of this 'universal' postal stationery are known, but these are beyond the scope of this book and are are not relevant to the study of Channel Islands Internee Mail. However, the dates of use of this 'universal' postal stationery by the Channel Islands Internees in the Internment camps is important to this study and has been recorded where possible.

A 'universal' 'Kriegsgefangenenpost' postcard used from Biberach in October 1944.

The 'Universal' Interniertenpost postcard

Type Un.Int.P/C.1.

Although I have given this postcard the term 'universal' it is in fact a very rare example of an Interniertenpost Postcard printing, but warrants the term 'universal' as it is recorded used from more than one of the Channel Islands Internment camps.

In the winter of 1944 conditions in Germany were chaotic, and the Internment camps did not escape from the effects of this chaos. The postal services for the Internees had virtually dried up and most of the various camps' stationery had long been exhausted. It was at this time that the Germans produced a 'universal' postcard intended for use in any of the Internment camps. At first only one or two examples were recorded from Wurzach used in November 1944, and it was thought that this was a printing peculiar to that camp, but more recently an example has been found used from Laufen in April 1945 and so the printing, although very rare, must be regarded as 'universal'.

An example of the 'universal' Interniertenpost Postcard used from Wurzach Internment camp in November 1944.

(a) At the top of the Postcard on the address side the capital 'P' of the word 'Postkarte' appears beneath the letters 'In' at the beginning of the word 'Interniertenpost'.

(b) In the 'Absender' panel the camp name is missing after the words 'Lager-Bezeichnung:'.

The 'Universal' Interniertenpost Lettersheet
Type Un.Int.L/S.1.

It is probable that a 'universal' lettersheet printing, as well as the postcard printing, was made by the Germans, but examples of such a lettersheet used from more than one Internment camp have yet to be recorded.

A lettersheet exists used from Laufen Internment camp in April 1945, which could well have been intended as a 'universal' printing as it bears no printing of the camp name in the 'Absender' panel. I have recorded it as Laufen printing Type Lf.L/S.4. because its recorded use is confined to that camp and even if it was intended as a 'universal' printing there may not have been enough time to distribute it to the other Internment camps as the example recorded was used only a few days before Laufen was liberated.

'Exceptional' stationery used in the Internment Camps.

In addition to the normal postcards and lettersheets printed for each Internment camp, certain 'exceptional' stationery was also printed in some camps. This stationery was 'exceptional' in that it was produced for a specific purpose, and was issued in excess of the normal monthly quota of postcards and lettersheets, but usually left no room for any private message beyond that of the Internee's signature.

The most common forms of 'exceptional' stationery were Christmas cards with some form of illustration on the message side, and 'Receipt of Package' cards with which the Internee could thank a relative at home for sending a parcel and at the same time list on the card the contents that he had found in the parcel.

Such examples of 'exceptional' stationery are more commonly found from the Prisoner of War camps (see illustration in chapter 'German Prisoner of War Camps'), but the Channel Islands Internment Camp at Laufen is also known to have issued such stationery. The examples originating from Laufen are described in detail in the following pages on Laufen Internment Camp mail.

I have also classified certain other unusual postcards or usages as 'exceptional' although they do not fall within my own classification of 'exceptional' printings.

Both Biberach and Wurzach camps issued postcards to their Internees that had originated in the camps during an earlier time when they were Prisoner of War camps. Such postcards have very different printings from the 'Interniertenpost' stationery and are described in detail in the relevant chapters following.

'Exceptional' usages of 'Interniertenpost' stationery took place in some camps, notably Laufen, where postcards and lettersheets from other camps were used in the camp for brief periods during shortages of the camps' own stationery; again, such usages are described in detail in the following pages.

Location of German Internment Camps.
European Boundaries as of 1939

DORSTEN TRANSIT CAMP MAIL

Mail from the Transit Internment Camp at Dorsten is very scarce for a variety of reasons.

In the main only the Internees deported from Guernsey actually went to Dorsten and these Internees were only there for six or seven weeks before being transferred and reunited with the other Channel Islands Internees in Southern Germany. During their six weeks at Dorsten the Internees were probably only permitted to send one postcard to their relatives and those that are recorded were written on 4 and 5 October 1942, but were not released by the Germans from the camp until 26 the 27 October 1942.

A Prisoner of War British Censorship 'Intercept' of 8 November 1942 records examining 38 first letter cards (postcards) on 6 November 1942. These postcards from Dorsten were written on 4 and 5 October, postmarked 26 October 1942 and censored in the camp by German Examiner No 13. A second batch of cards written on the same dates, but postmarked 27 October and censored this time by German Censor No 12 were examined by the British Censor on 12 November 1942. The British Government eventually announced that eight hundred of these postcards had arrived in England by 18 November 1942, and it is thought that less than that number had already been delivered in the Channel Islands on 9 November 1942. Given the knowledge that this maximum of fifteen hundred cards bear no mention of Internee camps or Internee mail, but were 'Kriegsgefangenenpost' Postcards of Stalag VIF, censored with Oflag VIE censor cachets, one can easily understand why it was not until 1979 that a card was actually identified and recorded from a Channel Islands Internee at Dorsten.

Since the discovery of that first postcard, two others have been recorded and all three are of a similar format and date. Doubtless others exist, but as they are easily mistaken for Prisoner of War mail and are also the earliest items of mail from the Internees, it is not surprising that few have survived until this day.

Some confusion arises when trying to identify Dorsten mail because the Channel Islands Internees state that they were in Stalag VIF at Dorsten, but this is a contradiction as Stalag VIF was Bocholt P.O.W. Camp, while Oflag VIE was Dorsten P O.W. Officer Camp. The confusion increases because the mail from the Internees is Stalag VIF postcards, but with the Oflag VIE censor cachet. These two camps were very close together in north Germany and some camps in the north of Germany were closing at this time and their inmates were being transferred further south to areas from which it was more difficult for them to escape. Dorsten camp was already empty when the first batch of Internees arrived and it could be that these two camps had been amalgamated using the name and censor cachets of Dorsten but the number and postal stationery of Bocholt.

Dorsten Postcard Printing
(Type Do.P/C.1.)

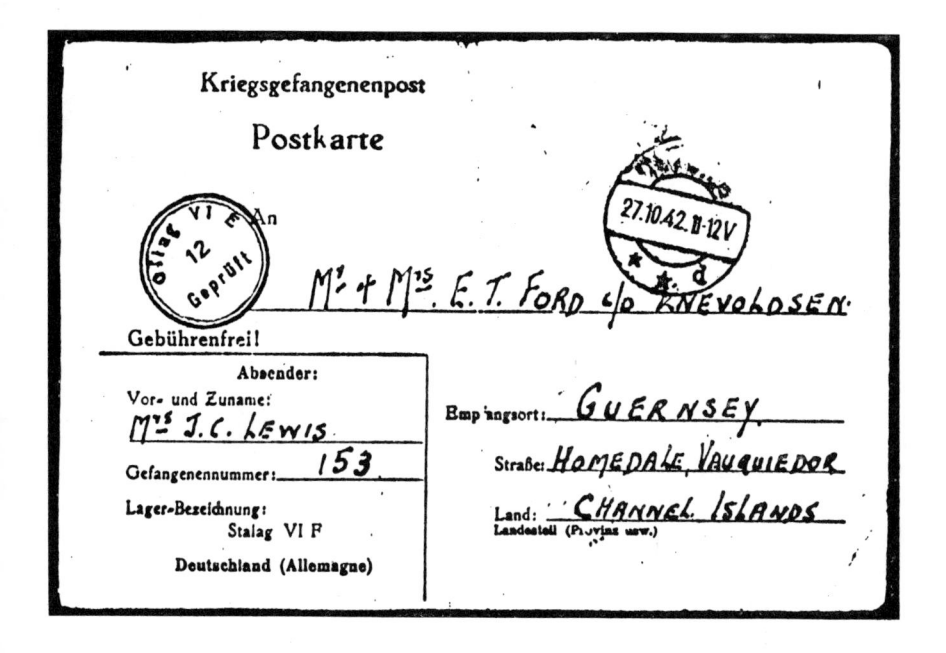

```
Kriegsgefangenenpost
       Postkarte

An
            Mr & Mrs. E. T. FORD c/o KNEVOLOSEN
Gebührenfrei!
        Absender:
Vor- und Zuname:              Empfangsort: GUERNSEY
Mrs J. C. LEWIS
Gefangenennummer: 153         Straße: HOMEDALE, VAUQUIEDOR
Lager-Bezeichnung:            Land: CHANNEL ISLANDS
        Stalag VI F           Landesteil (Provinz usw.)
   Deutschland (Allemagne)
```

The Postcard in use at Dorsten was a printing in common with most of the cards in use at other Prisoner of War camps. It bore the direction 'Kriegsgefangenenpost' (not 'Interniertenpost') and the camp designation 'Stalag VIF' in the 'Absender' panel.

It should be noted that Channel Islands Internee Mail can only originate from Dorsten during the six weeks from the beginning of October to the second week of November in 1942.

Dorsten Censor Cachet

Type Do.C.1: A double circle cachet; the thin inner circle has a diameter of 21 m.m., while the thick outer circle has a maximum diameter of 23.5 m.m. Inside the circle, in Roman letters, is the legend:

Oflag VE
12
Geprüft

The letters of 'Oflag VIE' are 1 m.m. and 2 m.m. high, the figures of '12' are 2.5 m.m. high and the letters of 'Geprüft' are 1.5 m.m. and 2.5 m.m. high.

This cachet was struck in violet and is recorded on Internee mail in October 1942.

UNRECORDED

Type Do.C.2: The British Censor recorded cards from Channel Islands Internees at Dorsten with a German censor cachet No 13 applied to them.

Details of this cachet are not known as one has yet to be recorded.

Dorsten Postmark

Type Do.P.M.1: A 'dumb' double circle postmark 26 m.m. wide and with the inner circle 15 m.m. wide. The inner circle is broken by an open bar 10 m.m. wide which crosses the centre of the postmark. Within this bar is the date followed by three code numbers one of which is a Roman figure; all these figures are 4 m.m. high. Below the bar and between the two circles appear two, five pointed stars and the letter 'd', while above the bar the two circles seem to be blocked in. The three examples recorded of this mark are all very poor strikes, but in a good example, this blocking could be a town name.

Type Do.P.M.1. is found struck in black and the only recorded date on Channel Islands Internee mail is 27.10.42. followed by the code letters 11–12 V, however the British Censor recorded this postmark used on the first batch of Channel Islands Internee mail from Dorsten on 26.10.42., but he did not record the code letters used with it.

BIBERACH INTERMENT CAMP MAIL

As with many of the other major Internment Camps and Prisoner of War Camps, Biberach Camp had its own individual Internee Post-Free Postcards and Lettersheets which had the camp's address preprinted in the 'Absender' panel on these cards and lettersheets.

The first messages sent from Biberach camp were on the 'universal' Kriegsgefangenenpost postcard or lettersheet; the earliest date recorded is 8 December 1942 and they remained in use until February 1943. The camp address was either handwritten in the 'Absender' panel or printed with Biberach cachet Type Bb.C.3.

In February 1943 Biberach introduced its own Interniertenpost Post-Free Postcards and Lettersheets. Six different printings of the Lettersheets and four different printings of the Postcards are recorded. No unusual items of stationery were used in the camp except for an 'exceptional' postcard printing in April 1943.

By October 1944 Biberach's own Printed Stationery was completely exhausted and so the 'universal' Kriegsgefangenenpost postcard was reintroduced and remained in use almost until the liberation of the camp in April 1945. Throughout this period Biberach cachets Type Bb.C.7. and Bb.C.8. were used to identify the camp in the 'Absender' panel on the card, while Biberach cachet Type Bb.C.3. was used as an identification cachet and a censor cachet.

Biberach had a proliferation of Cachets, nine types in all, and their use was somewhat indiscriminate as Identification cachets were also often used as Censor cachets.

Five different types of postmarks are recorded on mail from Biberach Internment camp, but many items of mail left the camp without being postmarked. Mail from Wurzach was usually brought to Biberach for censoring and so it also bears the Biberach postmarks.

Biberach Lettersheet Printings

There were six different printings of the 'Interniertenpost' Lettersheet used at Biberach camp. All the printings are basically the same although the first and last printings are the most individual. The length of the lettersheet averages

The printing on a Biberach Lettersheet.

about 340 m.m. and the width is 147 m.m., however there are length variations of up to 5 m.m. and as the same printing can be found with different sizes, the printings cannot be identified by size. All the lettersheets have ruled lines on one side for correspondence. The other side is headed 'Interniertenpost' and has an address panel of six lines and an 'Absender' panel of five lines printed on it. When the lettersheet is folded into three and the flap is tucked into a slit, it forms the closed lettersheet with the address panel on one side and the sender's name and camp address on the reverse. All the lettersheets have twenty four lines for correspondence except for Type 1 which has twenty five lines.

The main aid to identification of the six types of lettersheet is the 'Absender' panel on the reverse of the folded lettersheet.

The layout for this 'Absender' panel is five lines of printing in the following format:

Absender:
Vor-und Zuname: _____
Internierten Nr.:_____
Lager-Bezeichnung: Internierungslager Biberach/Riss.
Deutschland (Allemagne)

Type Bb.L/S.1.

Absender:

Vor- und Zuname: _____

Interniertennummer: _____

Lager-Bezeichnung: Internierungslager Biberach / Riss

Deutschland (Allemagne)

This is the most individual and easiest of the lettersheets to identify.

(a) There are 25 lines on the correspondence side.
(b) The beginnings of the first four lines of printing in the 'Absender' panel are all in line beneath each other.
(c) The third line has the full printing of the word 'Interniertennummer:'
(d) The last three words are 1 m.m. lower than the first two in the line: 'Lager-Bezeichnung: Internierungslager Biberach/Riss'

Because of its early use this is one of the less common forms and is recorded in use from February to May 1943.

Type Bb.L/S.2.

Absender:

Vor- und Zuname: _____

Internierten Nr.: _____

Lager-Bezeichnung: Internierungslager Biberach / Riss

Deutschland (Allemagne)

(a) There are 24 lines on the correspondence side.

(b) The beginnings of the first four lines of printing in the 'Absender' panel are all in line beneath each other.

(c) There are three dots after 'Nr.:' in the shortened 'Internierten Nr.:'

(d) The words in the line:
'Lager-Bezeichnung: Internierungslager Biberach/Riss' are all on the same straight line.

This lettersheet was in use from June until October 1943 and was reprinted and again used in June 1944.

Type Bb.L/S.3.

Absender:

Vor- und Zuname: _____

Internierten Nr. _____

Lager-Bezeichnung: Internierungslager Biberach / Riss

Deutschland (Allemagne)

(a) There are 24 lines on the correspondence side.
(b) The beginnings of the first four lines of printing in the 'Absender' panel are all in line beneath each other.
(c) There is only one dot after 'Nr.' in the shortened 'Internierten Nr.'
(d) The last three words are 1 m.m. lower than the first two in the line: 'Lager-Bezeichnung: Internierungslager Biberach/Riss'.
(e) There is a 'spur' on the end of the line after 'Vor-und Zuname:'. This line is also thicker than in other printings.

Types Bb.L/S.3. and Bb.L/S.4. were used partly concurrently. Type Bb.L/S.3. was in use from December 1943 until April 1944.

Type Bb.L/S.4.

Absender:

Vor- und Zuname: _____

In·ernierten N͟r - _____

Lager-Bezeichnung: Internierungslager Biberach / Riss

Deutschland (Allemagne)

(a) There are 24 lines on the correspondence side.

(b) The beginnings of the first four lines of printing in the 'Absender' panel are all in line beneath each other.

(c) The 'Nr' of the shortened 'Internierten Nr.' is faulty so that part of the 'r' and any dots are missing.

(d) The last three words are 1 m.m. lower than the first two in the line: 'Lager-Bezeichnung: Internierungslager Biberach/Riss'.

(e) The bottoms of the double letters 's' in 'Biberach/Riss' are partly missing.

This lettersheet was used partly concurrently with Type Bb.L/S.3. but Type Bb.L/S.4. was in use from January to April 1944.

Type Bb.L/S.5.

Absender:

Vor- und Zuname: _____

Internierten Nr.: _____

Lager-Bezeichnung: Internierungslager Biberach / Riss

Deutschland (Allemagne)

(a) There are 24 lines on the correspondence side.
(b) The beginnings of the first four lines of printing in the 'Absender' panel are all in line beneath each other.
(c) There are three dots after 'Nr.:' in the shortened 'Internierten Nr.:'
(d) The last three words are 1 m.m. lower than the first two in the line: 'Lager-Bezeichnung: Internierungslager Biberach/Riss'.
(e) There is a large 7 m.m. gap between the last three words and the first two in the line:
'Lager-Bezeichnung: Internierungslager Biberach/Riss'

This is quite an uncommon printing as I can only record examples used at the end of May 1944.

Type Bb.L/S.6.

Absender:

Vor- und Zuname: —————————————————————

Internierten Nr.: ——————————

Lager-Bezeichnung: Internierungslager Biberach / Riss

Deutschland (Allemagne)

(a) There are 24 lines on the correspondence side.
(b) The word 'Internierten' is 5 m.m. out of alignment with the beginnings of the other first four lines in the 'Absender' panel.
(c) There are three dots after 'Nr.:' in the shortened 'Internierten Nr.:'
(d) The last three words are 1 m.m. higher than the first two in the line: 'Lager-Bezeichnung: Internierungslager Biberach/Riss'

I can record this lettersheet used from August 1944 until February 1945 but it was probably in use until the liberation of the camp in April 1945 as unused examples of it exist.

Biberach Postcard Printings

Biberach had four distinctive printings of the Postcard, but their size was common, 149 m.m. by 97 m.m. and on the reverse they all had twelve lines for the message and the word 'Internierungslager' in the top left corner and 'Datum:' with a line, in the top right corner.

The identification of the four types of printing is made by the position of the wording on the address side of the card.

Type Bb.P/C.1.

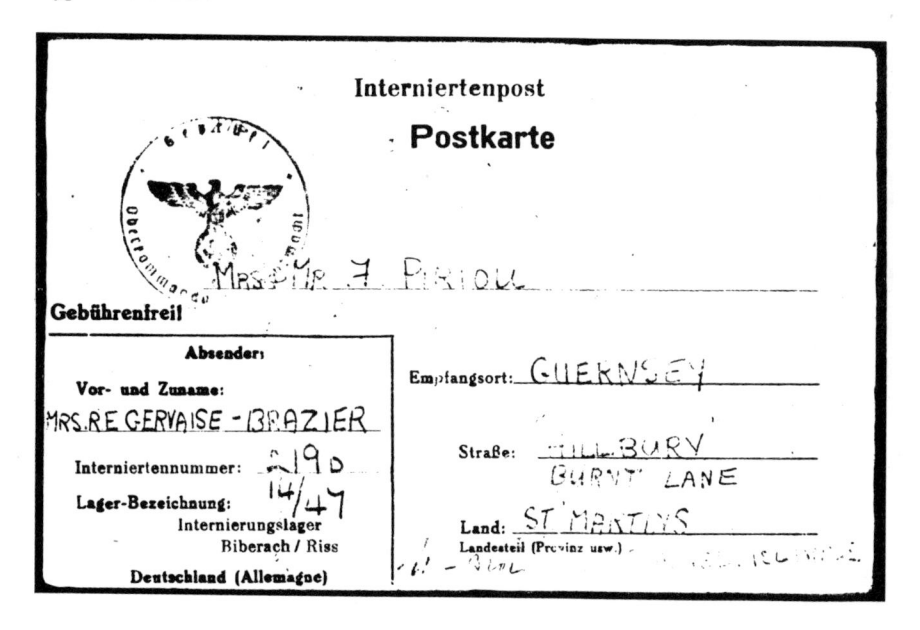

```
                    Interniertenpost
                      Postkarte

                         MR J PIRIOU
Gebührenfrei
        Absender:                Empfangsort: GUERNSEY
   Vor- und Zuname:
MRS R E GERVAISE - BRAZIER
                                 Straße: TILLBURY
   Interniertennummer: 2190              BURNT LANE
   Lager-Bezeichnung: 14/47
          Internierungslager    Land: ST MARTINS
             Biberach / Riss    Landesteil (Provinz usw.)
      Deutschland (Allemagne)
```

(a) At the top of the Postcard on the address side the capital 'P' of 'Postkarte' appears beneath the letters 'rn' near the centre of the word 'Interniertenpost'.

(b) In the three lines for the address there is a space of 4 m.m. between the word 'Straße:' and its following line.

(c) In the 'Absender' panel the camp address appears in two lines:—

'Internierungslager
Biberach/Riss'

This card is recorded in use from February to June 1943 and was used partly concurrently with Type Bb.P/C.2.

75

Type Bb.P/C.2.

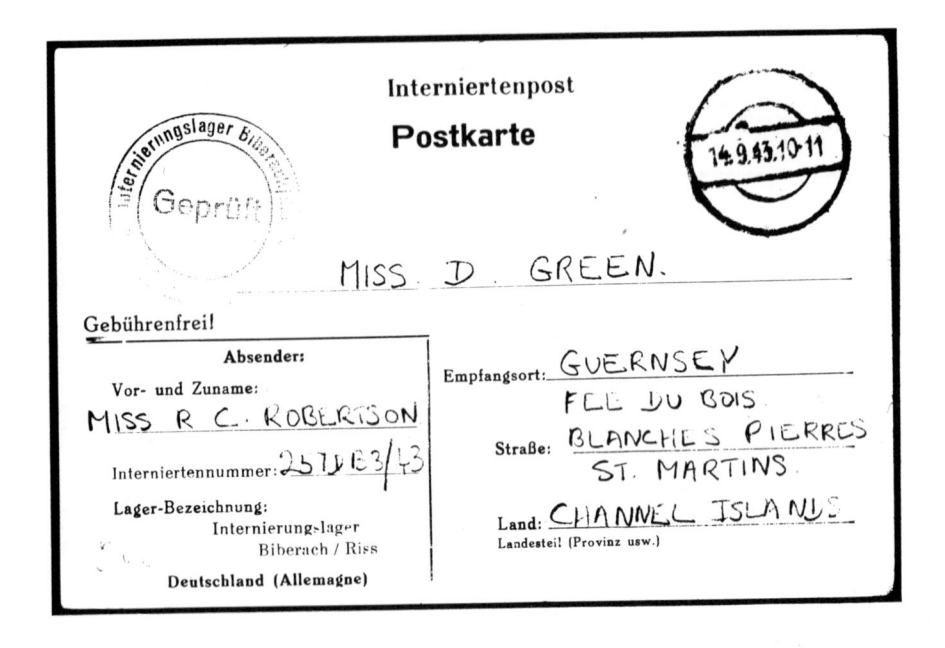

```
            Interniertenpost
              Postkarte            [postmark 14.9.43.10-11]
[stamp: Internierungslager Biberach / Geprüft]

                    MISS D. GREEN.

Gebührenfrei!
        Absender:              Empfangsort: GUERNSEY
Vor- und Zuname:                            FLL DU BOIS
  MISS R C. ROBERTSON           Straße: BLANCHES PIERRES
  Interniertennummer: 25TJB3/43          ST. MARTINS.
Lager-Bezeichnung:              Land: CHANNEL ISLANDS
   Internierungs-lager          Landesteil (Provinz usw.)
        Biberach / Riss
     Deutschland (Allemagne)
```

(a) At the top of the postcard on the address side the capital 'P' of 'Postkarte' appears beneath the capital 'I' of the word 'Interniertenpost'.

(b) In the three lines for the address there is a space of 4 m.m. between the word 'Staße:' and its following line.

(c) In the 'Absender' panel the camp address appears in two lines:

'Internierungslager
     Biberach/Riss'

This card is recorded in use in March and October 1943.

Type Bb.P/C.3.

(a) At the top of the postcard on the address side the capital 'P' of 'Postkarte' appears beneath the capital 'I' of the word 'Interniertenpost'.

(b) In the three lines for the address there is a space of 4 m.m. between the word 'Staße:' and its following line.

(c) In the 'Absender' panel the camp address appears as one single line:

'Internierungslager Biberach/Riss.'

This card is the most common and is recorded in use from October 1943 through to September 1944.

Type Bb.P/C.4.

```
                    Interniertenpost
                    Postkarte


                         _____

 Gebührenfrei!
         Absender:              Empfangsort:_____
   Vor- und Zuname:

                                Straße:_____
   Interniertennummer: _____
   Lager-Bezeichnung:           Land:_____
     Internierungslager Biberach / Riss    Landesteil (Provinz usw.)

       Deutschland (Allemagne)
```

(a) At the top of the postcard on the address side the capital 'P' of 'Postkarte' appears beneath the capital 'I' of the word 'Interniertenpost'.

(b) In the three lines for the address there is a space of only 1 m.m. between the word 'Straße:' and its following line.

(c) In the 'Absender' panel the camp address appears as one single line:

'Internierungslager Biberach/Riss'

This card is the scarcest of the Postcard Printings from Biberach and appears to be a reprint of Type Bb.P/C.3. I can only record its use in April 1945 at the time of the liberation of the camp, and as mint examples also exist amongst the effects of repatriated Channel Islands Internees, it is probable that this card was issued so close to the time of the liberation of the camp that few examples had a chance to be used.

Biberach 'Exceptional' Stationery

Although Biberach was a large Internment camp, the variety of stationery emanating from it was not very diverse. There were no true 'exceptional' printings of stationery as can be found from Laufen, and the only different item, besides the 'universal' Kriegsgefangenenpost lettersheets and postcards, is a postcard that was printed for use during an earlier period when the camp was an Officer Prisoner of War camp, before the Internees were sent there.

Type Bb.P/C.5.

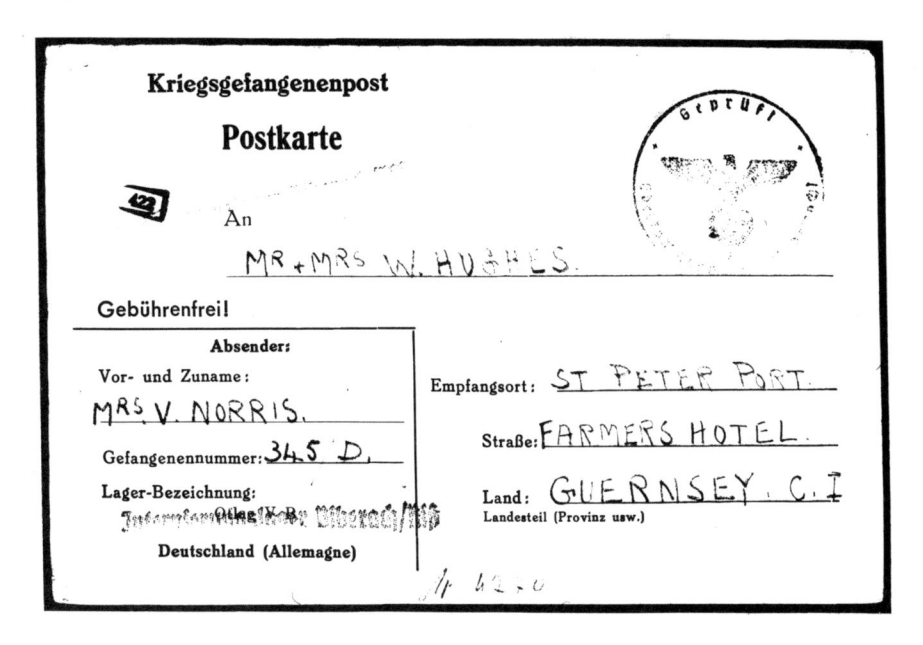

The postcard is easily identifiable as although it is headed 'Kriegsgefangenenpost' like all the 'universal' stationery, in the 'Absender' panel there is pre-printed the camp identification 'Oflag VB' of Biberach Officers' camp.

The only example recorded was used from the camp in April 1943, and the camp number 'Oflag VB' has been overprinted with Biberach Identification cachet Bb.C.3. This postcard is unusual in that it was not used during a shortage of other camp stationery, but was used concurrently with Biberach Postcard printings Bb.P/C.1. and Bb.P/C.2. As the writer of the card states, 'We are getting extra letters and cards now, so will be able to write you more often', it is probable that the camp authorities decided to use up old stocks of camp stationery that they still had in the camp.

It is interesting that the camp authorities did not issue this postcard when the Internees first arrived in the camp. All the recorded first messages are on the 'universal' Kriegsgefangenenpost postcards, and two printings of the camp's own Interniertenpost postcards were issued before they decided to use this card.

Biberach Cachets and Censor Cachets

Although I have recorded 9 cachets used on mail associated with Biberach camp, only three of these Bb.C.4., Bb.C.5. and Bb.C.6. are genuine censor cachets. All the others are identification cachets of the camp although some have obviously been used in a censorship capacity.

Type Bb.C.1: A 33 m.m. single circle cachet with a spread-winged eagle above a laurelled swastika in centre, and Gothic script around the edge of the circle reading: 'Internierungslager + Biberach/Riß +'. This cachet was printed in violet and is very rare, the only recorded examples being used in December 1942. It has the appearance of a military unit handstamp as normally applied to identify German soldiers' Feldpost Mail and I believe it was probably applied to a batch of Internee Mail in error, or else used in this early period as a 'stop-gap' measure before the camp had time to produce a proper cachet for censoring the Internee's Mail. It is known that the camps were rather taken by surprise with the arrival of the Channel Island Civilians and it was some time before adequate facilities were available.

Type Bb.C.2: A large double, straight line cachet in Gothic script. The top line reads 'Internierungslager', 57 m.m. long, and centred underneath is: 'Biberach/Riß', 41 m.m. long. The overall height of the cachet is 14 m.m., the capitals are 6 m.m. high and the lower case letters are 4 m.m. high. Printed in violet and seen in use in early 1943, this cachet is usually found used as the censor cachet in conjunction with Bb.C.3. in the sender panel of the letter or card.

Internierungslager Biberach/Riß

Type Bb.C.3: A straight line cachet 56 m.m. long in Gothic script with lower case letters 3 m.m. high and capitals 4 m.m. high, reading: 'Internierungslager Biberach/Riß'. This cachet is printed in violet and has been recorded in use from January to June 1943. This mark is sometimes used as a censor cachet in its own right, while in other examples it is seen used in conjunction with Bb.C.2. when it is then used in the sender panel of Kriegsgefangenenpost Lettersheets and Cards. It is interesting to note that in all the examples recorded, the cachet has never been seen used with a Biberach Town Postmark.

Type Bb.C.4. and Type Bb.C.4a: A 33 m.m. double circle cachet with 23 m.m. across the inner circle. This is the only genuine 'censor' cachet of Biberach with 'Geprüft' written in Roman script across the centre of the cachet and: 'Internierungslager Biberach/Riß *Postüberwachung*' between the two circles around the edge. This mark is printed in violet and is the most common of the Biberach cachets, seen in use from September 1943 through to February 1945. Probably more than one of these cachets were in use but it is not possible to differentiate between them as differences in measurement are less than 1 m.m. and the cachet itself was probably made of rubber and therfore liable to distortion. An individual cancellor can be identified by its squat appearance and a kink in the inner circle above the first 'ü' in the word 'Postüberwachung'. (Bb.C.4a.)

Type Bb.C.5: A 33 m.m. double circle cachet, identicial to Bb.C.4. but printed in blue-black and used to censor incoming mail to the camp.

D 22

Type Bb.C.6: Type Bb.C.6. is merely the code 'D22' in Roman script that is 5 m.m. high. Struck in blue/black in late 1944, this cachet is only recorded on incoming mail to the camp from the United Kingdom and is seen used in conjunction with Bb.C.5. The significance of this individual censor cachet code is not yet understood but its recorded use is rare and it was definitely applied at Biberach using the same ink as used with cachet Bb.C.5.

Type Bb.C.6a: A tidy-minded German Censor fooled me with the first example of this cachet that I saw, as he had neatly applied it beneath the word 'Geprüft' of cachet Bb.C.5. and for a while I thought I had identified a new censor cachet (Bb.C.6a.). However, other recorded examples show the use of Bb.C.6. with Bb.C.5. but in various positions on the covers so that there was obviously no actual cachet Bb.C.6a.

Zivilinternierungslager Biberach/Riß

Type Bb.C.7: A straight line cachet 61 m.m. long with Roman script 3 m.m. high and capitals of 4 m.m. reading: 'Zivilinternierungslager Biberach/Riß'. Printed in violet the cachet is seen used late in 1944 on Kriegsgefangenenpost Lettersheets and Cards in the sender's panel, where it identifies the camp. Bb.C.4. is the censor cachet usually seen in conjunction with this cachet.

Biberach an der Riß

Type Bb.C.8: A straight line cachet 34 m.m. long with Roman script 2 m.m. high and capitals of 3 m.m. reading 'Biberach an der Riß'. Printed in violet the cachet is seen used in late 1944 on Kriegsgefangenenpost Cards in the senders' panel, where it identifies the camp. Bb.C.4. is the censor cachet seen used in conjunction with this cachet.

Interniertenpoft

Type Bb.C.9: A straight line cachet 31 m.m. long consisting of the one word: 'Interniertenpoft' in Gothic script 4 m.m. high with capitals 5 m.m. high, and struck in violet.

Letters posted from the camp to addresses within Germany could be sent in plain envelopes. They would be censored in the normal way, probably with cachet Bb.C.4., and this single line 'Interniertenpost', cachet would be applied to denote that the letter could travel free of postage. Such letters are naturally very scarce since few internees would have cause to write to people in Germany, however at least one example is recorded addressed to an internee who was taken seriously ill and transferred to Biberach town hospital for treatment.

Biberach Postmarks

Although I have recorded five different types of postmarks on mail from Biberach camp, not necessarily all mail carries postmarks. In particular, early mail from the camp in 1942 and also 'Kriegsgefangenenpost' lettersheets and cards from the camp are found without any postmark.

Type Bb.P.M.1: A 'dumb' double circle postmark 28 m.m. wide and the inner circle, 16 m.m. wide. The inner circle is broken by an an open bar 9 m.m. wide which crosses the centre of the postmark. This bar consists of two lines, the top one of which displays damage and has a break of about 8 m.m. in it. Within this bar is the date followed by two, usually double digit numbers; all these figures being 3 m.m. high. The most common of the double digits is '10–11', so for a date in October 1943 the post mark would read 5.10.43. 10–11. Other double digit numbers recorded are 9–10, 10–10, 11–12, 15–16, 16–17 and 17–18 but these do not signify different postmarks as all the examples recorded are from the same postmark identified by the damage to the top line of the bar crossing its circle.

Type Bb.P.M.1. is the most common postmark that was in use, it is always found struck in black and is recorded on mail to the Channel Islands and to the United Kingdom from September 1943 through to May 1944.

Type Bb.P.M.2: A double circle postmark 28 m.m. wide with an unbroken inner circle 18 m.m. wide. Around the edge, between the two circles runs the inscription: 'BIBERACH (RISS)' in Roman Capitals 2.5 m.m. high with the letter 'a' in lower case at the bottom of the circle. Across the centre of the circle, but within the inner circle runs a bar consisting of two lines 9 m.m. wide, the bottom line of which displays damage with a break of about 3 m.m. Within this bar is the date followed by one double digit number, the figures of which are 3 m.m. high. The digits recorded are –9, 14 and 20.

84

This postmark Type Bb.P.M.2. is one of the local 'town' postmarks of Biberach. It is struck in black and is found on camp mail to destinations within Germany and also on mail to the United Kingdom in late 1944 (i.e. after the invasion of Europe by the Allies). It has not been recorded on camp mail to the Channel Islands.

Type Bb.P.M.3: A double circle postmark that is identical to Type Bb.P.M.2. but for the figure '1' at the bottom of the circle in place of the letter 'a', and for the lack of damage to the bottom line forming the date bar across the circle. The digits recorded after the date in the bar on this postmark have been 9, 11 and 12.

This postmark Type Bb.P.M.3. is another local 'town' postmark of Biberach. It is struck in black and has only been recorded on mail with a United Kingdom destination in late 1944. I have discovered one 'Interniertenpost' postcard from Wurzach camp in November 1944 addressed to Jersey, which has this postmark Bb.P.M.3. struck on it, but it is evident that it did not go straight to Jersey but went via the United Kingdom as it has a British Censor 'Crown over PASSED P.128' struck in crimson on it.

UNRECORDED

Type Bb.P.M.4: I have only been able to note this mark but have not had the opportunity to record it properly.

It is a postmark similar to Types Bb.P.M.2. and Bb.P.M.3. but with the 'Biberach (Riss)' inscription in a larger and more fancy type face, probably Gothic.

Again I believe this postmark Type Bb.P.M.4. was struck in black and was only in use on mail to the United Kingdom in late 1944.

Type Bb.P.M.5: On 23 April 1945, Biberach was liberated by troops of the 1st Free French Army, attached to the VIIth U.S. Army Group. Internee mail was no longer handled by the Germans and so some letters and cards from the camp received a French Army postmark rather than a Biberach postmark. Covers with the French Army postmark are very rare but one 'Interniertenpost' post card from the camp has been recorded addressed to the United Kingdom and dated 28 April 1945, five days after the camp's liberation.

85

The postmark is a single circle 27 m.m. wide, with the inscription running around the edge in Roman Capitals 3 m.m. high: 'POSTE AUX ARMEES' and with an eight pointed star at the bottom of the circle. The date is in the centre of the circle in two lines of numbers each 3 m.m. high. The first line has the day and month, 28–4 and the second has the year 45.

This postmark Type Bb.P.M.5. is of course not a 'true' Biberach postmark, but a postmark from another source found in use on mail from the camp.

WURZACH INTERNMENT CAMP MAIL

In the same manner that Biberach and Laufen Internment Camps had their own printed stationery, so Wurzach Internment Camp had its own individual Internee Post-Free Postcards and Lettersheets with the camp's address preprinted in the 'Absender' panel on both these types of stationery. The layout of the Lettersheets and Postcards is similar to those from Biberach and Laufen Camps (see introductions to 'Biberach Lettersheet Printings' and 'Biberach Postcard Printings') and there is only one 'exceptional' type of postal stationery recorded from Wurzach Camp.

The 'universal' Kriegsgefangenenpost Postcard and Lettersheet are unknown used from Wurzach camp and seem to have been replaced by the 'exceptional' Wurzach Camp stationery which actually originated in the Officer Prisoner of War Camp at Wurzach and so also bears the word 'Kriegsgefangenenpost'. This exceptional stationery was a bilingual, preprinted, reply postcard (described below as Type Wz.P/C.3.) which was first used when the Channel Islands Internees arrived at the camp and again later when supplies of the Wurzach Internment Camp Stationery ran out. The earliest surviving recorded messages from Wurzach of 30 December 1942 are on this 'exceptional' stationery and it was again in use in June and July 1943.

I have recorded three different printings of the 'Interniertenpost' Lettersheet, and two different printings of the 'Interniertenpost' Postcard from Wurzach, but this does not preclude the existence of others because although Wurzach camp was a major camp as far as the Channel Islands Internees are concerned, it was still a small Internee Camp, and examples of Internee Mail from the camp are not easily found today, so it is likely that not all types of stationery have been recorded.

Wurzach Internee mail was sent to Biberach Camp for censoring and so the Wurzach cachets that are found struck on Internee postcards and lettersheets are really Identification cachets rather than Censor cachets. Only three Wurzach cachets are recorded on the mail, but it is usually also overprinted with Biberach cachets which were applied during censoring. Some items of mail can be found originating from Wurzach but bearing only the Biberach censor's cachets, the collector should always be careful therefore to also check the printing of the card or lettersheet to help verify its origin.

As the Wurzach Internee mail was posted from Biberach after censoring in that camp, the only postmarks recorded on Wurzach mail are those found at Biberach. The few items of mail that are recorded posted straight from Wurzach bear no postmarks and so no Wurzach postmark has been recorded on Internee mail. This is a further complication in the identification of mail that has originated in Wurzach Internee camp.

Wurzach Lettersheet Printings

Type Wz.L/S.1.

Absender:

Vor- und Zuname: _____ _____

Internierten Nr.: ___ _____ _____

Lager-Bezeichnung: Internierungslager Wurzach / Allgäu

Deutschland (Allemagne)

(a) Above the address section of the lettersheet, the word 'Interniertenpost' has a damaged letter 'o'.

In the 'Absender' panel:

(b) The abbreviated word 'Internierten Nr.' appears.

(c) The camp name 'Internierungslager Wurzach/Allgäu', follows 3.5 m.m. after the words 'Lager-Bezeichnung:' and all the words are on the same level.

This lettersheet is probably the most common of the printings from Wurzach; it has been recorded in use from October 1943 until March 1944.

Type *Wz.L/S.2.*

Absender:

Vor- und Zuname: ___

Internierten Nr.:

Lager-Bezeichnung: Internierungslager Wurzach / Allgäu

Deutschland (Allemagne)

(a) Above the address section of the lettersheet, the word 'Interniertenpost' appears undamaged, although some examples may be found with damage to the first letter 'n'.

In the 'Absender' panel:

(b) The abbreviated word 'Internierten Nr.' appears.

(c) The camp name 'Internierungslager Wurzach/Allgäu', follows 8 m.m. after the words 'Lager-Bezeichnung:' and has lifted almost 1 m.m.

This lettersheet has been recorded in use in August 1944.

Type Wz.L/S.3.

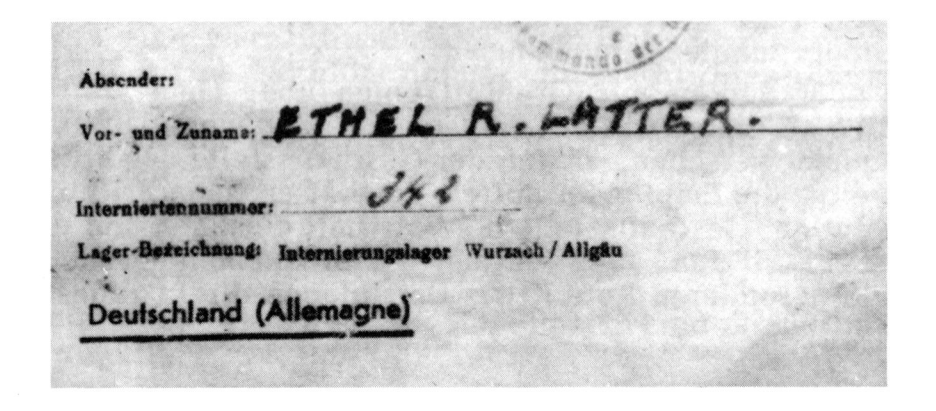

```
Absender:
Vor- und Zuname: ETHEL R. LATTER.
Interniertennummer: 342
Lager-Bezeichnung: Internierungslager Wurzach / Allgäu
Deutschland (Allemagne)
```

I have not been able to fully record an example of this printing, but the following information is taken from a photograph of this lettersheet which appears in:

'Neues Handbruch Der Briefmarkenkunde, Heft 39.
KANAL-INSELN (1940–1945)' by Heinz Mohle.

(a) Above the address section of the lettersheet, the word 'Interniertenpost' appears undamaged.

In the 'Absender' panel:

(b) The full word 'Interniertennummer' appears.

(c) The camp name 'Internierungslager Wurzach/Allgäu', follows about 3 m.m. after the words 'Lager-Bezeichnung:' and has dropped about 1 m.m.

I can only record the one example of this lettersheet that is photographed in the Handbook by Mohle. No date is given for the lettersheet, but as the full word 'Interniertennummer' appears in the 'Absender' panel and there is no Post Office datestamp on the letter it could well have been an early usage, probably before Type Wz.L/S.1. recorded above.

Wurzach Postcard Printings

Type Wz.P/C.1.

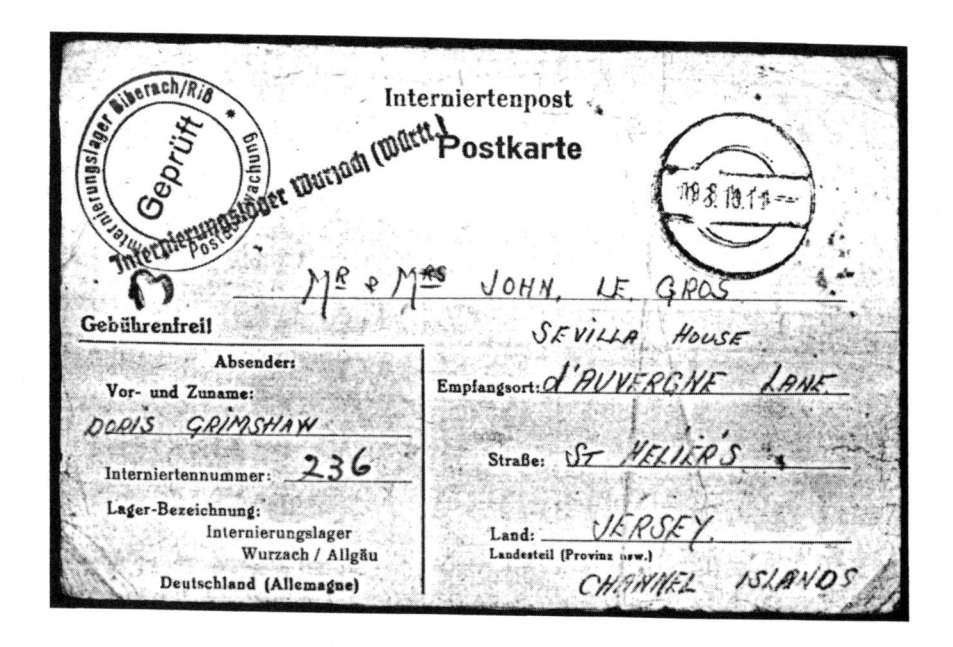

(a) At the top of the Postcard on the address side the capital 'P' of the word 'Postkarte' appears beneath the letters 'rn' near the centre of the word 'Interniertenpost'.

(b) In the 'Absender' panel the camp name 'Internierungslager Wurzach/Allgäu' appears in two lines underneath the words 'Lager-Bezeichnung:'.

This Postcard is recorded in use from May until August 1943.

Type Wz.P/C.2.

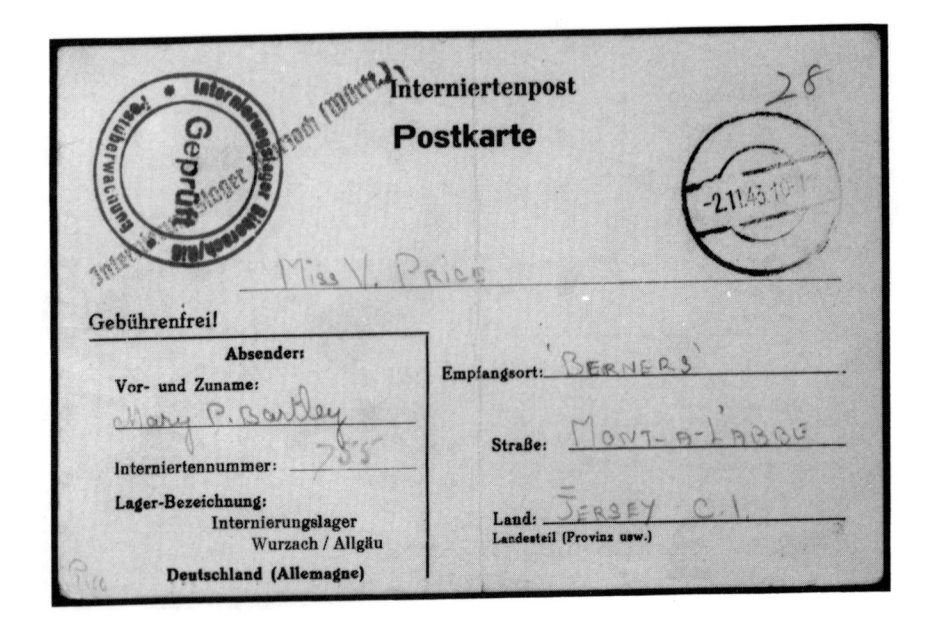

(a) At the top of the Postcard on the address side the capital 'P' of the word 'Postkarte' appears beneath the letters 'In' at the beginning of the word 'Interniertenpost'.

(b) In the 'Absender' panel the camp name 'Internierungslager Wurzach/Allgäu' appears in two lines underneath the words 'Lager-Bezeichnung:'.

This Postcard is recorded in use from September 1943 until February 1944.

Wurzach 'Exceptional' Stationery

Wurzach did not have any 'exceptional' stationery printed in the same way that Laufen did, but it did use one very unusual piece of stationery which had not been printed for the Internment Camp at Wurzach, but which was in use at the Officer Prisoner of War camp at Wurzach. It was a bilingual Postcard with a preprinted half for a return message to be sent back to the camp.

Type Wz.P/C.3.

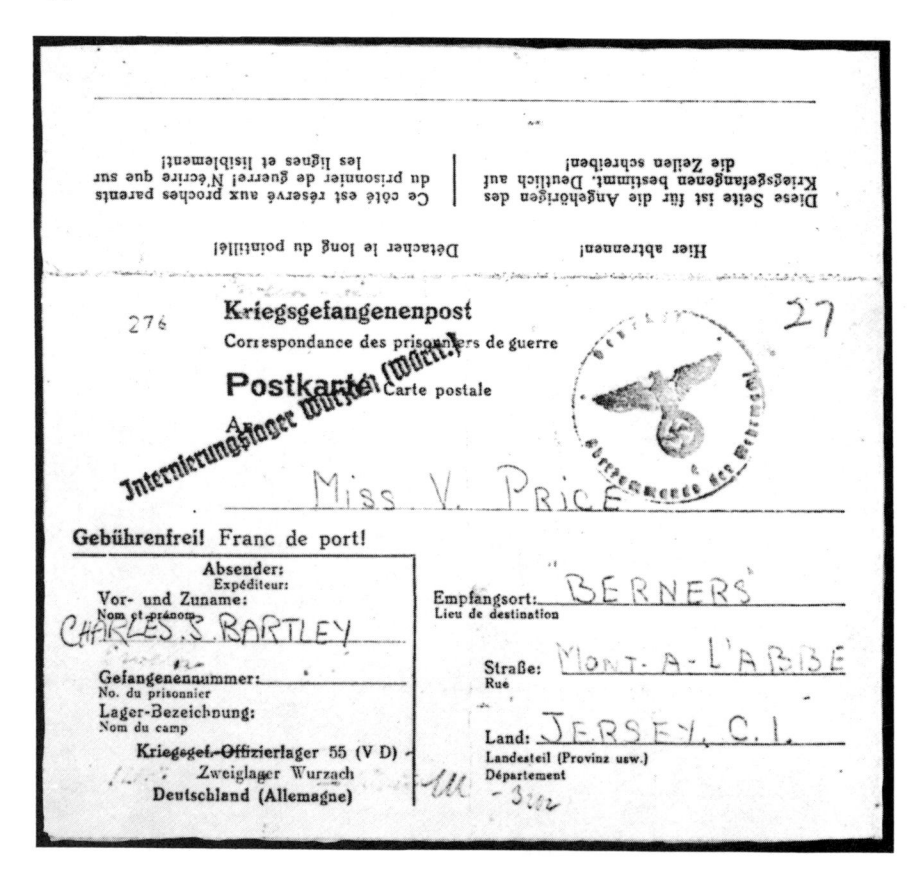

Identification of this 'exceptional' stationery is easy:

(a) The card is bilingual – French and German.

(b) The card is double the size of a normal camp Postcard 198 m.m. by 151 m.m.

(c) One half and its reverse, form a relatively normal Postcard for a message

93

from the camp, but the other half forms a preprinted card with the address of the camp printed on one side and space for a message to be sent back to the camp on the reverse. The card would have been cut or torn across the centre so that one half could be retained and the other half sent back to the camp.

[Illustration of a Kriegsgefangenenpost Antwort-Postkarte addressed to Kriegsgef.-Offizierlager 55 (V D), Zweiglager Wurzach, Deutschland (Allemagne), with the top portion showing the reverse (message side) of the other half upside down.]

Each of the two illustrations above show a bottom half with the address side of one of the cards, and part of the top half with the message side that belongs to the other card.

Examples of these cards used by Internees writing to the Channel Islands have been recorded used in December 1942 and again in June and July 1943. Normally, only one half of the Postcard is found, that is the half with the message from the camp. Although the half for the reply has been detached from these cards and presumably used, no used example from the Channel Islands back to Wurzach has been recorded.

Only one example has so far been recorded with both halves still uncut and it is from this example that the illustrations above have been made.

Wurzach Cachets and Censor Cachets

Three cachets have been recorded for Wurzach but none of them are strictly censor cachets as the first is a Military Unit handstamp as normally applied to soldiers' Feldpost Mail and the other two are camp identification cachets. Because Wurzach was a small camp, subsidiary to and close to Biberach its mail from the Channel Island Internees (apart from some early despatches) was often, if not always, forwarded to Biberach for censoring. Wurzach covers are therefore more often found with a Wurzach identification cachet and a Biberach Censor Cachet.

Type Wz.C.1: A 35 m.m. single circle cachet with a spread winged eagle above a laurelled swastika in the centre of the circle. Around the top edge of the circle in Gothic script 1.5 m.m. high with capitals 2 m.m. high, is the inscription 'Internierungslager' while around the bottom it reads 'Wurzach (Württ.)' and at the sides on either side of the eagle there is a small cross of 1 m.m. in each dimension. As with the Biberach Type Bb.C.1. this cachet has the appearance of a Military Unit handstamp as normally applied to German Soldiers' Feldpost Mail. It's early use in December 1942 when the Channel Island Internees first arrived at the camp, and its scarcity, give reason to believe that it may have been used in error on a batch of Internee Mail sent through the Feldpost, when it should normally only have been used on Military Feldpost Mail as an identification cachet. Another idea is that this cachet was used as a 'stopgap' measure before the issue of the identification cachet Wz.C.2. Although this cachet is an early mark in use when Wurzach changed status from a P.O.W. camp to an Interment camp with the arrival of the Channel Islanders, it is not a 'left-over' from the camps' P.O.W. days as the cachet definitely states 'Internierungslager' in the inscription.

As with the Eagle and Swastika cachets of Biberach and Laufen (Type Bb.C.1. and Type Lf.C.8.), this cachet Type Wz.C.1. was struck in violet.

The Eagle and Swastika cachets of the Internment Camps are very scarce and should not be confused with the more plentiful Eagle and Swastika cachets of the Oberkommando der Wehrmacht which were applied to the Internee Mail at the Primary Censorship Offices (ref. chapter – 'German Censorship') when the mails were in transit. (O.d.W. Eagle & Swastika cachets are easily identified as they are struck in crimson).

Internierungslager Wurzach (Württ.)

Type Wz.C.2: A Straight Line cachet 64 m.m. long with an inscription in Gothic script 3 m.m. high and with capitals of 4 m.m. The inscription reads: 'Internierungslager Wurzach (Württ.)'. This cachet is the most common of the Wurzach cachets used throughout the stay of the Channel Island Internees at the camp and it is seen struck in violet and often in conjunction with the Biberach Type Bb.C.2.

UNRECORDED

Type Wz.C.3: A Straight Line cachet identical to Type Wz.C.2. but found struck in black. I have not been able to record this cachet, but its existence was reported to me by O. W. Newport who had an example in his collection. It is possible that only one batch of mail received this cachet in black and that the cachet is in reality Wz.C.2., this would then account for its relative scarcity.

Wurzach Postmarks

No postmark has been recorded as being individual to Wurzach. Many of the early covers from Wurzach are found without any postmarks at all and the rest usually carry the 'dumb' Biberach Postmark type Bb.P.M.1. which has been applied after the cover was sent to Biberach for censoring. I have one 'Interniertenpost' Postcard from Wurzach addressed to Jersey and used in November 1944 which carries the Biberach Postmark Type Bb.P.M.3., but this is the only example I have ever seen of a postmark other than the 'dumb' one being used.

Note: Wurzach cards are often not identified as being such because they carry the Biberach Censor Cachet Type Bb.C.2. and the Biberach Postmark Type Bb.P.M.1., and the camps own identification cachet Wz.C.2. is very similar to the Biberach Cachet Type Bb.C.3. Final identification can usually be made from the camps stationery which nearly always carries the camp name. Even Kriegsgefangenenpost stationery used in the camp was of an individual bilingual type which had the camp name imprinted in the Absender panel; the other 'universal' German Kriegsgefangenenpost stationery has not been recorded used in the camp.

LAUFEN INTERNMENT CAMP MAIL

Although Laufen was not a large camp, holding only 454 Internees as compared to 1143 in Biberach, nevertheless its postal history is prolific and varied because the camp was not a family camp, but a camp for single males, and so all of its 454 Internees were over the age of sixteen years and therefore eligible for the full quota of Internee Postfree postcards and lettersheets.

Like the other major Internment Camps, Laufen Internment Camp had its own individual Internee Post-Free Postcards and Lettersheets which had the camp's address preprinted in the 'Absender' panel on this stationery. The layout of the Lettersheets and Postcards is similar to those from Biberach Camp (see introductions to 'Biberach Lettersheet Printings' and 'Biberach Postcard Printings') but Laufen Camp was unique among the Internment Camps in that it had a proliferation of 'exceptional' stationery which was specially produced for events like Christmas or the receipt of 'Next-of-Kin' Parcels.

The use of the 'universal' Kriegsgefangenenpost Postcard and Lettersheet during shortages of its own stationery is recorded from Laufen Internment camp in August 1943 and again in October and November 1944, but Laufen has another unique claim in that it also used Postal Stationery from other camps. Wulzburg (Ilag XIII) Lettersheets are recorded used from Laufen Camp in November 1942 and again in August 1943 and these should not be confused with the 'universal' Kriegsgefangenenpost Lettersheets as both bear the word 'Kriegsgefangenenpost' and not 'Interniertenpost'. The first messages recorded from Laufen in November 1942 are on Wulzburg Stationery.

Laufen also used 'Interniertenpost' Lettersheets from a different camp, this time Tittmoning (Ilag VII/Z) in August and September 1943, and during another shortage of stationery in February and March 1944 it used Tittmoning Postcards.

I have recorded with reprints, five printings of the Laufen 'Interniertenpost' Lettersheet and six printings of the 'Interniertenpost' Postcard. There were also five printings of 'exceptional' stationery at Laufen, and envelopes used by the Internees after Laufen was liberated as well as envelopes used by the Camp 'Kommandant' are recorded below.

Laufen had at least 16 cachets of various types, but all were used for their correct purposes and I have never been able to record a military cachet used on Internee mail or an Identification cachet used as a Censor cachet as was quite common in some other camps such as Biberach.

Only one postmark was in use in the town of Laufen and most Internee mail carries this postmark although some batches of mail have been recorded posted from other villages, notably Tittmoning.

Laufen Lettersheet Printings

Type Lf.L/S.1.

Absender:

Vor- und Zuname: _____

Gefangenennummer: _____

Lager-Bezeichnung: Ilag VII

Deutschland (Allemagne)

This first printing is the most individual and easiest of the lettersheets to identify.

(a) Above the address section of the lettersheet, the word 'Internierten-Post' is hyphenated.

In the 'Absender' panel:

(b) The word 'Gefangenennummer' appears (instead of the correct word 'Interniertennummer').

(c) 'Ilag VII' follows 5 m.m. after the words 'Lager-Bezeichnung:' and has dropped 1 m.m.

(d) The capital 'D' of 'Deutschland' displays damage.

This lettersheet has been recorded in use from April until June 1943.

Type Lf.L/S.2.

Absender:

Vor- und Zuname: _____

Internierten Nr. _____

Lager-Bezeichnung: Ilag VII

Deutschland (Allemagne)

(a) Above the address section of the lettersheet, the word 'Interniertenpost' appears as one word.

In the 'Absender' panel:

(b) The abbreviated word 'Internierten Nr.' appears but a colon does not follow it.

(c) 'Ilag VII' follows 3 m.m. after the words 'Lager-Bezeichnung:' and has only dropped ½ m.m.

(d) The words 'Deutschland (Allemagne)' are undamaged but heavily inked so that parts of the printing galley are also reproduced.

This is the most common of the lettersheet printings from Laufen, recorded in use from December 1943 until August 1944.

Type Lf.L/S.2(a).

A reprint of Lf.L/S.2. was made and is recorded used in February 1945. It is difficult to differentiate between the printings except that the reprint has a finer and not so heavily inked appearance and can usually be recognised because of its very late usage.

As any lettersheet used in 1945 is scarce, this lettersheet must naturally be quite rare.

Type Lf.L/S.3.

Absender:

Vor- und Zuname:

Internierten Nr

Lager-Bezeichnung: Ilag VII

Deutschland (Allemagne)

(a) Above the address section of the lettersheet, the word 'Interniertenpost' appears as one word.

In the 'Absender' panel:

(b) The abbreviated word 'Internierten Nr.' appears but a colon does not follow it.

(c) 'Ilag VII' follows 3 m.m. after the words 'Lager-Bezeichnung:' but all the letters have dropped unevenly so that the capital 'I' of 'Ilag' is higher than the other letters and the last 'I' of 'VII' is taller and thicker than the first two figures.

(d) The words 'Deutschland (Allemagne)' are undamaged and are not overinked so none of the printing galley is reproduced.

This printing is recorded in use from March until August 1944 and ran partly concurrently with Type Lf.L/S.2. although it is not as common as that printing.

Type Lf.L/S.4. (and Type Un.Int.L/S.1.)

Absender:

Vor- und Zuname. ____

Internierten Nr.: ____

Lager-Bezeichnung:

Deutschland (Allemagne)
_____

(a) Above the address section of the lettersheet, the word 'Interniertenpost' appears as one word.

In the 'Absender' panel:

(b) The abbreviated word 'Internierten Nr.:' appears and a colon follows it.
(c) The camp number 'Ilag VII' is missing.
(d) The words 'Deutschland (Allemagne)' are very damaged and have only a thin line beneath them.

This printing is very scarce and is only recorded in use in April 1945 shortly before the camp was liberated. Because the camp name is missing this lettersheet printing may have been intended as a 'universal' printing for all Internment camps (Type Un.Int.L/S.1.), but its use has not been recorded at any other camp which held the Channel Islands Internees.

A Postcard, also with the camp name missing, has been recorded in use at Wurzach camp in November 1944 and in Laufen in April 1945. It has been described earlier as a 'universal' printing (Type Un.Int.P/C.1.).

Laufen Postcard Printings

Type Lf.P/C.1.

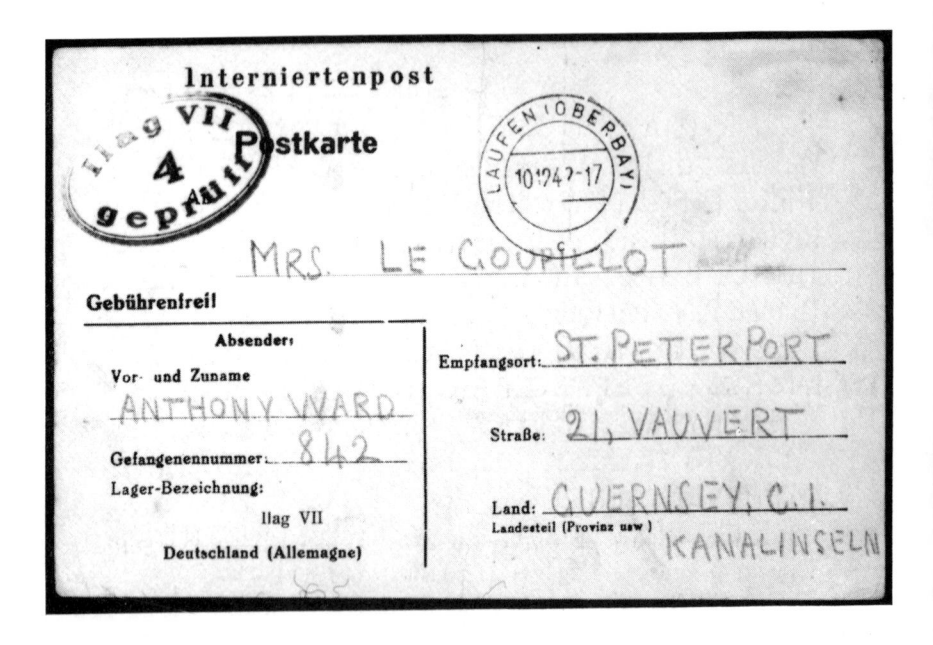

On the address side of the card:

(a) At the top of the Postcard, the word 'Interniertenpost' appears on the left side of the card.

(b) The capital 'P' of the word 'Postkarte' appears beneath the first pair of letters 'er' in the word 'Interniertenpost'.

(c) The word 'An' appears in the address section.

(d) In the lines for the address there is a space of 4 m.m. between the word 'Staße:' and its following line.

In the 'Absender' panel:

(e) The word 'Gefangenennummer' appears (instead of 'Interniertennummer').

(f) The capital 'I' of 'Ilag VII' appears underneath and after the words 'Lager-Bezeichnung:'.

(g) There is a gap of 5.5 m.m. between the base of the word 'Bezeichnung:' and the base of the word 'Ilag'; and there is a gap of 6 m.m. between the base of the word 'Ilag' and the base of the word 'Allemagne'.

On the message side of the card:

(h) Only the word 'Datum:' is printed but with a colon after it.

This card is recorded in use in early December 1942.

Type Lf.P/C.2.

> **Interniertenpost**
>
> **Postkarte**
>
> An
>
> Mrs. Ruth Mackesy
>
> Gebührenfrei
>
> Absender:
> Vor- und Zuname: THOMAS C.E MORTON
> Gefangenennummer: 1196
> Lager-Bezeichnung: KOUFEN O.B.B. Ilag VII
> Deutschland (Allemagne)
>
> Empfangsort: ST. PETER PORT
> Straße: HAVILLAND HALL FARM
> Land: GUERNSEY
> Landesteil (Provinz usw.)
> KANAL INSELN

On the address side of the card:

(a) At the top of the Postcard, the word 'Interniertenpost' appears on the left side of the card.

(b) The capital 'P' of the word 'Postkarte' appears beneath the first pair of letters 'er' in the word 'Interniertenpost'.

(c) The word 'An' appears in the address section.

(d) In the lines for the address there is a space of 4 m.m. between the word 'Straße:' and its following line.

In the 'Absender' panel:

(e) The word 'Gefangenennummer' appears (instead of 'Interniertennummer').

(f) The capital 'I' of 'Ilag VII' appears underneath and after the words 'Lager-Bezeichnung:'.

(g) There is a gap of 4 m.m. between the base of the word 'Bezeichnung:' and the base of the word 'Ilag'; and there is a gap of 8 m.m. between the base of the word 'Ilag' and the base of the word 'Allemagne'.

On the message side of the card:

(h) Only the word 'Datum' is printed and without any colon after it.

This card seems to be a reprint of Lf.P/C.1., the only changes being a slight change in the position of the word 'Ilag' and the missing colon on the message side.

This card is recorded in use from February to April 1943.

Type Lf.P/C.3.

> **Interniertenpost**
> **Postkarte**
>
> Ilag VII 13 geprüft
>
> Mrs. Ruth Mackesy
>
> Gebührenfrei!
> Absender:
> Vor- und Zuname: Thomas C.E. Morton
> Interniertennummer: 1196
> Lager-Bezeichnung:
> Ilag VII
> Laufen OB.B
> Deutschland (Allemagne)
>
> Empfangsort: St. Peter Port
> Straße: Haviland Hall Farm
> Land: Guernsey
> Landesteil (Provinz usw.) Kanal Inseln

On the address side of the card:

(a) At the top of the Postcard, the word 'Interniertenpost' appears in the centre of the card.

(b) The capital 'P' of the word 'Postkarte' appears beneath the letters 'In' at the beginning of the word 'Interniertenpost'.

(c) The word 'An' does not appear in the address section.

(d) In the lines for the address there is a space of 4 m.m. between the word 'Straße:' and its following line.

In the 'Absender' panel:

(e) The correct word 'Interniertennummer:' appears (not 'Gefangenennummer').

(f) The capital 'I' of 'Ilag VII' appears underneath the letters 'nu' in the words 'Lager-Bezeichnung'.

(g) There is a gap of 3.5 m.m. between the base of the word 'Bezeichnung:' and the base of the word 'Ilag'; and there is a gap of 9 m.m. between the base of the word 'Ilag' and the base of the word 'Allemagne'.

On the message side of the card:

(h) The word 'Internierungslager' is printed on the left side, and the word 'Datum:' followed by a colon is printed on the right side, both at the top of the card.

This card is recorded in use from April to July 1943 and then again in December 1943 when damage to the letter 'I' of 'Ilag' indicates that this later use is probably a reprint. (Lf.P/C.3a.).

Type Lf.P/C.4.

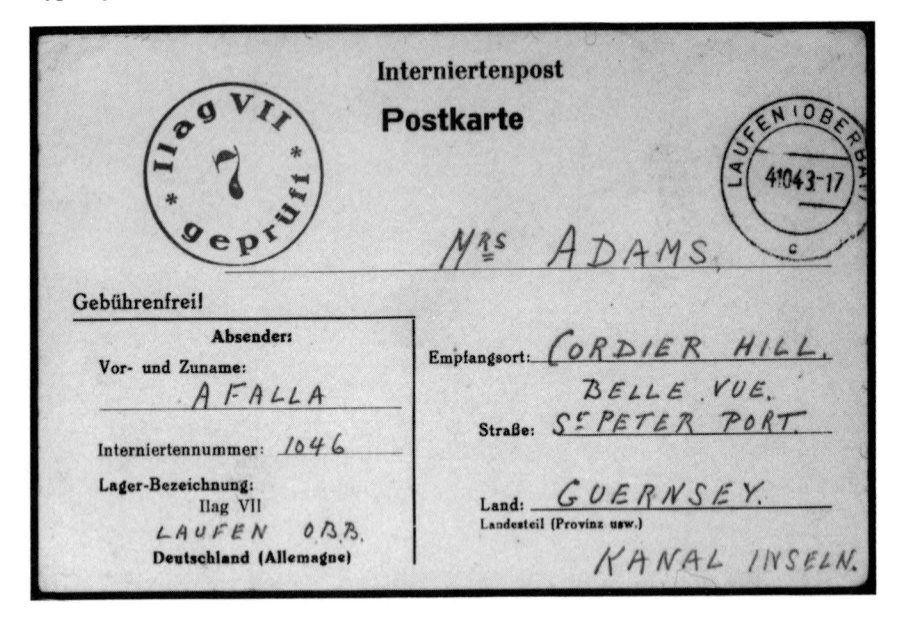

```
Interniertenpost
Postkarte

[Ilag VII geprüft stamp]              [LAUFEN OBERBAY 4.10.43-17 postmark]

                            Mrs ADAMS,

Gebührenfrei
        Absender:           Empfangsort: CORDIER HILL,
   Vor- und Zuname:                      BELLE VUE,
       A FALLA              Straße: ST PETER PORT
   Interniertennummer: 1046
   Lager-Bezeichnung:
          Ilag VII          Land: GUERNSEY.
       LAUFEN O.B.B.        Landesteil (Provinz usw.)
   Deutschland (Allemagne)           KANAL INSELN.
```

On the address side of the card:

(a) At the top of the Postcard, the word 'Interniertenpost' appears in the centre of the card.

(b) The capital 'P' of the word 'Postkarte' appears beneath the letters 'In' at the beginning of the word 'Interniertenpost'.

(c) The word 'An' does not appear in the address section.

(d) In the lines for the address there is a space of 4 m.m. between the word 'Straße:' and its following line.

In the 'Absender' panel:

(e) The correct word 'Interniertennummer:' appears (not 'Gefangenennummer').

(f) The capital 'I' of 'Ilag VII' appears underneath the letters 'ch' in the words 'Lager-Bezeichnung:'.

(g) There is a gap of 4 m.m. between the base of the word 'Bezeichnung:' and the base of the word 'Ilag'; and there is a gap of 9 m.m. between the base of the word 'Ilag' and the base of the word 'Allemagne.'

On the message side of the card:

(h) The word 'Internierungslager' is printed on the left side and the word 'Datum:' followed by a colon is printed on the right side, both at the top of the card.

This card is recorded in use from August 1943 through to February 1944 although one late example is recorded used on 29 July 1944.

Type Lf.P/C.5.

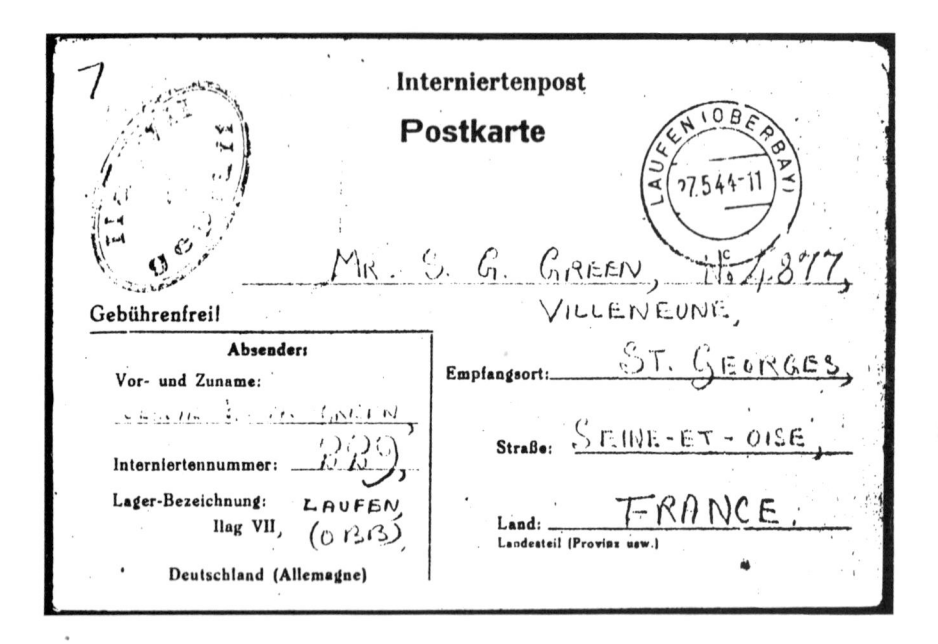

On the address side of the card:

(a) At the top of the Postcard, the word 'Interniertenpost' appears in the centre of the card.

(b) The capital 'P' of the word 'Postkarte' appears beneath the letters 'In' at the beginning of the word 'Interniertenpost'.

(c) The word 'An' does not appear in the address section.

(d) In the lines for the address there is a space of 4 m.m. between the word 'Straße:' and its following line.

In the 'Absender' panel:

(e) The correct word 'Interniertennummer:' appears (not 'Gefangenennummer').

(f) The capital 'I' of 'Ilag VII' appears underneath the letters 'ch' in the words 'Lager-Bezeichnung:'.

(g) There is a gap of 4.5 m.m. between the base of the word 'Bezeichnung:' and the base of the word 'Ilag'; and there is a gap of 8 m.m. between the base of the word 'Ilag' and the base of the word 'Allemagne'.

On the message side of the card:

(h) The word 'Internierungslager' is printed on the left side and the word 'Datum:' followed by a colon is printed on the right side, both at the top of the card.

This card is recorded in use in May 1944 and was probably a reprint of Lf.P/C.4. as the only changes are the position of the word 'Ilag' and a fuzziness in the lines of the address.

For some months before this card was introduced Laufen had used up its own stock of cards and had been using the 'universal' Kriegsgefangenenpost postcard and also supplies from Tittmoning Camp.

111

Type Lf.P/C.6.

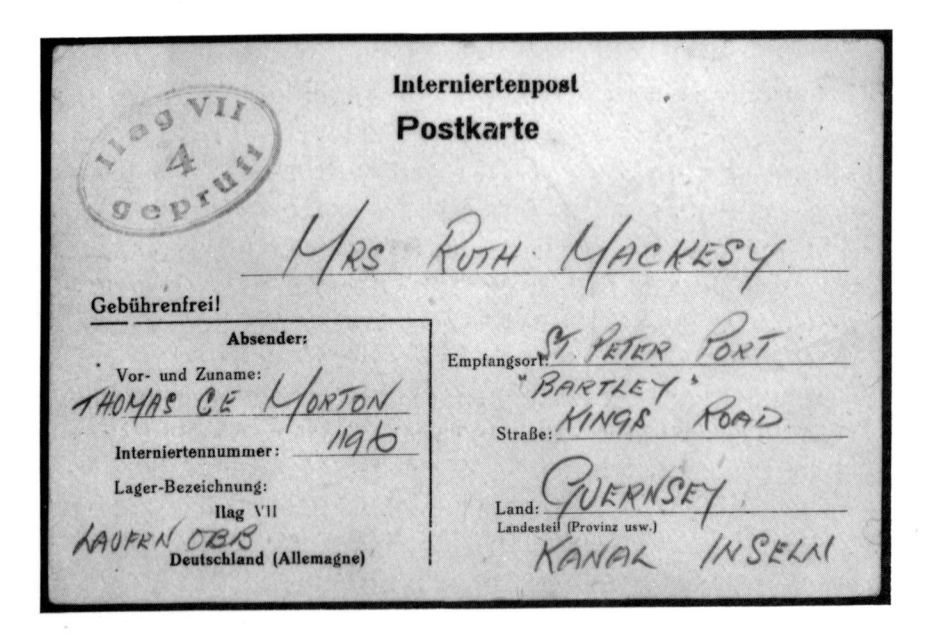

This card is easy to identify as it is the only card to have a different point (d) from all the other printings.

On the address side of the card:

(d) In the lines for the address there is no space (of 4 m.m.) between the word 'Straße:' and its following line.

In all other respects this card is identical to Type Lf.P/C.5.

This card is recorded in use in November 1944 and is a further reprint of Lf.P/C.4. and Lf.P/C.5., the only change being an improvement in the quality of the lines in the address section.

Laufen 'Exceptional' Stationery

Although various Prisoner of War Camps are known to have produced 'exceptional' stationery, such as Christmas cards (see illustration in chapter 'German Prisoner of War Camps'), Laufen was the only Internment Camp that is known to have used such stationery.

Laufen Internment Camp produced a Postcard for the Christmas of 1943 which carried a drawing of Schloss Laufen on the message side, while for the Christmas of 1944 a different design was used, this time the drawing was of the vaulted Canteen at Laufen. It also produced at least two printings of a bilingual 'Receipt of Package' Postcard with which the Internee could thank a relative at home for sending a parcel, and also list the contents that he had found in that parcel.

None of these special Postcards left room for a message as they were issued in excess of the normal monthly quota of message Postcards and Lettersheets, but the Internees usually managed to add a few words of greetings to the Christmas cards and I have a very humorous 'Receipt of Package' Postcard which thanks the addressee for sending '1 Cake' but instead of a list of contents, there follows the message 'Please do not send any more as they all go moldy' (s.i.c.).

One other Postcard which was special to Laufen Internment Camp was 'exceptional' for its lack of printing. The address side of this card was blank and so a home-made format has been drawn onto it while the message side has the normal preprinting of the two words 'Internierungslager' and 'Datum:' This type of card is recorded used at times when the normal camp stationery had run out.

Because they are so individual, identification of all these examples of 'exceptional' stationery is quite easy.

Laufen is also noted for its use of stationery from other camps. Wulzburg (Ilag XIII) Kriegsgefangenenpost Lettersheets and Tittmoning (Ilag VII/Z) Interniertenpost Lettersheets and Postcards are all recorded from Laufen. Their identification is easy when one looks at the camp address in the 'Absender' panel of these items.

Type Lf.P/C.7. (Christmas '43)

The Christmas Postcard for 1943 from Laufen is easily recognised because it bears a drawing of 'Schloss Laufen' on the message side.

Christmas Greetings from Schloss Laufen

The address side of this card is also quite individual as at the top of the card the word 'Interniertenpost' appears in a very fine print with lower case letters only 1.5 m.m. high and in the bottom right corner of the card there appears the printers' code 'N/0017'.

Type Lf.P/C.8. (Christmas '44)

The Christmas Postcard for 1944 from Laufen is also easily recognised because it bears on the message side of the card a drawing of the vaulted canteen at Laufen.

The address side of this postcard is even more individual than in any other postcard printing in that the 'Absender' panel which appears in the bottom left corner of all other Postcards, extends over the whole width of one end of the card in this printing.

Type Lf.P/C.9. (Bilingual-Package)

The message side of this Postcard is bilingual: English and Polish.

The address side of this postcard differs from all other types of Postcard in that the full camp name 'Laufen-Obb' is preprinted in the 'Absender' panel and the printers' code 'N/0148' appears in the bottom left corner.

This 'Receipt of Package' Postcard has been recorded used in May 1943 and February 1944.

Type Lf.P/C.10 (Bilingual-Package)

The message side of this Postcard is also bilingual: English and Polish, and it is similar to Type Lf.P/C.9. in all respects except that it is a later printing and can be identified by the printers' code '3/1453' in the bottom left corner of the card on the address side.

This 'Receipt of Package' Postcard has been recorded used in October 1944.

Type Lf.P/C.11. *(Blank Card)*

The message side of this card has the preprinted words 'Internierungslager' and 'Datum:' common to most printings of Laufen Postcards.

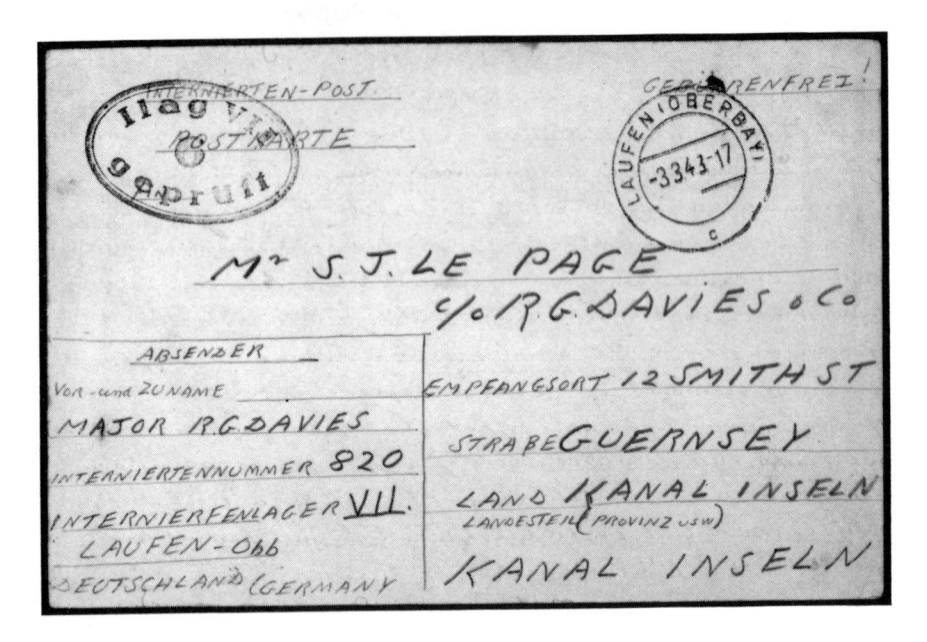

The address side of this Postcard, as has already been stated above, is 'exceptional' because there is no preprinting on it. Although these home-made cards could have been manufactured at any camp, none are recorded from the Channel Islands Internees at the other Internment Camps.

This type of home-made card is recorded used from Laufen Camp during shortages of the camp's own stationery in April 1944 and again in May 1945 at the time of Liberation. Few examples of home-made cards such as these have been recorded as Laufen often used supplies of cards from other camps as well as the 'universal' Kriegsgefangenenpost Postcard and Lettersheets.

Stationery from other Internment Camps in use at Laufen

During shortages of Stationery, all Internment Camps, including Laufen, are recorded as having used the 'universal' Kriegsgefangenenpost Postcards and Lettersheets intended for use in the P.O.W. Camps. Laufen however, is the only Internment Camp that is known to have used, on at least three different occasions, the preprinted Stationery belonging to other Internment Camps. Such stationery is easily identified by the Camp Number preprinted in the 'Absender' panel which has usually been changed to the Laufen number either by manuscript or the use of cachet Type Lf.C.6.

Type Lf.P/C.12. (Tittmoning Camp Postcard)

The printing of a Tittmoning Camp Postcard is very different from the Laufen printings, but final identification can be made by the Tittmoning Camp Number 'Ilag VII/Z' which appears in the 'Absender' panel.

The use of a Tittmoning Postcard at Laufen is scarce and is restricted to February and March 1944.

Type Lf.L/S.5. (Wulzburg Camp Lettersheet)

Absender:

Vor- und Zuname: *BILL ARROWSMITH*

Gefangenennummer: *1084*

Lager-Bezeichnung: Ilag XIII
LAUFEN O.BR.
Deutschland (Allemagne)

The printing of a Wulzburg Camp Lettersheet in use at Laufen is very easy to identify because the Wulzburg Lettersheets bear the word 'Kriegsgefangenenpost' on the front and 'Ilag XIII' in the 'Absender' panel, although usually both of these have been covered with Laufen cachets Type Lf.C.5. and Type Lf.C.6.

This lettersheet is recorded in use at Laufen in December 1942 and again in August 1943 but its use is not common.

Type Lf.L/S.6. (Tittmoning Camp Lettersheet)

Absender:

Vor- und Zuname: *WATON R.G.DAVIES*

Internierten Nr: *820*

Lager-Bezeichnung: Ilag VII Z
LAUFEN-OBB
Deutschland (Allemagne)

The Tittmoning Camp Lettersheet in use at Laufen is a somewhat more difficult printing to notice because as with Laufen Lettersheets it bears the word 'Interniertenpost' on the front and only the camp number 'Ilag VII/Z' on the reverse, in the 'Absender' panel, identifies it.

Unlike with the use of Wulzburg Lettersheets, no special cachets were used on the Tittmoning Stationery to re-identify it as Laufen mail. It was left to the Internee to obliterate the code letter 'Z' from the camp number which was the only difference between Tittmoning and Laufen Camp numbers.

This lettersheet was recorded in use at Laufen in September 1943.

Stationery of the Camp 'Kommandant' at Laufen

Mail from the Military personnel guarding the various Internment Camps was similar to any other soldiers' Feldpost mail and usually took the form of plain envelopes bearing a Feldpost cachet such as Laufen Type Lf.C.9. and a 'Unit' cachet such as Laufen Type Lf.C.8. or Biberach Type Bb.C.1. or Wurzach Type Wz.C.1. (see paragraph below: 'Laufen Military Feldpost Mail'). Such Military mail is scarce and also really beyond the scope of this book, but it is worth mentioning the example illustrated below because it bears a cachet found on Internees' Lettersheets and is a letter from the Camp 'Kommandant' at Laufen Internment Camp addressed to Berlin.

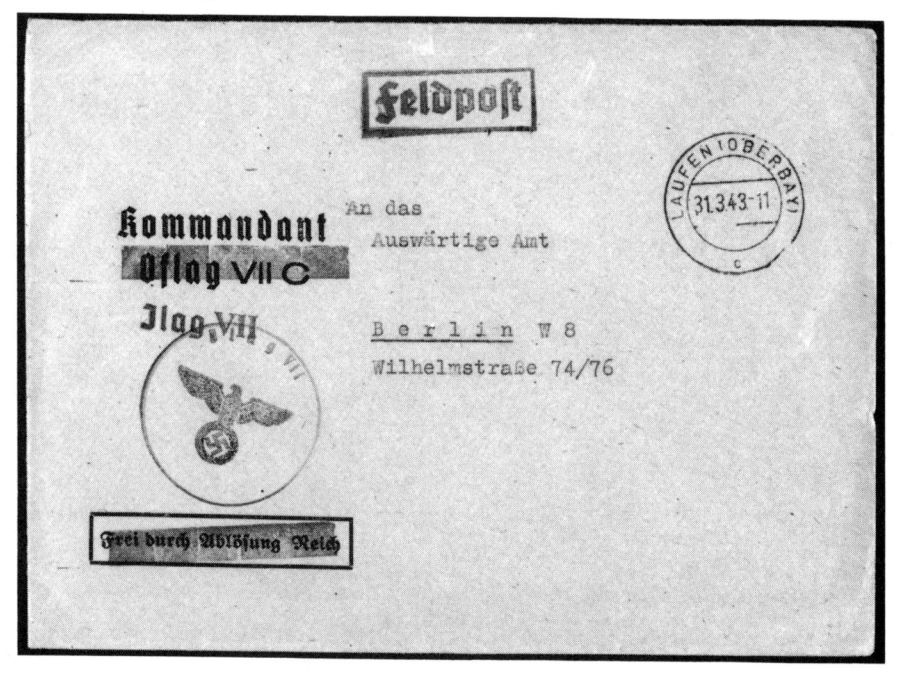

Type Lf.E.1. The envelope has a preprinted format which was intended for use at the old Officer Prisoner of War Camp at Laufen but which has been adopted for use by the Kommandant when the camp changed status to an Internee Camp. The old camp title 'Oflag VIIC' has been blocked out with a blue rubber stamp and the new camp title 'Ilag VII' has been inserted by the use of Laufen Cachet Type Lf.C.6. which can also be found on Internee's Lettersheets. The envelope bears two other cachets of Laufen, Type Lf.C.8. and Lf.C.9. used correctly here on Military mail. These cachets were not intended for use on the Internees' mail and to date have not been recorded used in that manner at Laufen although similar cachets are recorded used wrongly on Internees' mail at Biberach and Wurzach camps.

121

Post Liberation Stationery in use at Laufen

Supplies of Laufen's own stationery ran out in 1945 and so after the camp was liberated the Internees were issued with plain Envelopes and Postcards for writing to their relatives. The blank postcards have already been described above – Type Lf.P/C.11., and below is illustrated an example of an envelope in use from the camp at this time.

Type Lf.E.2.

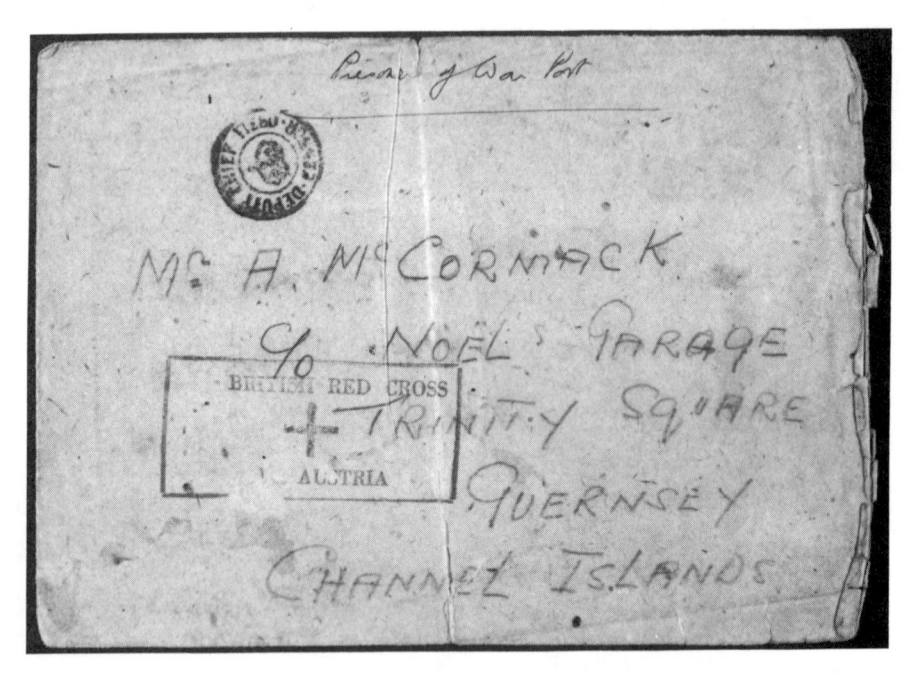

There is no need to describe the envelope as it is a plain buff envelope and the cachets are described elsewhere – Type Lf.C.10 and Lf.C.11. The Internee wrote his address on the reverse of the envelope, but it is interesting to note the manuscript endorsement 'Prisoner of War Post' which is in a different handwriting.

Very few examples of Post Liberation mail from Laufen are recorded, but the examples that are known carry this same endorsement which was probably applied by the Military Censor or the British Red Cross in Austria.

122

Laufen Cachets and Censor Cachets

Of the sixteen cachets recorded on mail from Laufen, only three were used for identification of the camp on Kriegsgefangenenpost Letter Sheets, nine were all censors' cachets, two were special cachets reserved for Military Feldpost Mail from the Camp Kommandant and the remaining two are very scarce cachets found used on mail from the Camp after it was liberated on 4 May 1945 by the 7th American Army, 40th Armoured Division.

The individual censor cachets are easily identified as each has a large number in the centre of an oval or circular frame. These numbers range from one to thirteen although I have yet to record numbers 2, 5, 8 and 9 actually used on an Internee's letter. It could be that these numbers were reserved for use in Censor Cachets for Prisoner of War mail, (as opposed to Internee mail) as Laufen was originally a camp for Officers – an 'Offizierlager' – Oflag VII C. This theory can be substantiated as I have seen a cachet with number 5 used on a 'Kriegsgefangenenpost' Postcard from Oflag V11C/H (i.e. Laufen) in February 1941, almost two years before the Channel Island Internees arrived at the camp. This number 5 is a censor cachet very similar to Laufen Type Lf.C.3. recorded below except that it carries the inscription 'Oflag VII C' instead of 'Ilag VII' and of course the number 5 is in the centre instead of number 10.

The Oflag censor cachet number 5 in use at Laufen (Oflag VIIC/H) before it became an Internment Camp.

Type Lf.C.1: Censors 1, 3, 4 and 6 are double ringed oval cachets 38 m.m. wide, with the number in the centre 5 m.m. high and 'Ilag VII geprüft' around the edge, 'Ilag VII' being above the number and 'geprüft' beneath it.

Type Lf.C.2: Censors 7 and 11 are single circle cachets 32 m.m. wide, with the numbers in the centre 9 m.m. high and 'Ilag VII geprüft' around the edge of the circle written in thick Roman script. In the inscription, 'Ilag VII' is above the number and 'geprüft' beneath it; there are also two stars which appear each side of the number.

Type Lf.C.3: Censor 10 is similar to Lf.C.2. in that it is a single circle cachet 32 m.m. wide, with the number in the centre and 'Ilag VII geprüft' around the edge. However, it is distinctive in that the number is 10 m.m. high, the inscription is written in thin Roman script and there are no stars either side of the number.

Type Lf.C.4: Censors 12 and 13 are very distinctive. They are 32 m.m. single circle cachets with the numbers in the centre 9 m.m. high. Around the edge, the inscription reads in Roman Capitals 'JLAG VII' (not Ilag), with 'geprüft' underneath the central number and in lower case Roman script. Censor 12 is the rarest of the Laufen Censor cachets as only one example has been recorded, this was as a receiving mark on a postcard into the camp from the hospital in Salzburg. Censor 13 is also very scarce, I have seen the mark on camp documents and photographs, used as a receiving censor on inbound letters, and on mail to England in late 1944, but as yet I can only record it on one batch of mail to the Channel Islands at Christmas time in 1944.

Colours and Dates of Use

All the above Laufen Censor Cachets are found used in a violet or blue/violet colour and they all seem to have been in use at the same time as the dates of use that I have recorded cover from November 1942 through to November 1944. The possible exception is Lf.C.4. Censor 13 which as I have already stated, I have only seen used in October 1944.

When the Censor cachets are used on mail coming into the camp, they tend to be struck in a blue/black colour and more rarely in a black colour.

I have one unusual example of Lf.C.2. Censor 11 which is struck in crimson on a letter to the United Kingdom on 28 August 1944. It is the only example I have seen of another colour being used but I cannot explain why as there appears nothing significant about the letter. No other Censor cachet from any of the Channel Islands Internee camps has been recorded struck in crimson except those of Kreuzburg Internment camp.

Identification Cachets

The following three cachets were used to identify Laufen Camp on Kriegsgefangenenpost Lettersheets when the camps own printed stationery was exhausted. These cachets always appear used in conjunction with one of the above censor cachets and I have never seen one used in place of a censor cachet as one often finds on the Biberach camp mail.

Jnternierten-Post

Type Lf.C.5: A straight line cachet 67 m.m. long with Roman script 3 m.m. high and capitals 5 m.m. high. The inscription is mis-spelt and reads: 'Jnternierten-Post' and is printed above and in place of the original heading printed on the lettersheet 'Kriegsgefangenenpost'. Underneath this cachet appears a thick bar 59 m.m. long and 5 m.m. high which is used to obliterate the original 'Kriegsgefangenenpost' heading.

Both the cachet and the bar are struck in violet and are usually seen in conjunction with Lf.C.6. and one of the Laufen censor cachets.

Jlag VII

Type Lf.C.6: A straight line cachet 24 m.m. long with Gothic script 3 m.m. high and capitals 5 m.m. high and Roman Numerals 4 m.m. high. The inscription reads 'Jlag VII' and is printed on the reverse of Kriegsgefangenenpost Lettersheets at the bottom of the Senders panel on the 'Lager-Bezeichnung' line to identify the camp and often to obliterate the printed name of another camp. This cachet has been recorded used in conjunction with Lf.C.5. in August 1943 and earlier in November 1942 when it was used in conjunction with Lf.C.5. and Lf.C.7.

It is also known on Feldpost Mail from the Camp Kommandant of Laufen where it is used to alter the designation of pre-printed envelopes from the old camp name of 'Oflag VIIC' to Ilag VII when the camp changed status from an Officer P.O.W. camp to an Internee camp.

The cachet is printed in the same violet colour as the other cachets with which it is seen used.

Laufen/Obb.

Type Lf.C.7: A straight line cachet 49 m.m. long with Roman script 4 m.m. high and capitals 6 m.m. high. The inscription reads 'Laufen/Obb.' and the cachet has a very temporary hand-made appearance as none of the letters are level.

The cachet was struck in violet and has only been recorded in November 1942 when it was used in conjunction with Lf.C.5. and Lf.C.6. on Kriegsgefangenenpost Lettersheets to identify the camp in the Absender panel of the sheets. The cachet was obviously a 'stop-gap' measure used to identify the camp when it first became an Internee Camp in 1942 with the arrival of Channel Island men and before the camp had a chance to print its own 'Interniertenpost' stationery. In later years when the camp ran out of its own lettersheets and had to resort to using the universal Kriegsgefangenenpost Lettersheets, Lf.C.5. and Lf.C.6. were brought back into use but Lf.C.7. was no longer in evidence which makes it the scarcest of all the Laufen cachets found on Internee's mail.

Laufen Military Feldpost Mail

Laufen had two other cachets which were reserved for Soldiers' Mail from the camp and which so far have not been recorded on Internee Mail. One is of particular interest (Lf.C.8.) because it is an eagle and swastika cachet in the same style as Biberach Type Bb.C.1. and Wurzach Type Wz.C.1. but whereas the Biberach and Wurzach Military cachets have been found used in error on Internee mail, we find Lf.C.8. used here, in the manner in which it was intended, on Feldpost mail. The other cachet reserved for Soldiers' Mail (Lf.C.9.) is a common boxed 'Feldpost' cachet used to indicate free postage through the field post office.

Only one cachet has been recorded used on both Internees' Mail and Military Mail and that is the Identification cachet Lf.C.6. recorded above.

Type Lf.C.8: A 37 m.m. diameter single circle cachet, with a spread-winged eagle above a laurelled swastika in the centre, and the legend 'Jlag VII' in Gothic script around the top edge of the circle with capitals of 2.5 m.m. and letters of 2 m.m. and 1.5 m.m.

The cachet is printed in the violet ink common to the other Laufen cachets and has been recorded used in March 1943.

Type Lf.C.9: A rectangular boxed cachet consisting of the one word 'Feldpost' and used to identify post-free military field post office mail. The box is 35 m.m. long and 12.5 m.m. high and the legend 'Feldpost' is in a thick Gothic script with capitals 8 m.m. high and lower case letters 6 m.m. or 5 m.m. high.

The cachet is struck in the violet ink common to the other Laufen cachets and is seen used in conjunction with Type Lf.C.8. in March 1943.

Post Liberation Cachets on Laufen Mail

When Laufen was liberated on 4 May 1945 the Internees, although well looked after, could not be given their freedom by the Americans until all Internees had been carefully screened by security. For many, repatriation did not take place for several months and so mail still left the camp although now no longer subject to German censorship. Letters from the camp during this period of its history are very scarce, but the two items that I have seen, which are addressed to Guernsey (one card and one envelope) both bear the same cachets from the occupying powers. These two items are not camp stationery, nor do they carry any of the Laufen cachets already recorded above or a Laufen Postmark.

Although the two cachets struck on these items are obviously not strictly Laufen marks, one being a British military censor and the other a Red Cross cachet, their use so far as it relates to the Channel Islands, is only recorded on mail originating from Laufen and this I feel, justifies their inclusion here.

Type Lf.C.10: A double circle British Military Censor cachet bearing a crown in the centre and the legend 'DEPUTY CHIEF FIELD . CENSOR .' around the edge between the two circles. The circles have diameters of 21 m.m. and 11 m.m. respectively and the letters which are Roman Capitals are 2 m.m. high, while each side of the word 'CENSOR' there appears a dot. This cachet is struck in black.

Type Lf.C.11: A rectangular boxed Red Cross cachet bearing a cross in the centre with the legend 'BRITISH RED CROSS' above the cross, and 'AUSTRIA' beneath it. The box itself has dimensions of 56 m.m. by 26 m.m. and the cross in the centre is made from two bars 10 m.m. long and 1 m.m. thick. The legend is in Roman Capitals that are 2.5 m.m. high. The whole cachet is struck in a dull pink/maroon ink.

Laufen Postmarks

Laufen had only one postmark in use throughout the War and it was a town postmark very similar to the Biberach Type Bb.P.M.2.

Very little Laufen Camp mail was forwarded without a postmark but it is possible to find some, especially if it is the 'Kriegsgefangenenpost' Lettersheets.

Type Lf.P.M.1: A double circle postmark 28 m.m. wide with an unbroken inner circle of 19 m.m. width. Around the edge, between these two circles runs the inscription 'LAUFEN (OBERBAY)' in Roman Capitals 2.5 m.m. high, while at the bottom of the circle is a small letter 'c'. Across the centre but within the inner circle is a bar 8.5 m.m. wide consisting of two lines which display progressive deterioration. In 1942 the top line of this bar is complete and only the bottom one shows a break, but in late 1943 the top line is also displaying damage and by 1944 only half the bottom line remains while the top line has a break of over 5 m.m. Within this damaged bar is the date in figures followed by a horizontal 'dash' and then a number. These figures are 4 m.m. high and the numbers recorded are: 8, 10, 11, 12, 17 and 18.

This Postmark is found on mail to the United Kingdom as well as to the Channel Islands and I can record that it was still in use after the war on mail from Laufen in December 1946.

Type Lf.P.M.2: This postmark is not strictly a Laufen postmark, but the postmark of the town of Tittmoning situated near Laufen, and found on batches of mail from Laufen camp between 5 April 1943 and 13 April 1943.

Type Lf.P.M.2. is similar to Type Lf.P.M.1. and Type Bb.P.M.2., in that it is a town postmark with a double circle 28 m.m. wide; the inner circle being unbroken and 19 m.m. wide. Around the edge, between the two circles runs the inscription: 'TITTMONING' in Roman Capital letters 2.5 m.m. high, with the letter 'a' in lower case at the bottom of the circle. The outer circle displays damage in three positions. Across the centre of the circle, but within the inner circle runs a bar consisting of two unbroken lines 8 m.m. apart. Within this bar is the date in figures followed by a horizontal 'dash' and a double digit number. The figures are all 3.5 m.m. high and the only dates recorded so far are 5.4.43 and 13.4.43., both followed by the digit 15, although other dates could exist. The postmark is struck in black.

Covers from Laufen bearing this postmark are obviously very scarce and the ones so far recorded have been addressed to Guernsey and England.

Type Lf.P.M.3: This postmark is also not strictly a Laufen postmark, but the postmark of the town of Munchen-Pasing which has been discovered struck on a Postcard from Laufen Camp on 7 July 1943.

Type Lf.P.M.3. is similar to Type Lf.P.M.2. in that it is a town postmark with a double circle; the outer circle is 29 m.m. wide and and the inner circle is unbroken and 19.5 m.m. wide. Around the edge, between the two circles runs the inscription: 'MUNCHEN-PASING' in Roman Capital letters 2.5 m.m. high, with the letter 'k' in lower case at the bottom of the circle. Across the centre of the circle, but only within the inner circle runs a bar consisting of two lines 9 m.m. apart, both these lines display damage. Within this bar is the date in figures followed by two small horizontal 'dashes' and the number '0'.

The postcard recorded with this postmark is so far unique and has the date 07.7.43--0. It is addressed to Jersey and has a further claim to fame in that it has been censored at the German Transit Censor Office in Berlin.

KREUZBURG INTERNMENT CAMP MAIL

Kreuzburg Internment Camp was a large camp which held Internees of several nationalities, but it held only a few Channel Island Internees and for a relatively short time. Because of this, although Kreuzburg Camp is known to have had its own printings of Internee Post-Free Lettersheets and Postcards in the same manner as other Internment Camps, very few examples have survived that were used to the Channel Islands, indeed no more than twenty such covers are recorded. As a Channel Islands-associated Kreuzburg cover, is therefore so scarce there is little point in trying to identify the further relative scarcity of the different printings in use at Kreuzburg Camp, especially as these would not be represented in the few covers that are recorded from Channel Island Internees. Suffice it to say that Kreuzburg Camp did have its own printings of the Internee Lettersheet and Postcard and that these have been recorded in use to the Channel Islands throughout 1944, although in October 1944 examples of the 'universal' Kriegsgefangenenpost Lettersheet are also recorded from the camp.

Kreuzburg Lettersheet Printings (*Type Kr.L/S.1.*)

Kreuzburg Postcard Printings (*Type Kr.P/C.1.*)

These are recorded and can be identified by the camp name 'Ilag VIII Z' which appears in the 'Absender' panel on both Lettersheets and Postcards.

Kreuzburg Cachets and Censor Cachets

Three Censor Cachets and one Identification Cachet have been recorded for Kreuzburg on Channel Island Internee Mail was well as one other cachet which takes the form of an instructional marking.

Type Kr.C.1: A circular 'cog-wheel' cachet, superficially similar to that of Compiègne and St. Denis Camps, was 29 m.m. in diameter to the outside points of the cogs and with a thin circle inside the cogs of 25 m.m. diameter. Inside the circle and round the top edge in thick letters 2 m.m. high with capitals of 4 m.m., is written the legend: 'Ilag VIIIZ', while around the bottom edge of the circle in thinner letters but of the same heights as the others is written the one word 'Geprüft'. In the centre of the circle, and 5 m.m. high, is a large figure '2'.

This mark was struck in Crimson and has been recorded in early 1944.

Type Kr.C.2: A triangular cachet with a flat top and point down. The top of the triangle is 28 m.m. long, the left side is 27 m.m. and the right side is 25 m.m. long. The cachet has a horizontal three line inscription in the centre. The top line reads, in Roman script with lower case letters 1 m.m. and capitals 2 m.m. high, 'Ilag VIIIZ'. The second line has a thicker script with lower case letters 1.5 m.m. high and capitals 2 m.m. and reads 'Geprüft', while underneath this is the number '4', the figure being 4 m.m. high.

This mark was struck in crimson and has been recorded in late 1944.

132

```
   ┌─────────────┐
   │   Ilag VIII │
   │      21     │
   │   Geprüft   │
   └─────────────┘
```

Type Kr.C.3: A fancy shield shaped cachet of overall height 29 m.m. and width 26 m.m. with a three line horizontal inscription in the centre. The first line reads 'Ilag VIII' with the small letters 3 m.m. high and the capitals 4.5 m.m. high, the second line has the number 21 in figures 4.5 m.m. high, and the last line reads 'Geprüft' in a thin Roman script with small letters 2 m.m. high and capitals of 3 m.m.

This mark was struck in crimson and has been recorded in early 1944.

Note: Although only a few Channel Island Internees were sent there, Kreuzburg was a large camp and from the identification numbers inside the recorded Censor Cachets – 2, 4 and 21, it seems highly probable that the camp used several more censor cachets even if it did not have all the numbers up to 21. However, as covers from the camp sent by Channel Islanders are quite scarce, perhaps few others than those cachets recorded above were actually used on Channel Island Mail as these were probably reserved for censors dealing with only the English Language.

Ilag VIII Z

Type Kr.C.4: Type Kr.C.4. is an Identification Cachet which has been recorded used on the 'universal' Kriegsgefangenenpost Lettersheets from the camp in the 'Absender:' part, on the 'Lager-Bezeichnung;' camp name line. It is a straight line cachet, 24 m.m. long, which reads in Gothic Script and Roman numbers: 'Ilag VIIIZ'. The capital letters are 4 m.m. high and the lower case letters are 2.5 m.m. high and the cachet is recorded struck in crimson. Censor cachet Kr.C.2. is the one normally seen used in conjunction with this Identification cachet.

Nicht im Jlag VIII

Type Kr.C.5. Type Kr.C.5. is not a Censor Cachet or Identification Cachet but an instructional mark that has been discovered on a cover sent to Kreuzburg to a Channel Island Internee who was thought by the sender to be in that camp, but who was actually interned at Laufen. The address 'Kreuzburg' on this cover has been crossed out in manuscript and a cachet applied which reads 'Nicht im Jlag VIII' (Not in Ilag 8). The cachet is a single straight line cachet, 35 m.m. long, with Gothic script that has lower case letters 2.5 m.m. high and capitals 4 m.m. high. The cachet is struck in violet.

Kreuzburg Postmarks

Type Kr.P.M.1: The only Kreuzburg postmark recorded in use on Channel Island covers is a 'dumb' double circle mark 29 m.m. wide with the inner circle 17 m.m. wide. Across the centre of the whole mark runs a bar consisting of two parallel lines 9 m.m. wide which extend to the edges of the outside circle and leave two small semi-circles one above and one below the bar formed by the inner circle. Each of these semi-circles is filled in and decorated by nine solid verticle lines. Progressive damage to the ends of the lines forming the bar has given the appearance to some of the later marks that there is no central bar only a 'phantom' bar formed by the two semi-circles, however closer examination usually reveals traces of the damaged lines. Across the circle in the centre of this bar runs the date in figures followed by a code consisting of a number, a short horizontal 'dash' and then another number and letter; all these figures being 3 m.m. high. The codes so far recorded are 4–5N, 12–IN and 12–IV. The close spacing of the dates and the following code can often give a rather confused look to this mark, for example, one date that I have recorded is 28 April 1944 with the code 4–5N which in the postmark gives the following: '28. 4.4 4.4–5N'

LIEBENAU INTERNMENT CAMP MAIL

Because the German Censors at Liebenau only dealt with the Greek and Italian language, mail from any Channel Islanders interned in the camp had the word 'English' endorsed on the front by the writer and was taken to Biberach for censoring. A Liebenau card is therefore found with a Biberach Censor Cachet and Biberach Postmark and can usually only be identified by the printing of the card which is not a Biberach printing but states the camp name 'Liebenau (Krs. Friedrichshafen)' in the 'Absender' panel. Although a Liebenau card from a Channel Islander is very scarce because so few of the Internees were actually sent to the camp, there are probably in existence more cards than the six that have so far been identified. This is because inaccurate identification has been made from the Censor Cachet and Postmark without due reference to the printing of the card or letter which indicates its true origin.

Liebenau Postcard Printings

Type Li.P/C.1.

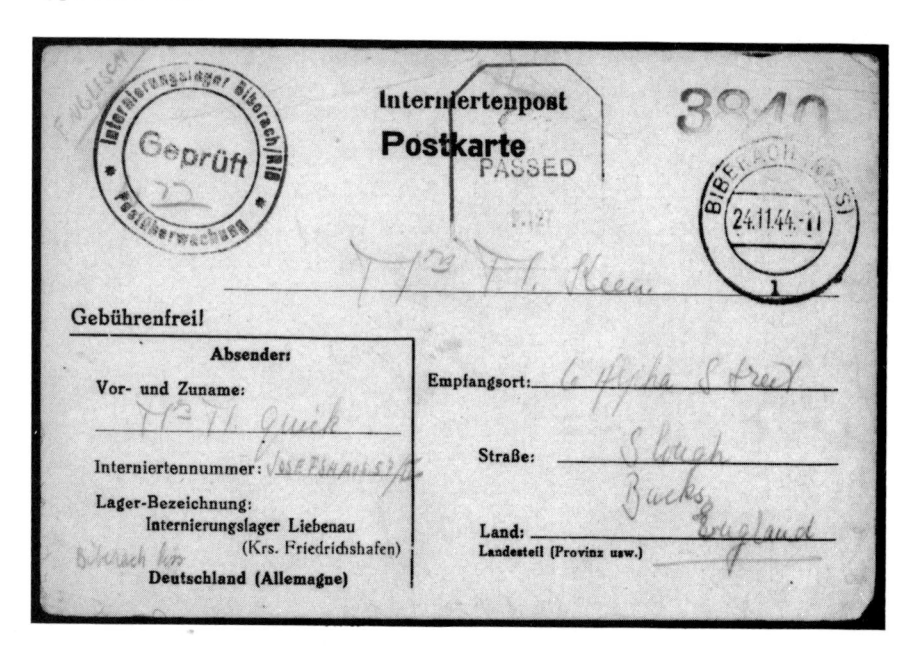

The Liebenau postcard recorded is an 'Interniertenpost Postkarte' similar to the Wurzach Type Wz.P/C.2. and the Biberach Type Bb.P/C.3. It has the capital 'P' of 'Postkarte' directly beneath the capital 'I' of 'Interniertenpost', and in the Absender Panel the address of the camp forms two lines:

135

'Internierungslager Liebenau
(Krs. Friedrichshafen).'

with the 'K' of 'Krs' underneath the 'a' in 'Internierungslager'

Note: There are doubtless other printings of Liebenau postcards but I have only had the opportunity to record this one.

Liebenau Lettersheet Printings (*Type Li.L/S.1.*)

Although Lettersheets from the camp probably exist, I have not as yet seen one from a Channel Island Internee.

Liebenau Censor Cachets

No Liebenau Censor Cachet has been recorded on a card used by a Channel Islander. The Censor Cachet found on the cards is Biberach Type Bb.C.4.

Liebenau Postmarks

A Liebenau Postmark has not been recorded on a card used by a Channel Islander. The only Postmark so far recorded is Biberach Type Bb.P.M.3. used in November 1944 with the digit 11 after the date. Other Biberach postmarks must however be in existence.

COMPIÈGNE AND ST. DENIS FRONTSTALAG CAMPS MAIL

As has already been stated in PART 1 of 'ISLANDERS DEPORTED', Compiègne and St. Denis were 'sister' FRONTSTALAG Camps near Paris in France which shared the same camp number – '122'. To quote from my own writing:

> 'The address of Compiègne on mail from the camp is always given as "Compiègne (Oise) France", but sometimes with the addition of any one of the following: "Z122", "Stalag 122", or "Front Stalag Z122", while the address of St. Denis is always "Grande Caserne, St. Denis (Seine) France", but again ocassionally with the addition of "Z.I. Larger 122" or "Teil Larger 2", the latter I believe being a subdivision of the camp for men only.'

The confusion that arose from the similarity of the number and the addresses of the two camps is evident from the following Foreign Office Memo written in 1942.

Memo K.W. 15/46   5/5/42   F.O.
From Mr. Filliter with Ref. to St. Denis.
P.O.W. Dept. British Red Cross Society, Lady W. Gore told me this morning that their Foreign Relations Dept. telegraphed to Geneva asking them to find out whether the camps at St. Denis and Compiègne were both called Frontstalag 122. The reply has now come back saying that they both have the same number although they are quite a long way away from each other.
(A short time ago there was an intercept from a man at Frontstalag 122 Compiègne saying that he was an American taken from the Channel Islands to this camp.)

Compiègne and St. Denis Lettersheet and Postcard prinings

There are probably far more examples of Internee Mail from Compiègne camp available to collectors for research than there are from St. Denis camp where so few Channel Islanders were interned, but mail from both camps is very scarce as even Compiègne in its most dense period only held the Channel Islands Internees for a relatively short time. Because of this, most of the letters and postcards from the two camps are individual, if not unique in themselves, and so it is impracticable to make an analysis of the types and printings of the postal stationery represented by the few examples recorded from Channel Islanders.

As early as 1940, St. Denis camp was holding a few male Channel Islands Internees and these were provided with buff coloured cards with the black imprint 'F.M.' on the address side and the camp address on the top right corner of the message side. The imprint 'F.M.' signified 'Franchise Militaire' as the cards were remnants of an earlier period when the camp was French, before it became a German Frontstalag. All later items of mail from St. Denis camp and all those from Compiègne that have been recorded are on the 'universal' Kriegsgefangenenpost Lettersheets and Postcards although one example of these printings was also on a buff coloured card.

An example of the buff coloured card with imprint 'F.M.' in use at St. Denis camp in 1940.

Compiègne and St. Denis Censor Cachets

The similarity of the Censor Cachets used at Compiègne and St. Denis Camps and the run of numbers used in them makes one feel that the mail from both camps was either censored at a central location or that the Censor Cachets were taken from one run but allocated to each camp on a random basis. This is born out if one refers to the following table of Censor Cachets recorded:

Censor No.	Box Type	Cog Type	Diamond Type	Camp	122 Included?
1				NOT YET RECORDED IN USE	
2	small letters			St. Denis	
3	small letters			St. Denis	
4				NOT YET RECORDED IN USE	
5	large letters			St. Denis	
6	large letters			Compiègne	
7				NOT YET RECORDED IN USE	
8		large		St. Denis	122
9		small		Compiègne	122
Blank		small		Compiègne	122
Blank			large	Compiègne	122

The scarcity of mail from these camps makes it difficult to complete detailed research. Whereas some cachets have yet to be recorded in use, none have as yet been recorded used on mail from both camps which tends to negate the idea of a central censorhsip. Until new evidence can prove otherwise I have therefore described the censor cachets as if they were restricted in their use to only one of the camps.

Having written the above, I then discovered in the Public Records Office at Kew, some of the International Red Cross Reports on St. Denis Camp. From the following extracts dealing with mail, found in those reports, it can be seen that for one period at least, from May to October 1943, the censorship of the mail was centralised at Compiègne, but this gave rise to such delays in the delivery of the St. Denis mail that eventually each camp was again given its own censorship service. It is coincidental, but probably not significant that this was also the exact period when Compiègne was acting as a transit camp for the second deportation of Internees from the Channel Islands in 1943.

International Red Cross Report on St. Denis Camp 27 May 1943
Point 14 Mail.

According to an order from the new Camp Kommandant, who is at the same time Commander of the American Internees Camp at Compiègne, since 1 May all letters are censored at Compiègne. The Internees complain that the result is a delay in the delivering of the mail. That question was thoroughly discussed with both camp authorities at St. Denis and Compiègne and the Inspector was told by the German Officer in charge of the censoring that these delays will disappear as soon as the period of organisation is over. The High German Authorities in France were asked and agreed to keep an eye on that question and to take the necessary steps should the new system prove unsatisfactory.

St. Denis is a British Camp.

International Red Cross Report on St. Denis Camp   4 August 1943
Sect 14 Mail.

Mail for St. Denis is still censored in Compiègne, both camps being under the same command, and the Internees complained again that it means a delay of about a week in the delivery of the letters to the Internees and probably in the despatching of the letters too. The Camp Authorities in Compiègne with whom the matter was thoroughly discussed, denied it, and the Camp Commander said that the delay is not more than four days. The German Officer in charge of censoring declared that he is unable to improve the situation in that respect as long as he has not more censoring staff at his disposal, on the other hand an application for more personnel would certainly meet with a refusal in the present stage of the war. Telegrams are censored in the camp itself and delivered at once.

International Red Cross Report on St. Denis Camp   4 Oct 1943
Correspondence.

Following our appeals on this subject and thanks to the sympathy of the new Colonel and the action of the Camp Leader (Lagerfuerhrer), on the very day of our visit the Censorship service arrived from Compiègne. It is reinstalled now in the camp at St. Denis. This change should have a happy effect on the handling of correspondence, the mail from Paris, in particular will be speedier as up to now even pneumatics have had to go through Compiègne and took many a long day to arrive in the camp.

International Red Cross Report on St. Denis Camp   5 Nov 1943
Mail.

Mail was stated to be very satisfactory since the Censor's office has been brought back to this camp.

Even though the censorship service was centralised at Compiègne during the time that the majority of the Channel Islands Internees were there, still no example has been recorded of the same censor cachet being used on mail from both camps, and so I have continued to describe below the cachets as if they were unique to the mail of one camp only.

Compiègne Censor Cachets

```
┌─────────────┐
│  GEPRÜFT    │
│    N° 6     │
└─────────────┘
```

Type Cm.C.1: A rectangular boxed cachet 39.5 m.m. long and 15.5 m.m. high. Within the box is the one word 'GEPRÜFT' in Roman Capitals 5 m.m. high while underneath is 'No. 6', the capital 'N' and the figure '6' being 3 m.m. high.

This cachet is known struck in violet in 1943 and is almost identical to St. Denis Type St.D.C.3.

Type Cm.C.2: A circular 'cog-wheel' cachet, 27 m.m. in diameter to the outside points of the cogs with a thin circle inside the cogs of 24 m.m. diameter. Inside the circle and around the top edge in Roman Capital Letters 2.5 m.m. high is the legend 'FR.STALAG'. and across the circle in three lines, one underneath each other is:

<u>122</u>
GEPRÜFT:
9

This mark was struck in crimson and has been recorded in use in 1943.

Type Cm.C.3: A circular 'cog-wheel' cachet, identical to Type Cm.C.1. except for the omission of the number 9 in the centre of the cachet.

This cachet was struck in blue/black and has been recorded in use in 1943.

Type Cm.C.4: A horizontal diamond cachet with a double border of one thick line enclosing a thin line. The mark is 58 m.m. wide and 25 m.m. high. Across the centre in two lines of Roman script with lower case letters 2 m.m. high and capitals 3 m.m. high is written:

'Frontstalag 122
Geprüft'

This cachet is struck in violet but it has not been possible to record its dates of use.

St. Dennis Censor Cachets

Type St.D.C.1: A rectangular boxed cachet 41 m.m. long and 19 m.m. high. Within the box is the one word 'GEPRÜFT' in Roman Capitals 4 m.m. or 4.5 m.m. high, while underneath is 'No. 2' the capital 'N' and the figure '2' being 4 m.m. high.

This cachet is known struck in crimson in 1944 and is similar to Compiègne Type Cm.C.1. as well as St. Denis Types. St.D.C.2. and St.D.C.3.

Type St.D.C.2: A rectangular boxed cachet very similar to Type St.D.C.1. The box is 40 m.m. long and 18 m.m. high, while the word 'GEPRÜFT' inside the box has Roman Capitals 4 m.m. high. The 'No. 3' which appears beneath 'GEPRÜFT' is in thin figures which are only 3 m.m. high.

This cachet is recorded in use in 1944 and was struck in a crimson/maroon.

```
┌─────────────┐
│  GEPRÜFT    │
│   N° 5      │
└─────────────┘
```

Type St.D.C.3: A rectangular boxed cachet very similar to Compiègne Type Cm.C.1. The box is about 40 m.m. long and ranges from 16 m.m. to 17 m.m. high. The word 'GEPRÜFT', within the box, consists of Roman Capitals 5 m.m. high and beneath this is a rather squat 'No. 5' in figures 3 m.m. high.

This cachet is recorded struck in scarlet in 1941.

```
     STALAG
  FR.  122
    GEPRÜFT:
       8
```

Type St.D.C.4: This cachet is almost identical to the two circular 'cog-wheel' cachets of Compiègne – Types Cm.C.2. and Cm.C.3. except that it is much larger and carries the number '8' where the other two carry '9' or are blank. The example that I can record is a rather poor strike and so although the outside circle of 'cogs' has a diameter of over 30 m.m. I cannot ascertain its exact measurement or if it is made from one or two circles. The legend 'FR.STALAG' and '122 GEPRÜFT: 8' is made from Roman Capitals of at least 3 m.m. in height.

The whole cachet is struck in a very weak violet ink and I can record its use in July 1943.

Compiègne and St. Denis Postmarks

Compiègne and St. Denis Camps seem to have been without any postmarks of their own as nearly all the lettersheets and postcards that I have recorded from the two camps used by the Channel Island Internees are devoid of any type of postmark. In May of 1944 one postcard from St. Denis Camp is recorded as having received a Paris postmark of the Gare du Nord, but this was probably applied after the card has passed through the hands of the German censors in Paris as the card also carries a Paris Abwehr Durchlaufstempel 'A.x.' in circle. The postmark is identified and illustrated below with a St. Denis reference number because it was found on a card from St. Denis Camp but it is not a St. Denis Camp postmark.

Type St.D.P.M.1: A single circle Paris postmark with the legend 'PARIS GARE DU NORE PROVINCE.A' around the edge of the circle, and the date in two lines in the centre of the circle, 20-5 with 44 beneath. The legend is in Roman Capitals and these and the date figures are all 3 m.m. high. The circle has a diameter of 27 m.m.

The postmark is struck in black.

TITTMONING CAMP

Following the discovery of some Internee postcards addressed to Guernsey and bearing a Tittmoning town postmark of 5 April 1943 (Laufen Type Lf.P.M.2.), it was conjectured that some Channel Islanders were interned at Tittmoning Camp which prior to 1943 was OFLAG VIIC. I have not been able to discover any evidence to substantiate this theory, in fact all the evidence points to the fact that the postcards in question were sent by Internees from Laufen Camp and that for some unexplained reason a batch received the town postmark of Tittmoning. None of them bear any Tittmoning Censor Cachets. More recently other examples of cards with the Tittmoning Postmark have been recorded and from the dates noted – 5 April 1943 through to 13 April 1943 – it seems more likely that for some reason the Laufen Post Office was closed for two weeks in April 1943 and that all mail was taken to Tittmoning Post Office for despatch.

The cards in question are from known and recorded Laufen Internees who, in the Absender panel on the cards, give their Laufen Internee Numbers. The cards themselves are all Laufen Postcards Printing Type Lf.P/C.3. and the censor cachet on them is the Laufen Type Lf.C.3. number 10. One of the Internees has even written 'Laufen (O.B.B.)' on top of his card on the message side!

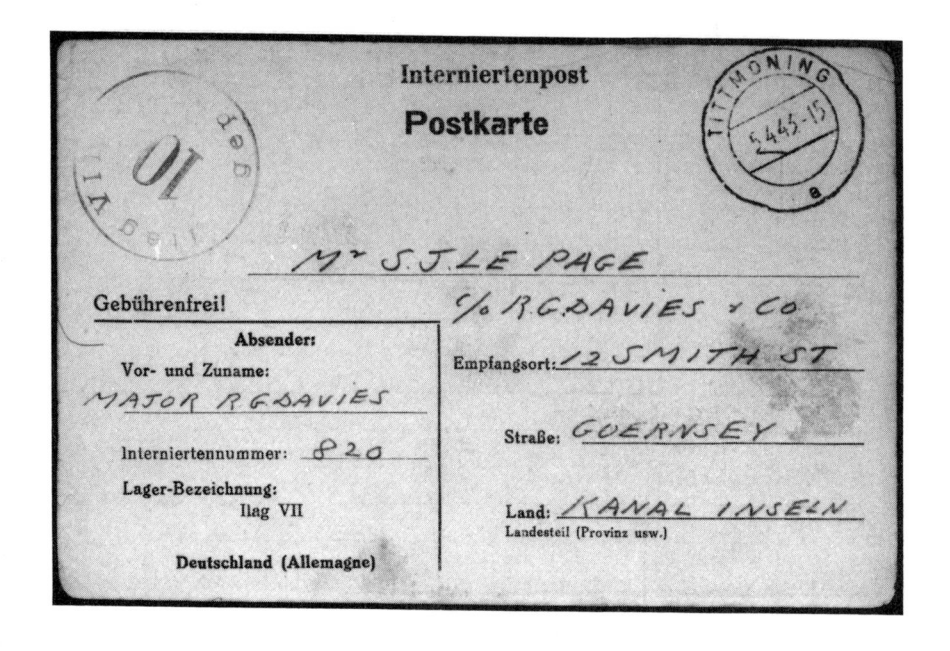

Don McKenzie who also has one of these cards in his collection suggested that they could have been Laufen cards sent for use at Tittmoning Camp during a

145

shortage of that camps' own cards as the writer of Don's example makes reference to the shortage of cards at the camp (although he does not name the camp). This however, would still not explain the use of the Laufen Censor Cachet Type Lf.C.3. on the cards, and anyway, it is known that at this time Laufen Camp was itself short of cards and a few months later had to revert to using the universal 'Kriegsgefangenenpost' Lettersheets and cards for a while, before new stocks of their own cards arrived.

It is on record that Tittmoning Camp held at least one Channel Islands P.O.W. but in my various researches I have not been able to find any reference to Channel Islanders being interned at Tittmoning, and whereas Laufen cards with this Tittmoning postmark are obviously very scarce I can find nothing to convince me that these cards have originated from Tittmoning Camp.

The town postmark of Tittmoning is described in detail as Laufen Postmark Type Lf.P.M.2.

OTHER CAMPS

Other camps exist where, for a short time, no more than a handful of Channel Islanders might have been interned, often having been moved there for one reason or another from one of the larger Channel Islands camps already described. In the majority of cases, examples of mail from Channel Islanders in these other camps is either non-existent, or else very rare, perhaps only one example being recorded.

What details are known of the camps or mail have been recorded in full in PART 1 of 'ISLANDERS DEPORTED' and the reader should refer there for information on the following camps. The camps have not been recorded again in this part of the book because in the main no examples of Postal Stationery or Censor Cachets have yet been found to record.

Ilag XVIII Spittal Drau Austria

Marlag und Milag Nord Ilag Westertimke

Stalag VIIIB Teschen

Oranienburg

Ilag XIII Wulzburg: Weissenburg/By.

Swiss Internment Camps

Penal Prisons and Concentration Camps

Section III

Censorship, Postal Markings, The Red Cross and Miscellaneous Documents and Ephemera associated with the Internees.

German Censorship.

MAP: Location of German Censor Offices.

Channel Islands Censor Cachet.

The 'Mysterious' Four Digit Cachet.

German Prisoner of War Camps (and Civilian Internee Camps).

Italian Prisoner of War Camps.

British Censorship.

British Post Office Markings.

French Post Office Markings.

Swiss Postmarks, Cachets and Censor Lables.

Cachets and Postmarks from the Rest of the World.

Unidentified Cachets.

The Red Cross.

Miscellaneous Objects, Documents and Ephemera.

GERMAN CENSORSHIP

Mail from the United Kingdom to an Internment Camp was censored on arrival at the camp as was mail from the Channel Islands, while Internee mail from the camps to the United Kingdom or to the Channel Islands was subjected to censorship before leaving the camps. Mail from Internees at certain small camps, before its despatch to destination, was taken to nearby larger camps where censors were competent in dealing with the language of the Internees of the smaller camp. The prime examples of these are letters from the Channel Islands Internees at Liebenau and Wurzach camps which were taken to Biberach for censoring. Censoring of the Internees' mail at the camps is dealt with in detail, with examples of all the known censor cachets used, in the individual chapters on each Internment Camp preceding this chapter.

Besides the censorship cachets applied at the camps, which tend to be struck in a violet or blue-black colour, many letters to and from the camps display other styles of German censorship which take the form of red or crimson cachets as well as machine censor marks, censor tapes and chemical wash tests for hidden writing. These other forms of German censorship have been applied at one or other of the fourteen Primary Censorship Offices set up throughout Germany and the Occupied territories to deal with foreign mail in transit.

Identification of the various German censor markings used during World War II is a complicated and confusing feature of the study of the Channel Islands Internee mail service. Luckily for the researcher only a limited number of the numerous German censor markings are identified as having been used on the Channel Islands Internee mail service and indeed it is highly unlikely that all the marks would have been used. Before recording the known censor markings found on Channel Islands Internee mail it is worth describing the structure of the German censorship administration.

Notes on the structure of the German censorship administration were made available to me by Don McKenzie who utilised three main sources. The first was 'Postzensur-Vol.II' by Karl Kurt Walter, which covers the broad spectrum of German censorship, from civilian mails, P.O.W. and Internee mails to Concentration camp mails, etc. The second book is titled 'Zensurpost aus dem III Reich, Die Überwachung des Auslandbriefverkehrs während des II. Weltkrieges durch deutsche Dienststellen.' by Karl Heinz Riemer, and this deals exclusively with the censorship, by German offices, of mail to or from foreign lands. The third source was further information contained in the bulletins published by the American based, 'Third Reich Study Group'.

The basic administration of censorship in Germany was operational prior to the outbreak of hostilities in September 1939, as a peacetime censorship was already in force and was thus able to rapidly expand to cater for the increased demands of wartime censorship. The mails subject to censorship may be broken into six classes as follows:—

(i) Foreign mails to/from German nationals.
(ii) Mails to/from the occupied territories.
(iii) Military Feldpost.
(iv) Red Cross mails.
(v) Concentration camp mails.
(vi) P.O.W. and Internee mails.

Whilst this chapter is intended to illuminate the sixth class only, it is of course also relevant to all Channel Islands occupation mails. It should be remembered that ultimately Germany was in a state of war with 54 countries, excluding colonies but including the governments in exile of such countries as Czechoslovakia and Norway. This situation, together with Germany's geographical location in central Europe, necessitated a rather complex and ponderous censorship machine.

The original administration, with headquarters in Berlin, was sub-divided into seven offices, each of which was located in a different city and was detailed to handle specific foreign mails. These seven offices were later augmented by a further six offices which were located in the occupied territories. Four of the original seven went on to administer sub-offices which were also located in the occupied territories. Finally, a second Berlin office was opened in 1944. Therefore there was a total of fourteen primary offices and four sub-offices, these being in addition to the censor departments, already mentioned above, in the Internee camps and P.O.W. camps.

Each of the Primary Censorship Offices was allocated a code letter or 'kennbuchstaben' e.g. Frankfurt had code letter 'e' and Paris had code letter 'x'. These code letters are often, but not always, found in the handstamps, machine stamps or censor tapes of each of the Primary Offices. The marks of the sub-offices were similar to those of their Primary Office and they used the same code letter as the Primary Office.

Location of German Censor Offices.

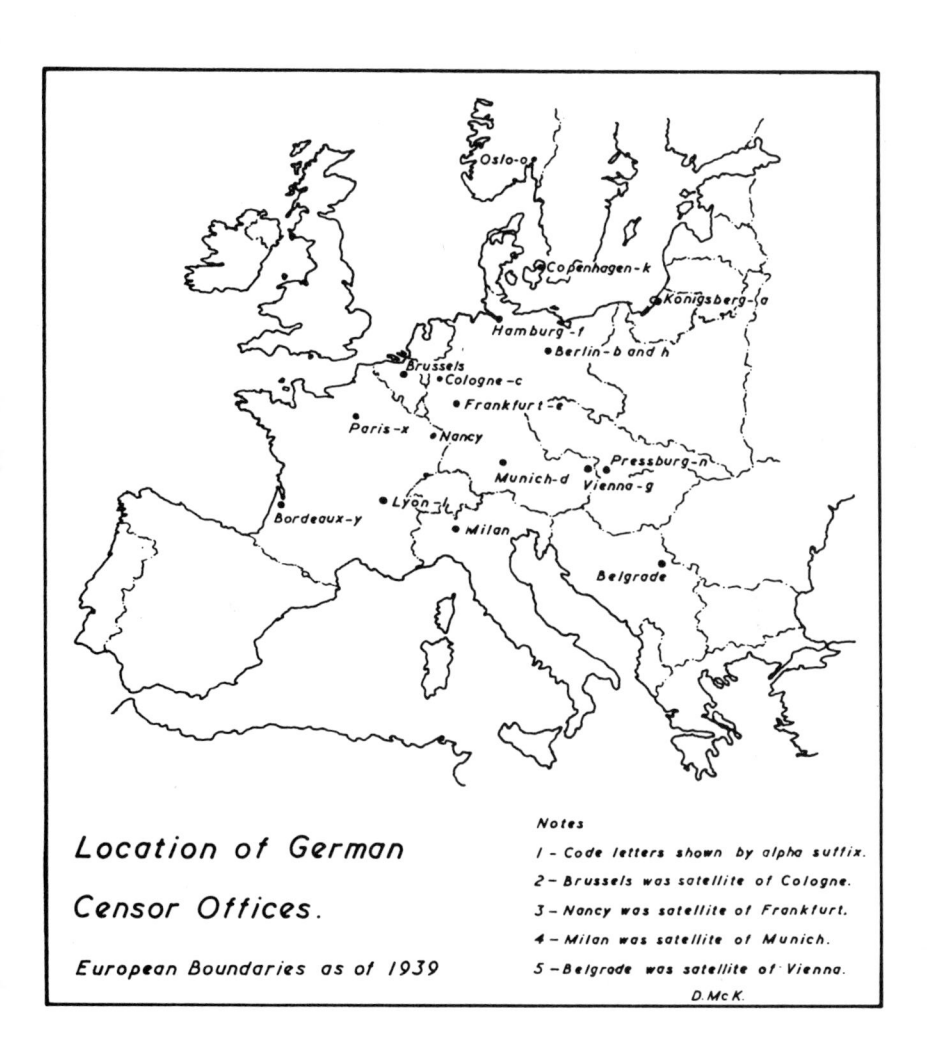

European Boundaries as of 1939

Notes
1 - Code letters shown by alpha suffix.
2 - Brussels was satellite of Cologne.
3 - Nancy was satellite of Frankfurt.
4 - Milan was satellite of Munich.
5 - Belgrade was satellite of Vienna.

D. McK.

The following list itemises the fourteen primary offices and gives their code letters, locations, foreign mails handled and the locations of their sub-offices:

Code Letter	Office Location	Foreign Mail Handled	Sub-Office	Note
a	Konigsberg	Baltic States, U.S.S.R.		
b	Berlin	Air mail in transit to/from North and South America, Red Cross Mails.		
c	Cologne	Holland, Belgium, Luxemburg, Northern France.	Brussels	
d	Munich	Italy, Spain, Portugal, Ireland, Switzerland.	Milan	
e	Frankfurt A.M.	Switzerland, North and South America, Southern France.	Nancy	
f	Hamburg	Scandinavia.		
g	Vienna	Balkans, Hungary, Turkey.	Belgrade	
h	Berlin	German P.O.W. mail.		1
k	Copenhagen	Sweden, Finland, Norway.		2
l	Lyon	To/from Southern France.		3
n	Pressburg			
o	Oslo	Sweden, Finland, Denmark.		4
x	Paris	To/from Paris, Red Cross mails.		5
y	Bordeaux	To/from South West France.		6

Notes:
1 Office opened in the spring of 1944.
2 Office opened in May 1940.
3 Office opened in the winter of 1942.
4 Office opened in the winter of 1940.
5 Office opened in the winter 1940.
6 Office opened in the summer of 1942.

All of these offices were initially administered by the German army, or more specifically, the High Command, the 'Oberkommando der Wehrmacht', with this name appearing on nearly all of the markings. In February 1944, the 'S.S.' or 'Schutzstaffel' replaced the Abwehr as the body responsible for military intelligence and shortly thereafter, following the unsuccessful attempt on Hitler's life by a member of the army on 20 July 1944, the 'S.S.' assumed responsibility for postal censorship from the Oberkommando der Wehrmacht. Heinrich Himmler, Reichfuhrer S.S., delegated responsibility to Dr. Ernst

Kaltenbrunner, head of the National Central Security Office or 'Reichssicherheitsaupamt' (R.S.H.A.). Censorship of internal or domestic mails was performed by Bureau IV, the State Secret Police or 'Geheimestattspolizei' (Gestapo). Censorship of foreign mails was by the Security Police or 'Sicherheitsdienstpolizei' (S.D.), whose head was Dr. Walter Schellenberg. Following the change of control, new hand stamps were prepared on which the word 'Zensurstelle' (censor office) replaced 'Oberkommando der Wehrmacht'.

During the period of O.K.W. administration, the Berlin Office, the largest of all, had a staff of over 3,000 people to deal with foreign mails only, the department being known as the Auslandsbriefprufstelle. The staff was seconded from the War Ministry, Army, Navy and Airforce, together with foreign language experts from the Foreign Office. The numbers were made up as follows:

250 Army Supervisors	Mainly inactive officers.
785 Male censors	
2,000 Female censors	
175 Civil Servants	From the Post Office or Gestapo, etc.
42 Workers	Cleaning staff, etc.

This 3,000 plus staff was divided in to 9 groups:

1 Sorting Group. (Gruppe Sortierung)	Sorting the mails into categories, i.e. Personal, Commercial, P.O.W., Foreign Language, etc.
2 Personal Post Group. (Gruppe Privatpost)	Censoring personal or private letters.
3 Commercial Post Group. (Gruppe Handelpost)	Censoring commercial or business letters.
4 Fieldpost Group. (Gruppe Feldpost)	Controlling and censoring the civil mails to/from neutral or occupied countries, carried by the Feldpost system, but not the normal military Fieldpost mails.
5 P.O.W. Group. (Gruppe Kriegsgefangenenpost)	Censoring the letters to/from German P.O.W. held by the Allies, but not the letters of Allied P.O.W. held by the Germans, these were normally censored at the individual P.O.W. or internment camp.

6	Chemical Group. (Gruppe Chemische Untersuchung).	Testing letters with chemicals and/or optical machines for hidden messages.
7	Card Index Group. (Gruppe Zentralkartei)	Card indexing the names and addresses of all private and commercial mail users, including addressees.
8	Intelligence Group. (Gruppe Auswertung)	Evaluating the contents of the mails for news which may have been of either direct or indirect military significance.
9	P.O.W. Intelligence Group. (Gruppe Kriegsgef. - Briefauswertung)	Evaluating the contents of all mails from German P.O.W. held by the Allies, for news of military significance.

From the list of Primary Offices given above and the details of the Foreign Mail that each handled one would surmise that Internee mail passing between the camps and the United Kingdom could attract censorship markings of any of the Primary Offices at Berlin, Cologne, Munich or Frankfurt; while Internee mail passing between the camps and the Channel Islands might be expected to attract censorship at Cologne or Paris. Research, however, does not bear out these suppositions.

From all the letters that I have recorded, mail between the Internee camps and the Channel Islands or the United Kingdom only attracted censorship at the Primary Offices with the first despatches from Biberach in December 1942 through to the despatches just before D-Day in June 1944. I cannot record any letters after this date being censored at the Primary Offices. It must be remembered that in November 1944 the International Red Cross took over the delivery of Internee mail to the Channel Islands from the German Feldpost and this might account for the cessation of censorship at the Primary Offices, although presumably the mail could still be subject to censoring at the offices in Berlin or Munich which dealt with the Red Cross and Switzerland mails. What is perhaps even more surprising is that only the Internee mails to and from the camps of Biberach, Wurzach and Kreuzburg seem to have been subjected to this extra censorship and that the only Primary Office where they received it was at Frankfurt from December 1942 until March 1944. Indeed, with some despatches from Wurzach camp censorship did not take place as the mail was not taken to Biberach for censoring and so the only censorship the letters have received was at Frankfurt.

A very few examples of letters from Laufen have received a 'Durchlaufstempel', transit censor cachet, 'A.e.' in circle, of Frankfurt. The 'Durchlaufstempel' was a transit mark applied to foreign destined mails at a Primary

Office to indicate usually that the mail had passed through that Office but had not been opened or examined. The capital 'A' in the mark stood for 'Auslandsdienstprufstelle' or Foreign Letter Examination Office, and the small letter was the code letter or 'Kennbuchstaben' of the Primary Office; in this case the small letter was 'e' for Frankfurt. This is the only form of German censorship, outside of the camp censorship, recorded on Laufen mail and therefore any mail from Laufen that has been censored at a Primary Office must be relatively scarce. Letters from Laufen, Biberach, Kreuzburg and St. Denis en-route to the Channel Islands in 1944 have received a 'Durchlaufstempel' transit censor cachet, 'A.x.' in circle, of Paris, but these were all at about the time of the D-Day landing in June and just before the liberation of Paris.

Mail to and from the camps can therefore display two forms of German Censorship markings applied at a Primary Office besides the markings applied in the camps. These two forms of marking are either:

1. Markings to signify that the mail has been opened and examined at the Primary or Secondary Office – these take the form of Hand cancels with an Eagle and Swastika motif, Censor Tapes with the Eagle and Swastika motif and machine cancels also with the Eagle and Swastika motif. Chemical washes obviously indicate examination and very small numbers in a box indicate an individual censor. (See below: 'Frankfurt Censor Cachets').

2. 'Durchlaufstempel' or transit censor cachets which indicate that the mail has passed through a Primary or Secondary Office but has not necessarily been examined.

It is possible to summarise the probability of censorship of Internee mail at the Frankfurt or Paris Offices by one of these methods as follows:

(a) *Laufen*

Laufen Internee mail was seldom censored at a Primary Office. The few examples recorded display only a 'Durchlaufstempel' or transit type of censor mark.

(b) *Biberach*
- (i) Early despatches from Biberach to the United Kingdom or Channel Islands were nearly always censored at Frankfurt.
- (ii) Despatches in 1943 from Biberach to the Channel Islands were usually censored at Frankfurt.
- (iii) Mail in 1943 between Biberach and the United Kingdom (i.e. both ways) was often but not always liable to censorship at Frankfurt.
- (iv) Mail in 1944 between Biberach and the Channel Islands or the United Kingdom was unlikely to be censored at a Primary Office.

(c) *Wurzach*

Mail from the camp during 1943 was often censored at Frankfurt.

(d) *Kreuzburg*
Little mail from the camp is recorded, but at least one letter in early 1944 was censored at Frankfurt.

(e) *Liebenau*
Very little mail is recorded, but as it was all routed through Biberach there is a high possibility that some could also have been censored at Frankfurt.

(f) *Compiègne and St. Denis*
Therse camps were in France and therefore there was no reason for mail from them to be censored at Frankfurt. One card from St. Denis is known to have received a Paris transit mark.

(g) *All camps*
Any mail in the Spring of 1944 en-route to the Channel Islands via Paris might receive a 'Durchlaufstempel' transit censor cachet, 'A.x.' in circle, of the Paris office.

Internee mail was not censored at the Primary Offices after the control of censorship passed from the 'Oberkommando der Wehrmacht' (O.K.W.) to the 'Schutzstaffel' (S.S.) on 20 July 1944 and therefore any of the censor markings found on Internee mail that have been applied at a Primary Office bear the legend 'Oberkommando der Wehrmacht' and not 'Zensurstelle'.

Those German censor markings of Frankfurt and Paris that have been recorded used on Channel Islands Internee mail are described below:

Frankfurt Censor Cachets

Type Fk.C.1: A 34 m.m. single circle cachet with a spread-winged eagle above a laurelled swastika in centre. Above the tips of each wing of the eagle there appears a small + and beneath the swastika is the code letter 'e' of Frankfurt. In Gothic script with small letters 1.5 m.m. high, around the edge of the circle is the word 'Geprüft' above, and the words 'Oberkommando der Wehrmacht' below. This cachet is printed in red and is recorded on some of the first letters from Biberach in December 1942 and early 1943. It is also recorded used in conjunction with a censor tape on a letter from England to Biberach in April 1943.

Type Fk.C.2: This cachet is almost identical to Type Fk.C.1. but for some minute but quite distinct differences. It is a 35 m.m. single circle cachet with a spread-winged eagle above a laurelled swastika in centre. Above the tips of each wing of the eagle there appears the small + but the cachet does not carry any code letter beneath the swastika. The cachet bears the same legend as Type Fk.C.1. but it is clearer because the small letters of the Gothic script are 2 m.m. high. This cachet is printed in red and is recorded used on Internee mail from March until July 1943.

Note: The uninitiated often mistake Frankfurt Censor cachets Types Fk.C.1. and Fk.C.2. for the very rare Eagle and Swastika cachet of Biberach, Type Bb.C.1. In appearance they are superficially similar, but the inscriptions of each are totally different and of course, the Biberach cachet is struck in violet while the Frankfurt cachets are struck in red.

159

Type Fk.C.3: A 'Maschinen-Prufstempel' or machine censor cancel consisting of six parallel lines and a single circle of 28 m.m. diameter with an Eagle and laurelled swastika in the centre beneath which is a small code letter 'e'. Around the edge of the circle in Gothic script with small letters 2 m.m. high appears the word 'Geprüft' with two small crosses on each side of it, while below are the words 'Oberkommando der Wehrmacht'. As the machine is of the continuous repeating type, usually at least two strikes of the cancel appear on a letter or card. This cachet was printed in red/brown and is recorded on Internee mail in February 1943 although it was in use at Frankfurt on other types of mail from February 1942 until February 1944. Its use on Internee mail is very scarce; one item is recorded to England and another to Jersey from Wurzach.

Type Fk.C.4: A 'Durchlaufstempel' transit censor mark, consisting of the letters 'Ae' in a circle. The circle has a diameter of 20 m.m. and the capital 'A' is 11 m.m. high, while the small 'e' is 7.5 m.m. high. Karl Heinz Riemer records the use of this handstamp at Frankfurt from September 1940 until December 1943, but I can only record its use on Internee mail in October 1943 when it was struck in red on a letter from Laufen. Obviously its use on Internee mail is very rare.

Type Fk.C.5: A 'Durchlaufstempel' transit censor mark consisting of the letters 'Ae' in a circle. The circle has a diameter of 21 m.m. and the line forming the circle as well as the two letters is much thicker than in Type Fk.C.4. The capital 'A' is 10 m.m. high and the small 'e' is only 3.5 m.m. high. Karl Heinz Riemer records this handstamp in use at Frankfurt from September 1943 until August 1944 and I can record it struck in red on Internee mail from Biberach in October 1943 and in violet on Internee mail from Laufen in March 1944. As with Type Fk.C.4. this cachet is very rare used on Internee mail.

| 248 |

Type Fk.C.6: A small boxed cachet consisting of a three digit number with figures 2.5 m.m. high, inside a box with dimensions of about 9 m.m. by 4.5 m.m. (Different boxes can vary up to 1 m.m.). The cachet is struck in violet and the most common numbers recorded inside the box and used on Channel Islands Internee mail are 248 and 411 while 214, 353 and 417 are also known. These small boxed cachets were the individual marks of the different censors at Frankfurt and are always seen used in conjunction with the larger cachets, Types Fk.C.1., Fk.C.2. and Fk.C.3.

276

Type Fk.C.7: A cachet consisting only of a two or three digit number with figures 3 m.m. high. The cachet is struck in red and the most common number recorded used on Channel Island Internee mail is 276 although 15, 17, 425 and 457 are also known. As with Type Fk.C.6., these cachets belonged to individual censors and were used in conjunction with cachet Fk.C.1. They were struck inside the circle of cachet Type Fk.C.1. and so can easily be mistaken as being part of that cachet.

Whereas the use of the boxed cachet Type Fk.C.6. in violet is quite common, the use of this un-boxed cachet Type Fk.C.7. in red is relatively scarce.

Frankfurt Censor Tapes

A variety of censor cachets from the Primary Offices are recorded used on Channel Islands Internee mail but only one censor tape has been recorded. The correct name for these tapes is 'Verschlußstreifen' and Karl Heinz Riemer records seven different types in use at the Frankfurt Office although only three were in use during the Internment of the Channel Islanders. Of these three, I can only record one used on Channel Islands Internee mail and this is found on mail from the United Kingdom into the Camps. It is used to re-seal a letter that has been opened and examined by the censor and always has at least one censor cachet used in conjunction with it.

Type Fk.C.T.1: An off-white gummed tape 40 m.m. wide. Printed on this tape in grey/black is a 35 m.m. circle with and Eagle and Laurelled Swastika and the inscription 'Oberkommando der Wehrmacht', in Gothic script above the Eagle, and the code letter 'e' with two small bars each side of it beneath the Eagle, 15 m.m. to the left of this circle is the word 'Geöffnet' in Gothic script, and 28 m.m. to the left of this word is a straight line 8 m.m. long. As these three inscriptions, the line, the word and the circle, were repeated along a continuous roll of tape it is possible to find them on a letter in a variety of combinations although of course always in the same order. This tape is recorded by Karl Heinz Riemer as being in use from January 1941 until December 1943 but I can only record it on Internee mail in May 1943. The tape has been tied to the letter with cachet Type Fk.C.1.

Paris Censor Cachets

As stated before, the only censor cachet of the Paris Primary Censorship Office that has been recorded on Channel Island Internee mails is a 'Durchlaufstempel', transit censor cachet which was in use in the Spring of 1944.

Type Ps.C.1: A 'Durchlaufstempel', transit censor mark consisting of the letters 'A.x.' in a circle. The circle has a diameter of 20 m.m. and the capital 'A' is 6 m.m. high, while the small 'x' is 3.5 m.m. high. This cachet was only in use between March and August 1944 and I can record it during this period of use struck in red on Internee mail from Laufen, Biberach, Kreuzburg and St. Denis. Because of its very limited period of use it is a rare marking on Internee mail.

Channel Islands Censor Cachet

As has already been stated in previous chapters, mail between the Channel Islands and the Internment camps was never censored in the Islands by the Germans as it always received censorship in the camps and more rarely at one of the Primary Censorship Offices. The one exception to this norm is the very limited amount of mail that left the Channel Islands for the Interment camps on the Red Cross relief ship 'Vega' early in 1945. Information contained in these letters could hardly affect the progress of the war but the German Authorities in the Islands did give them cursory censorship and then occasionally applied a 'Dienststelle' (Security Office) Censor cachet to the letters before handing them over to the International Red Cross Officials on board the 'Vega'.

This 'Dienststelle' Censor cachet had been in use in the Islands throughout the Occupation as it was the Security Office cachet of the VII Feldkommandantur 515, Administration Headquarters of the Channel Islands located in Victoria College School House, St. Helier, Jersey. It is known used on some items of Feldpost mail and Don McKenzie records it used on a Red Cross Message on 6 June 1941, but in these examples a Feldpost Number is included in the cachet whereas on the Internee Mail the space on the cachet for the Feldpost Number is left blank.

```
Geprüft
Dienststelle
Feldpost Nr.
    1 c
```

Type Ch.Is.C.1: A rectangular boxed cachet, 47 m.m. long and 29 m.m. high with four lines of Roman script within this box. The four lines of script read:

Geprüft
Dienststella
Feldpost Nr.
1 c

The letters of 'Geprüft' are 4 m.m. and 3 m.m. high while those of 'Dienststella' and 'Feldpost Nr.' are 3 m.m. and 2 m.m. high.

This cachet was struck in crimson on Internee Mail from Jersey during the early months of 1945.

Evidence of Examination and Censorship

Two forms of examination and censoring of Internee mail exist. The first is a chemical wash which is painted on the card either in lines or all over it. This wash leaves a blue, pink or more rarely, a grey stain and its purpose was to show up hidden writing on the letter or card. The second form of censoring is seen when a writer has written a passage which offended the censor, then the offending words were painted over with a fugitive, non-waterproof black ink.

Mail to England from the camps sometimes bears these two forms of censoring but mail to the Channel Islands seldom does. The reason for this is self-evident as England was the enemy, but the Channel Islands were occupied territory and so mail to the Islands always remained within the German Feldpost system. I also believe that if a message addressed to the Channel Islands contained truely offensive or dangerous information, it was removed from the mail and destroyed which was quite convenient and possible for the Germans to do as the Internee mail to the Channel Islands was not inspected or handled by the International Red Cross or the Protecting Power until November 1944. This idea can be substantiated as Frank Stroobant in his book 'One Man's War' mentions that when he was camp leader, the German Authorities at Laufen showed him letters that they had removed from the mail because the letters contained false statements about the welfare of the Internees in the camp and they did not want these letters to cause unfounded consternation in the Channel Islands.

I do have a letter from Laufen to Guernsey which has been censored, the only example that I have ever seen, but this was written in November 1944 when the Red Cross had taken over the transportation of the mail from the Internment Camps. The letter has further unique qualities in that it was censored by the S.S. and bears the 'mysterious four digit cachet' 3961 (see following chapter), but the cachet is struck in purple which is again unique as this mark has only been seen struck in red before. Following this the letter passed through the hands of a British Censor who has applied a boxed cachet Type U.K.C.3. reading 'THE BRITISH EXAMINER IS NOT RESPONSIBLE FOR THE MUTILATION OF THIS CARD'. This is the only recorded example of the use of this British cachet on a Channel Islands Internee letter.

A card from Biberach tested with blue and pink chemical washes.

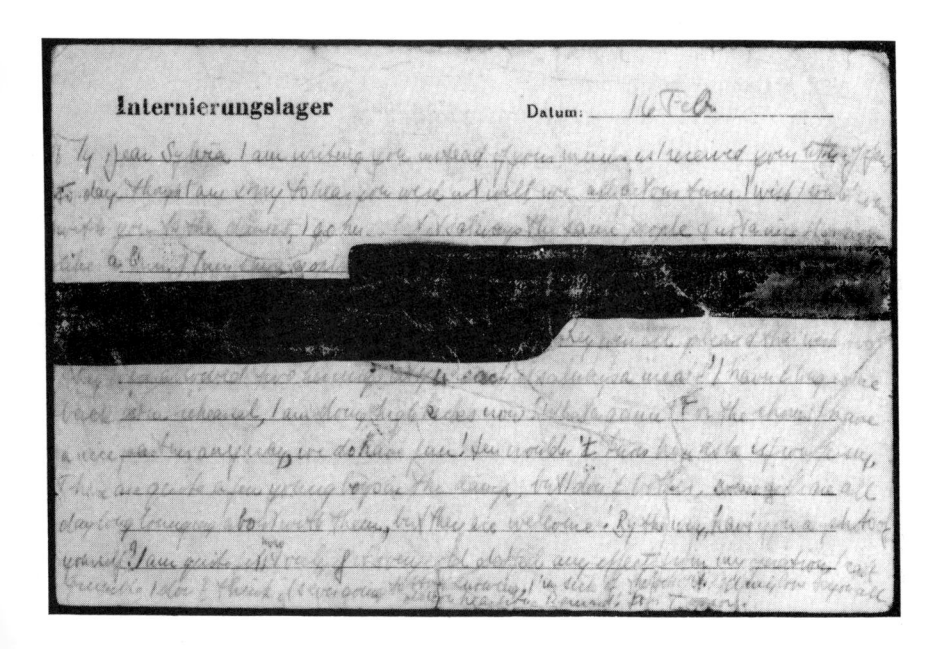

A card from Biberach showing evidence of censoring with black ink.

THE 'MYSTERIOUS' FOUR DIGIT CACHET

In the summer of 1944 a new cachet started appearing on the mail from all the Internee camps. It consisted of a simple four digit number struck in red and made up from figures that were 8.5 m.m. high.

5706 **5412**

Two examples of the four digit cachet.

At first glance it looked as if each cachet was different and possibly printed by some 'continuous counting' handstamp, in which case one would expect the lower numbers to appear in July and August while the higher numbers should appear later in November and December, but simple research does not bear this out. The numbers have no logical chronological sequence as can be seen from the following examples:

July 3774
August 4567 and 9641
September 3526 and 9673
October 3840 and 5555
November 3840, 3961 and 5412
December 5706 (used twice on different dates)

and further, it will be seen from a second glance at these examples that two numbers have been used twice: 3840 in October and November, and 5706 twice in December.

If the numbers had been printed by a continuous counting handstamp that had been reused at least once to get two sets of numbers the chances of finding one duplicate, let alone two duplicates, in such a small sample would be well over 18,000 to 1.

The numbers do not seem to relate to any particular camp; 5706 is recorded on two items of mail from Kreuzburg camp, but 3840 is recorded on mail from Laufen and Liebenau camps, while the other numbers display no logical correlation to the camps.

As we can assume that the mark was not applied in the camps; where could it have been applied, by whom and for what reason? Let me say at the outset that I do not have a conclusive answer to these questions, but after several years of discussion and thought I feel that I now have a likely solution.

Three significant acts took place in the history of the Channel Islands Internees' mail service at about the time that this marking first began to appear.

They are:
1. The D-Day landings on 6 June 1944.
2. The change of control of censorship from the 'Oberkommando der Wehrmacht' (O.K.W.) to the 'Schutzstaffel' (S.S.) during July 1944 following the attempt on Hitler's life by a member of the Army.
3. The take-over in transmission of all Internee Mails by the Red Cross in November 1944.

For a long time I though the third act was the answer and that this was a continuous counting cachet of the Red Cross, applied especially to Internee Mail when the Red Cross took over the transmission of all Internee Mail from the German Feldpost; this could also account for the marking appearing on mail addressed to the United Kingdom as well as the Channel Islands. I had to disregard this theory as more examples of the cachet were recorded and especially with earlier dates of usage. The earliest example I can now record is on a letter from Laufen camp dated 29 July 1944 which is well over three months before the Red Cross became involved with Channel Islands Internee Mail.

Several researchers favoured the significance of the first point, believing that the marking was one belonging to the Allied Armies or even the British Censor, especially as it is struck in a similar colour to that of the British 'Crown over Passed P.W. – ' Censor cachets. I never liked this idea, particularly as the four digit cachet appears on letters to the Channel Islands which should not necessarily have entered the hands of the Allies. More important still, covers with this cachet form only a small proportion of the Internee mail at this time going to either England or the Channel Islands, but as the British cacheted almost every piece of mail that passed through their hands this mark would have to be much more prolific if it belonged to the British censor.

It is only recently that the true significance of the second point listed above has dawned on me. In the chapter 'German Censorship' I have explained at length the importance of the Transit Censor Offices run by the 'Oberkommando der Wehrmacht' and I have described the cachets from these offices which are recorded on Channel Islands Internees' mail. When the control of censorship changed from the 'O.K.W.' to the 'S.S.' on or about 20 July 1944, the handstamps used to cachet mail no longer bore the legend 'Oberkommando der Wehrmacht', but carried the word 'Zensurstelle' of the 'S.S.' and because none of these cachets bearing the word 'Zensurstelle' had been found on Channel Islands Internees' mail, I assumed that the 'S.S.' did not censor the Internees' mail at the Transit Offices as the 'O.K.W.' had previously done. Now the facts seem to indicate differently:

(a) This four digit cachet is struck in a red colour similar to that used for Transit Office censor cachets.

(b) This four digit cachet being quite scarce, is found in similar proportions to contemporary uncacheted mail as earlier covers were found with Transit Office censor cachets in proportion to those that were not censored at a Transit Office.

(c) This four digit cachet is very scarce on Laufen camp mail and earlier Transit Office censor cachets are almost unknown on Laufen camp mail.

(d) The 'S.S.' took over censorship from the 'O.K.W.' on about 20 July 1944 and the earliest recorded example of the four digit marking is on a letter posted on 29 July 1944.

(e) Although several different four digit numbers are recorded, some are the same and not enough have been recorded in chronological order to suggest a continuous counting handstamp. This parallels with the individual Censors' cachets in use at the 'O.K.W.' Transit Office in Frankfurt which were high numbers e.g. 214, 248, 357, 411, etc., several different ones were recorded on Internee mail but many were recorded more than once.

I now believe that this four digit cachet is probably a previously unrecorded cachet of the 'Schutzstaffel' (S.S.) Censorship and that the different numbers belonged to individual censors. It has always seemed strange that censorship at the Transit Offices of Internee mail should cease in July 1944 with the change over of control of censorship to the 'S.S.', but these unidentified four digit cachets probably hurriedly produced and without the word 'Zensurstelle' could explain how that misconception might have arisen.

Footnote: An example of the four digit cachet has recently been discovered struck in purple ink. This is the only example known of this colour and it is used on a letter from Laufen to Guernsey written in November 1944. The significance of the colour difference could be in the fact that the letter has been censored by the German Censor and some offending words have been obliterated with black ink. All the examples of this mark struck in red are on letters which display no other signs of censoring by the Germans.

GERMAN PRISONER OF WAR CAMPS
(AND CIVILIAN INTERNEE CAMPS)

At least one Channel Islands service man is known to have been a Prisoner of War in Changi Camp, Singapore, several others are recorded as Prisoners of War in Italy, and one Channel Islands family were in a Civilian Internment Camp in Italy and later transferred to Biberach, but the majority of Prisoner of War and Civilian Internee mail having a Channel Islands connection originated in one or other of the German Camps. Therefore, to aid the researcher and dispel some of the confusion that arises when Prisoner of War mail is found addressed to the Channel Islands and is often assumed to be from a Channel Islands Internee rather than a service man, an attempt has been made to give below a comprehensive listing of all the German Prisoner of War camps. Official documents covering this subject and period are not available to the public, consequently the camp listings are almost certainly incomplete but I am grateful to Don McKenzie who has made available to me his unpublished research which forms the basis for these lists and was in its turn based on the work of Karl Kurt Wolter.

It is virtually impossible to be specific on all the camps which housed Channel Islands service men but I have underlined the names of those camps in the lists which I know did at some time in their existence, hold Channel Islands Prisoners of War.

There are several reasons why so many different camps held Channel Islands Prisoners of War and one of these was given to me when visiting the Jersey Militia Museum. The Guernsey and Jersey Militias fought alongside other British troops in both World Wars, but the War Office learned a hard lesson from World War I when so many young Channel Islands males were killed at the same time. Although the Channel Islanders might prefer to fight together, it was the policy of the War Office in the Second World War not to have all the Channel Islands troops in one regiment, then if one company met with disaster, not all the Channel Islands young males would be killed. The Channel Islands troops were therefore split up and fought in many different campaigns and with various regiments, hence those that were captured were taken at different times and places and so found themselves in a variety of camps.

Another reason why so many camps are recorded as holding Channel Islands Prisoners of War comes from the fact that the Prisoners of War were frequently moved from one camp to another. In my own collection of wartime mail I have a correspondence from one man on letters from three diffeent camps, and I have before me another letter from a Channel Islands Prisoner of War in Oflag VIB which states:

'I have been to a number of places in Germany since my captivity, also Czechoslovakia and Poland. It is a change moving about from place to place but am simply longing to get back again to Guernsey.'

* * * *

'Replying to a question by Lord Portsea, in the House of Lords, on the 3 December 1941, Lord Croft, Joint Parliamentary Secretary, War Office, said that six officers and seventy eight other ranks, who were in the Channel Islands at the time of the enemy occupation, had been reported to have been taken prisoner. All these men were regarded as Prisoners of War and their families were treated in exactly the same way as other Prisoners of War in respect of allowances. These remittances could not be paid to wives and dependents in enemy territory (i.e. the occupied Channel Islands) but it had been arranged that grants and allotments should be banked until it was possible to release the accumulated sums'.

That news item appeared in 'The Times' in December 1941 and the letter written at Oflag VIB from which I have quoted above was written by one of those six officers mentioned in the news article, a Captain Alfred Connors. It has always been thought that these service men in the Channel Islands at the time of the German invasion were left at liberty for several days by the Germans, but Captain Connors in an earlier part of the same letter written on 10 March 1942 states:

'Well Sis, as regards myself I was taken prisoner when the Germans landed on the evening of 30 June 1940 and have been a Prisoner of War ever since. Two Years the end of June.'

By the end of the war, Captain Connors would have been a prisoner for five years and probably 300 more Channel Islands Service men besides these original eighty four would have been captured, so it is perhaps not so suprising that such a large number of camps are recorded as holding Channel Islands Prisoners of War. The Channel Islanders however, formed only a very small proportion of the approximate 1,500,000 captives held by the Germans in 216 camps during the period of 1939-1945. A Prisoner of War letter from a Channel Islander is therefore very scarce and also about four times rarer than a letter from a Channel Islands Internee.

The 216 German camps were divided into seven categories, each of which held a different class of prisoner and was given an identification number as well as a name. Two facts should be noted about these camps; the first is that 36 camps were used exclusively for holding Italian prisoners after their status changed from ally to enemy following the Italian surrender in the late summer of 1943, and the second fact is that the same camp can appear in two of the lists below, this applies particularly to six of the Internee camps, which also appear in the list of Officer camps. The seven categories of camps are as follows:—

(i)	Prisoner of War camps	—	Stammlager (Stalag)
(ii)	Officer camps	—	Offizierlager (Oflag)
(iii)	Internee camps	—	Interniertenlager (Ilag)
(iv)	Naval camps	—	Marinelager (Marlag)
	Army camps	—	Militarlager (Milag)
	Air Force camps	—	Luftlager (Luft)
	Transit camps	—	Durchgangslager (Dulag)
(v)	Penal camps	—	Straflager (Stralag)
(vi)	Labour camps	—	Arbeiter-Lager (Arlag)
(vii)	Labour Battalions	—	Arbeitsbataillone (Arbat)

During World War I, the German authorities did not regard the location of Prisoner of War and Internee camps as being worthy of being classified as secret. From 1939 to 1945 an attempt was made to keep all camp locations for military personnel, a secret, but the secrecy was not so strict for the Internment camps. Letters from Biberach had the camp name preprinted on them while letters from Laufen usually only had the camp number, but then the postmark of Biberach was often a dumb cancel while that of Laufen was always the normal town cancel with the name 'Laufen – (Oberbay).' Censorship regulations were enforced by the Germans however, when reports from such letters were printed in the Channel Islands newspapers. Camp names were only indicated by their Title letter 'B_____' Biberach, 'L_____' Laufen, etc. even though everybody in the Islands obviously knew what the letters represented. For Prisoner of War mail however, the censorship regulations were more stringent and dictated that only dumb post-office cancels should be used to postmark the mail; nevertheless, it is known that some covers do exist bearing a town cancel, these are scarce and for the collector of Prisoner of War mail they justify an appreciable premium.

In total, approximately 1,500 million pieces of mail were transmitted. This mail from the camps was similar to that described in the various chapters on the Internment Camps. Each camp had its own individual Lettersheets and Postcards with the camp number, but rarely the name or location, preprinted on them, and as they were all Prisoner of War camps the stationery of course carried the heading 'Kriegsgefangenenpost'. Such printings of this stationery were numerous and varied, but in times of shortages of the camps' own stationery or when a camp was in the process of being set up, then use was made of the 'universal' Kriegsgefangenenpost stationery which had no camp designation preprinted on it and to which I have made frequent reference in the preceding chapters. Some camps also issued 'exceptional' stationery. An amusing example from Oflag VIB and addressed to the Channel Islands for the Christmas of 1941 is illustrated overleaf.

> BUT I ASSURE YOU, MY DEAR CHAP — I REALLY AM FATHER CHRISTMAS!

'Exceptional' stationery from Oflag VIB for Christmas 1941.

Each camp had its own censor office which stamped all mail. The censor cachets used were non uniform, indeed within individual camps the cachets were of completely different form. They invariably carried the camp number, which was made up of the Roman numerals I to XXI with usually a suffix letter, A to K. In addition, most cachets have the individual censors number shown in Arabic numerals. The censor cachets were stamped in a variety of colours at different camps, but in the lists below an attempt has been made to record most of the types and colours of the various camp's censor marks.

The following abbreviations are used for the censor mark types and colours:

s/l	straight line	r	red
b	box or frame, often with a peculiar shape	b	blue
c	circle	l	lilac
dc	double circle	bl	black
o	oval	v	violet
x	other	g	green
(v)	(used as a suffix) various types		

Camp names underlined are recorded, from this research, as having held Channel Islanders at some time during the war.

P.O.W. Camps – Stammlager (Stalag)

These camps were for other ranks and the following table lists those in existence at the end of 1943. In the following year, camps IIIE, VE, VIH, XIIB, XIIC, XIIE, XXIB, XXICH and XXICZ had been closed.

Camp No.	Location	Censor Marks	Colours
IA	Stablack	b,c.	v.
IB	Hohenstein	o.	b,r.
IE	Prostken	b.	v.
IIA	Neubrandenburg	s/l,b(v),dc, trapezoid.	bl.
IIB	Hammerstein	b,c,dc,shield.	v.
IIC	Greifswald	b(v),o.	r.
IID	Stargard	b(v).	v.
IIE	Schwerin	b.	v.
IIIA	Luckenwalde	b(v),dc. box-in-box.	r,b,v.
IIIB	Furstenberg	b,c,dc.	bl,v.
IIIC	Alt-Drewitz	b,x.	v.
IIID	Lichterfelde-Sud	s/l,b,c.	bl,v.
IIIE	Kirchau	heptagon.	v.
IVA	Hohenstein	b,o. hexagon.	bl,v.
IVB	Muhlberg	b(v),o(v), octagon	r,v.
IVC	Wistritz	b,c(v).	bl,v.
IVD	Torgau	b(v),dc,o(v), shield.	v.
IVE	Altenburg	s/l.	
IVF	Hartmannsdorf	b(v),c(v).	bl,v.
IVG	Oschatz	b(v),c.	r,b,bl,l,v.
VA	Ludwigsburg	c, circle with flag.	r.
VB	Villingen	c(v).	
VC	Offenburg	b(v),c.	r,bl,l.
VD	Strasburg	s/l.	
VE	Muhlhausen Els	s/l.	

Camp No.	Location	Censor Marks	Colours
VIA	Hemer	b,c,o.	bl,v.
VIB	Neu Versen	b(v).	l.
VIC	Bathorn	s/l,c.	bl.
VID	Dortmund	o(v).	r,v.
VIF	Bocholt	b.	bl.
VIG	Bonn	c.	v.
VIH	Arnoldsweiler	c.	bl.
VIJ	Krefeld-Fichtenhain	Trapezoid (v).	v.
VIK	Paderborn	b.	v.
VIIA	Moosburg	b,c.	r,b,v.
VIIB	Memmingen	b.	r.
VIIIA	Gorlitz	b(v),o. triangle.	r,bl,v.
VIIIB	Teschen	b(v),o(v).	r,bl,v.
VIIIC	Sagan	b,c.	r.
IXA	Ziegenhain	s/l,b(v),c, segment.	r,v.
IXB	Wegscheide	b,c, rhomboid.	v.
IXC	Bad Sulza	s/l,b,c.	r,b,v.
XA	Schleswig	s/l.	
XB	Sandborstel	s/l.	
XC	Nimburg/Bohm	b.	v.
XIA	Altenbrabow	s/l(v),b(v).	v.
XIB	Fallingbostel	b(v),c,o(v).	bl,v.
XIIA	Limburg	a(v),b(v).	bl,v.
XIIB	Frankenthal	b(v),c.	r,bl,v.
XIIC	Wiebelsheim	c, triangle.	r,b.
XIID	Trier	b(v),c,o.	r,b,bl.
XIIE	Metz	s/l.	
XIIF	Forbach	s/l(v),b, triangle.	b,v.
XIIIA	Bad Sulzbach	s/l,c.	r,v.
XIIIB	Weiden	s/l,b.	r,bl.
XIIIC	Hammelburg	c.	r,v.
XIIID	Nurnberg-Langwasser	b.	v.

Camp No.	Location	Censor Marks	Colours
XVIIA	Kaisersteinbruch	b(v),o.	bl,v.
XVIIB	Gneizendorf (Krems)	b.	r,bl.
XVIIIA	Wolfsberg	c(v).	bl,l,v.
XCIIIA/Z	Spittal	s/l.	
XVIIIB	Oberdrauburg	s/l.	
XVIIIC	Markt-Pongau	c(v).	bl,v.
XVIIID	Marburg	o.	v.
XXA	Thorn	b(v), Trapezoid, flag, rhomboid, cross.	bl,v.
XXB	Marienburg	b(v).	r,v.
XXIA	Schildberg	s/l,b,c, octagon, heart-shape.	bl,v.
XXIB	Schubin	s/l.	
XXICH	Wollstein	c.	b.
XXICZ	Gratz	b.	v.
XXID	Posen	s/l,c,o.	bl,v.

Another short listing of camps identified by arabic numerals are known to have existed in 1944.

317	Markt Pongau		
344	Lamsdorf	b.	bl.
357	Thorn (later Fallingbostel)		
371	Stanislau	c.	r.
383	Hohenfels		
398	Pupping		

P.O.W. Camps – Offizierslager (Oflag)

The following table gives those in existence during 1943. Not less than 24 were closed during 1944, including IIA, IIC, IID, IIE, IIIA, IIIB, IIIC, IVA, VIB, VID, VIIB, VIICH, VIIIB, VIIIC, VIIIG, VIIIHH, IXAH, IXAZ, IXB, XA, XVIIIB, XVIIIC, XXIB, XXIC. In addition, six camps were reclassified as Internment Camps, VB, VC, VII, VIIC/Z, VIIIA, VIIIH/Z.

Camp No.	Location	Censor Marks	Colours
IIA	Prenzlau	b.	r.
IIB	Arnswalde	s/l.	v.
IIC	Woldenberg	s/l.	
IID	Grossborn	b(v),o, triangle,octagon.	b,v.
IIE	Neubrandenburg	s/l.	r.
IIIA	Luckenwalde	s/l.	
IIIB	Furstenberg	c.	v.
IIIC	Lubben	b(v),dc.	v.
IVA	Hohnstein	s/l.	
IVB	Konigstein	b(v).	g,b,v.
IVC	Leipzig-Colditz	b,c.	r.
IVD	Elsterhorst	s/l(v),b.	bl,v.
VA	Weinsberg	c(v).	b,bl.
VB	Biberach	See under Internee Camps	
VC	Wurzach	See under Internee Camps	
6	Tost/Oppeln	b.	bl.
VIA	Soest	dogs head in circle.	r.
VIB	Dossel-Warburg	s/l,b.	r,v.
VIC	Osnabruck	s/l.	
VID	Munster	s/l.	
VIE	Dorsten	c.	v.
VII	Laufen	See under Internee Camps	
VIIA	Nurnau	b,c.	r,v.
VIIB	Eichstatt	s/l,b.	r.
VIIC,CH	Laufen	c.	b,v.

178

Camp No.	Location	Censor Marks	Colours
VIICZ	Tittmoning	See under Internee Camps	
VIIIA	Oppeln	See under Internee Camps	
VIIIB	Silberberg	s/l.	
VIIIC	Juliusburg	s/l.	
VIIID	Hoyerswerda	s/l.	
VIIIE	Johannisbrunn	b.	r.
VIIIF	Mahrisch Trubau	shield.b.	bl,r.
VIIIG	Freiwaldau	s/l.	
VIIIH/H	Oberlangendorf	triangle.	v.
VIIIH/Z	Kreuzburg	See under Internee Camps	
IX A/H	Burg Spangenberg	b.	v.
IX A/Z	Rosenburg/Fulda	b.	b.
IX B	Weilburg	s/l.	
10	Hohensalza	o.	v.
XA	Tuchel, spater Itzehoe	s/lb(v).	b,v,bl.
XB	Nienburg	s/l,b(v).	r,b,v,bl.
XC	Lubeck	s/l(v),b,o.	r,bl.
XD	?	s/l.	b.
XIA	Osterode	s/l.	
XIIB	Mainz	b(v).	v,bl.
XIIIA	Hammelburg	b.	bl.
XIIIB	Nurnberg	s/l.	b.
XVIIA	Edelbach	b.	r.
XVIIIA	Lienz	s/l.	
XVIIIB	Wolfsberg	s/l.	
XVIIIC	Spittal	c.	v.
XXIA	Grune/Lissa	s/l,dc.	r,bl.
XXIB	Schubin	s/l.	v.
XXIC	Schokken	b.	r.

Oflag 6, Tost/Oppeln and 10, Hohensalza are the only two having Arabic numerals in the handstamps.

Oflag IVB, Konigstein/Sachsen was reserved for officers of General's rank.

Internee Camps – Interniertenlager (Ilag)

These were the camps for enemy (Allied) aliens.

Camp No.	Name Location	Censor Marks	Colours
	Bad Neuenahr		
VB	Biberach	s/l(v),dc(v).	v,b.
VC	Wurzach/Wurtt	s/l,dc.	v,bl.
	Liebenau		
VII	Laufen Obb.	c(v),o(v),s/l(v).	v,b,r.
VII C/Z	Tittmong Obb.		
VIII	Oppeln O.S.		
VIIIZ	Kreuzburg O.S.	dc,triangle, heart.	r.
10	Tost O.S.		
XIII	Wulzburg: Weissenburg/By	b(v)	r.
Frauenlager	Dongelberg/Belgium		
XVIII	Spittal Drau Austria (1944)		

Naval, Army, Airforce and transit Camps – Marine-, Militar-, Luft and Durchgangslager, (Marlag, Milag, Luft and Dulag)

The names are self-explanatory in that the first three camps were for P.O.W.'s from each of the three armed forces. The Transit camps housed prisoners of all services, usually newly captured, for short periods prior to them being sent to another camp.

The abbreviation 'Hulag' in all probability translates to Sub camp or satellite camp.

Camp Name	Location	Censor Marks	Colour
Marlag and Milag Nord	Wilhelmshaven	3 lines framed (v).	v.
Marlag and Milag Nord	Barmstedt-Bremen	3 lines.	v.
Dulag Nord	Wilhelmshaven		
Dulag Luft	Oberursel		
Luft 2	Bad Vogelsand		
Luft 3	Sagan	2 lines framed.	bl.
Luft 6	Heydekrug	30mm circle.	bl.
Hulag VA	Konstanz		
Hulag VC	Offenburg		

Labour Camps–Arbeiter-Lager (Arlag)

After the Italian surrender to the Allies in September, 1943, the Germans took prisoner all Italian servicemen who would not continue fighting under Mussolini. These prisoners were transferred to camps, generally located in urban areas, where they had to work in German industry.

Camp Name	Location
Gemeinschaftslager	Berlin, Borsigwalde
Gemeinschaftslager 15	Berlin, Schoneberg
Gemeinschaftslager Ahorn	Potsdam-Babelsberg
Gemeinschaftslager Loss	Stassfurt
Gemeinschaftslager No. 4914.01.14	Stassfurt
Gemeinschaftslager Mappes	Aglasterhausen
Gemeinschaftslager zur Eiche	Munich
Gemeinschaftslager Ringsee I	Ingolstadt
Gemeinschaftslager Rostock III	Rostock
Gemeinschaftslager Mitte I	Eberswalde
Gemeinschaftslager Goldene Wiege	Hamburg-Harburg
Gemeinschaftslager Ostbau	Odertal
DAF Gemeinschaftslager Schiesstand	Hamburg
DAF Gemeinschaftslager Lederstrasse	Hamburg-Stellingen
DAF Gemeinschaftslager G	Berlin, Malchow
OT Lager	Bremen
OT Ital.u.Baum.	Trznietz
OT Ital.Hafendorf	Kapfenberg
OT West	Golsen
OT Zenit	Karlsruhe-Durlach
OT 6	Eberbach/Neckar
OT 32	Brux
Wohnlager 2	Nattenbek
Wohnlager 31	Brux
Waldlager Britz	Angermunde
Reichbahnlager 5	Traun/Linz
Arbeitslager Berengelfeld	Danzig
Arbeitslager Wiesen	Dirschau
Arbeitslager Schutzenhaus	Magdeburg
Arbeitslager	Steinburg/Elsass
Arbeitslager	Bevensen
Arbeitslager	Holzminden
Arbeitslager	Langenlois
Arbeitslager	Radenthein
Arbeitslager	Zwickau/Aussig
Arbeitslager	Oranienburg
Arbeitslager	Dusseldorf-Oberkassel

This list is by no means complete. Usually the camp identification was given by a single stamp which cannot be considered a censor mark. Mail which was censored usually received both a handstamp and a machine stamp. The handstamp 34-36 m.m. dia., in red or black, was the eagle and swastika surrounded by 'Oberkommando der Wehrmacht', the word 'Gepruft' was contained in an external segment at the top, a small cross was at the bottom. The machine stamp in black was that of Munich containing A over d in a circle within two horizontal lines.

ITALIAN P.O.W. CAMPS
(for Allied Service men)

The camps were in use prior to the Italian surrender in 1943. Not all the locations are recorded because the list was taken from a Red Cross Map of Prisoner of War Camps in use in 1943.

Camp No.	Location	P.M.No.	Camp No.	Location	P.M.No.
P.G.5.	Serravalle	3100	P.G.75	Bari	3450
P.G.10	?	3300	P.G.77	?	3300
P.G.12	Candeli	3200	P.G.78	Sulmona	3300
P.G.21	Chieti	3300	P.G.82	Arezzo	3200
P.G.29	Viano	3200	P.G.85	Tuturano	3450
P.G.35	Padula	3400	P.G.87	Settore	3400
P.G.38	Poppi	3200	P.G.91	Avezzano	3300
P.G.47	Modena	3200	P.G.102	Nr. Aquila	3300
P.G.49	Reggio Nelle Emilia	3200	P.G.103	?	3100
P.G.52	Chiavari	3100	P.G.106	Vercelli	3100
P.G.53	Sforza Costa	3300	P.G.107	?	3200
P.G.54	Fara-in-Sabina	3300	P.G.113	?	3200
P.G.55	?	3200	P.G.115	Marciano	3200
P.G.57	Gruppignano	3200	P.G.118	?	3200
P.G.59	Servigliano	3300	P.G.120	?	3300
P.G.62	Grumillina	3200	P.G.122	South of Rome	3300
P.G.63	Aversa	3400	P.G.129	?	3300
P.G.65	Gravina	3450	P.G.133	?	3100
P.G.66	Capua	3400	P.G.136	Bologna	3200
P.G.70	Monturano	3300	P.G.145	?	3300
P.G.73	Carpi	3200	P.G.146	?	3100
			P.G.148	Verona	3200

BRITISH CENSORSHIP

British Censor markings do not present the complicated and confusing intricacies inherent in the German Censorship structure, but the British Post Office and the War Office remain reluctant to divulge the workings of the Postal Censorship or the significance of the various hand cachets and tapes used. Mail that has been examined by the British Censor bears either one of the numerous 'Crown over Passed' hand cachets, or if the item was a sealed letter that has been opened by the censor then it will have been resealed with one of the 'P.C.90'. Postal Censorship tapes.

Mail from the United Kingdom, addressed to German Internment Camps was subject to censorship by the British Postal Censor before leaving England. It was not normal policy to forward a letter if it contained a passage that offended the British Censor. More usually the letter would be returned to the sender with a British Postal Censorship leaflet explaining why the letter was returned and asking for it to be re-written with the offending sentences omitted.

Mail entering the United Kingdom from an Internment Camp was also subject to immediate censorship before delivery could be made. When the Channel Islanders were deported and their first batches of cards arrived from Dorsten, the British Censors compiled a complete report from these, of conditions in the Islands and in the camp, as well as the names of all the Internees that they could glean from the cards. At other times they would photograph letters if they contained any possible information that might prove useful. This information was then passed on to interested Government and Military departments without the receiver ever realising that the letter had been tampered with. Several examples exist in the Red Cross Archives in the Public Record Office at Kew of reports of casualties and deaths in the Channel Islands that were taken from the Internees' letters by the Postal Censor and passed on to the Red Cross and M.I.12. If a letter from the Internee displayed signs of censoring by the Germans, then the British Censor would try and restore the deletion to discover what the information was that the German censor had tried to destroy. Sometimes the British Censor was successful, other times he was not, but either way he would re-delete the passage after he had inspected it and then send on the letter to the addresses with a Postal Censorship Leaflet enclosed or a Cachet stating that the British Censor was not responsible for the mutilation of the letter.

Mail passing between the Channel Islands and the German Internment Camps did not enter British hands and so did not receive British Censorship; however, some items of mail from the camps, addressed to the Channel Islands were misrouted via England and these were censored by the British Censor before being returned to the Continent. Other items of mail captured by the advancing Allied Armies in Europe in 1944 were taken to England where they were censored by the British Censor, but were not delivered in the Channel Islands until after the end of the war.

Two different types of 'Crown over Passed' hand cachets and two distinct types of the 'P.C.90.' Tape have been recorded used on Channel Islands Internee Mail passing between the Internment Camps and the United Kingdom or the Channel Islands, but only one example of a rare Censor's handstruck, instructional cachet, has been recorded on Channel Island Internee mail.

United Kingdom Censor Cachets

Type U.K.C.1. (P.O.W.): An elongated octagon cachet, each example of which is of a different size, but the average measurements are 35 m.m. by 27 m.m. Inside the octagon is a crown over the word 'PASSED' in capital letters 3 m.m. high, and beneath this are the letters 'P.W.' followed by a three or more often, four digit numeral.

The letters 'P.W.' are thought to indicate 'Prisoner of War' as this type of cachet is normally found applied to the mail of enemy Prisoners of War and British Prisoners of War as well as the mail of Internees. The exact number of these cachets in use and the significance of their individual numbers is not known, but the following list, which is by no means complete, gives the numbers that I have been able to record on mail associated with the Channel Islands Internees.

426	3096	3874	6064	9196
914	3142	4615	6207	9491
2194	3235	4868	6515	9497
2763	3246	4920	7549	9505
2845	3257	5185	7819	9526
3033	3510	5888	7996	

Cachet Type U.K.C.1. was in use throughout the period of internment of the Channel Islanders and was nearly always struck in crimson. 'P.W.5185' is significant in that it is the only example recorded struck in blue and maroon.

Type U.K.C.2 (Civil): An elongated octagon cachet, of identical format to Type U.K.C.1. except that the 'P.W.' is replaced by the single letter 'P'. This is a Civil censor cachet, struck in crimson and more usually found on Red Cross Message forms. Don McKenzie in his book 'The Red Cross Mail Service for Channel Island Civilians 1940–45' erroneously mentions 500 of these cachets being in use; there were in fact only 300, but of these, only five have been recorded used on Channel Islands Internees' mail, and these were only used during September to December 1944. The numbers recorded are: P127, P128, P152, P213 and P236.

The limited period of use and the few numbers recorded make this a very scarce U.K. Cachet on Internee mail, but one could ask why this Civil Censor should appear at all on what is basically Prisoner of War mail.

A possible explanation is that most of the letters on which this mark is found are addressed to the Channel Islands in late 1944. Presumably they were taken to Switzerland by the Red Cross with the intention of being sent to the Islands via Lisbon on the 'Vega'. They obviously did not go by the 'Vega', having received this Civilian U.K. Censor cachet and so they were probably redirected from Lisbon to the U.K. As mails received from the Red Cross, via Lisbon, were usually Red Cross civilian message scheme forms which were censored with a 'Crown over Passed over P numeral' mark, this could explain how Internee mail (PW) received a Civil (P) censor mark.

A probably unique example of this cachet 'P152' has been recorded struck in purple and used in conjunction with cachet Type U.K.C.3. described below.

188

```
┌─────────────────────────────┐
│  THE BRITISH EXAMINER       │
│  IS NOT RESPONSIBLE         │
│  FOR THE MUTILATION         │
│  OF THIS CARD.              │
└─────────────────────────────┘
```

Type U.K.C.3. (Instructional): A boxed cachet showing some distortion, but with average dimensions of 50 m.m. by 21 m.m. Inside the box appears four lines of legend in Roman Capitals 2.5 m.m. high:

    THE BRITISH EXAMINER
     IS NOT RESPONSIBLE
    FOR THE MUTILATION
      OF THIS CARD.

The cachet is struck in crimson and is used on a letter in conjunction with cachet Type U.K.C.2. 'P152' which is struck in purple.

Only one example of this cachet has been recorded on mail from Channel Islands Internees and this is on a letter from Laufen posted on 4 Nov. 44. The letter bears other unique cachets; Type U.K.C.2. 'P152' struck in purple and the four digit cachet '3961' of the German S.S., but also struck in purple. The letter shows evidence of censorship by deletion and this in itself is very unusual as the letter is addressed to Guernsey and not England as one might expect from such censorship.

British Military Censor Cachet

One other type of British Censor cachet should be mentioned and this is the double circle cachet bearing a crown and the legend 'DEPUTY CHIEF FIELD CENSOR' belonging to the British Military forces in occupation in Germany at the end of the war. This cachet has been recorded on post-liberation mail from Laufen Internment Camp and although in reality it is a British Censor cachet, I have recorded it in detail as Laufen Cachet Type Lf.C.10. because so far its only recorded use as far as Channel Islands Internees' mail is concerned, is on Laufen mail.

Don McKenzie in his book 'The Red Cross Mail Service for Channel Island Civilians 1940-45' records a similar cachet (his Type 7.3.) struck in violet on Channel Island Red Cross message forms of M.E.F. origin from the VIIIth Army.

United Kingdom 'P.C.90' Censor Tapes

Numerous variations of the 'P.C.90' tapes exist and only a very limited sample are represented on mail associated with the Channel Islands Internees, but they all have in common the legend 'OPENED BY/EXAMINER (NUMBER)' and elsewhere on the tape, the code 'P.C.90'.

The use of the 'P.C.90' tape is most commonly found on sealed envelopes leaving the United Kingdom for an Internee Camp, as the Postcards and Lettersheets from the camps facilitated censorship and so did not need to be resealed with a tape. It is interesting to note that the German Censors also used cachets and tapes but that whenever they used a censor tape, it was always 'tied' to the envelope by at least one strike of the censor's cachet whereas one never finds a British 'P.C.90' tape 'tied' to the envelope with one of the octagonal cachets.

Type U.K.C.T.1.

```
51-2107—G.W.D.                    P.C. 90

        OPENED BY
      EXAMINER 3068
```

A white tape 50 m.m. wide and 87 m.m. long bearing a printer's code in the top left corner and 'P.C.90' in the top right corner, while across the centre in thick capital letters 9 m.m. higher are the words:

OPENED BY
EXAMINER 3068.

Similar tapes have been recorded for Examiner 8967 and Examiner 3796 while the printer's codes in the top left corner have been '51-2107 G.W.D.' and '51-2116 G.W.D.'.

A variation to this tape is one with exactly the same format of printing but with very much thinner lettering which possibly results from being produced by a different printer. On this finer printing, Examiners '5126' and '2,827' have been recorded, while the printer's code was '51-8959.W.H.H. Ltd.'

Type U.K.C.T.2.

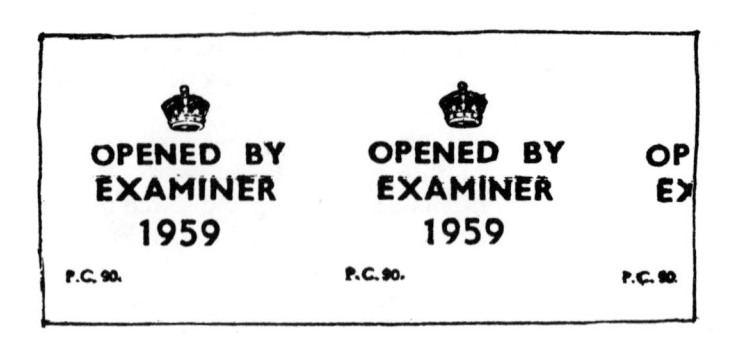

> ♛   ♛
> **OPENED BY**   **OPENED BY**   **OP**
> **EXAMINER**   **EXAMINER**   **E**
> **1959**   **1959**
> P.C. 90.   P.C. 90.   P.C. 90.

A white tape 38 m.m. wide, coming from a continuous roll and so having no uniform length. There are five lines of printing on this tape:

> (a crown)
> OPENED BY
> EXAMINER
> 1959
> P.C.90.

The crown is 6 m.m. high, the capital letters are 3 m.m. high and the numbers are 3.5 m.m. high, while 'P.C.90' is only 1.5 m.m. high. There is no printer's code on this type of censor tape.

Examiner numbers 1959 and 9497 have been recorded on Channel Islands Internee's mail, but the use of this tape is rare compared with Type U.K.C.T.1.

United Kingdom Censorship Leaflets

Any mail returned to the sender in the United Kingdom by a British Censor, would contain a British Postal Censorship Leaflet as would certain items of mail from the Internment Camps delivered in England. These leaflets, each identified by a code number in the top right corner which began 'P.C.---' were issued for many different reasons but the purpose of each one was only evident when reading it. If more than one topic was covered in the leaflet the censor might cross out a section which did not apply, or underline a section which he wanted particular attention applied to. He would also initial the leaflet and write his own reference code on it.

Only two types of these leaflets have been recorded used in association with the Internee mail service.

The first example, with code 'P.C.199', is illustrated below:

```
                BRITISH POSTAL CENSORSHIP              P.C.199
    Mail to Prisoners of War and Internees in enemy, enemy-occupied
                    and neutral territories

        This letter is returned to you because the passage(s)
    underlined contain(s) information which may be of value to the
    enemy. It is suggested that your letter be re-written with
    the omission of the matter underlined.

        No details of aircraft, air stations, operations (air crews
    or ground staff), equipment, movements etc. of the R.A.F. should
    be mentioned in letters to Prisoners of War and Internees.

        The enemy is anxious to find out all he can about the R.A.F.
    Do not help him.

        The return of this letter must not be referred to in any
    letters to Prisoners of War and Internees.
                                              EMS  7.18.

    40M21799-1 6000 AM PRP
```

The leaflet was contained in a letter addressed to an Internee which was returned to the sender because he had made some mention of R.A.F. operations. The censor has underlined the important parts of the leaflet.

The second type, with code 'P.C.223' has already been described and

193

illustrated in the chapter 'The Development of the Mail Services for the Channel Islands Internees'; it deals with forbidden enclosures in a letter to an Internee and is an example of a type where the censor has deleted a non-relevant section.

Such leaflets were also used on the Prisoner of War, the Civilian Red Cross and the Neutral Territories Mail Services, and so it is not possible to prove that a certain leaflet relates to Internee Mail unless one also has the original offending letter to which it refers.

BRITISH POST OFFICE MARKINGS

The events of the war in Europe in late 1944 and the rapid advance of the Allied Armies in 1945 completely disrupted the postal system on the Continent and especially in Germany. German Feldpost routes were destroyed or intercepted, the civilian postal service within Germany was interrupted and even the Red Cross at Geneva, through the Swiss Post Office, found it impossible to get all their mail delivered.

Mail from England was intercepted and returned to the sender in England. Mail from the Channel Islands destined for the Internment Camps, was brought to England. Red Cross mails which could not be forwarded into Germany were sent to England, and mail from the Internment Camps, whether it was addressed to England, the Channel Islands or Europe, was all brought to England. This placed a new and heavy burden on the British Post Office.

Letters from an English address could easily be returned to the sender, and mail from the Internment Camps addressed to England could be delivered after it had been intercepted in Europe, but mails addressed to the Channel Islands from the Internment Camps and letters from Guernsey or Jersey that could not be forwarded by the International Red Cross to the camps, all had to remain in England and wait for the Channel Islands to be liberated before they could be delivered or returned there.

A variety of hurriedly produced 'Instructional' rubber cachets were brought into use to explain the return or late delivery of a letter or card from Europe. It is uncertain where these markings were applied, indeed some which refer to the International Red Cross may even have been applied on the Continent, but I have recorded them all as U.K. cachets as they are all written in English and it seems probable that they were applied by the British Post Office. The cachets were recorded in use in 1945, although some were probably introduced in 1944, and they can be found on Prisoner of War mail as well as Internee mail. I have recorded eight distinct types and doubtless others exist, but they are all scarce markings as far as the mail service for Internees is concerned and in most cases only a few examples have been recorded.

One British Post Office postmark has special significance for the Internee mail service, it is a Manchester Post Paid mark and is described in detail after the 'Instructional' marks.

United Kingdom Post Office Cachets

All the following cachets are instructional markings.

```
THIS LETTER FORMED PART OF UNDELIVERED
MAILS WHICH FELL INTO THE HANDS OF
THE ALLIED FORCES IN GERMANY. IT IS
UNDELIVERABLE, AS ADDRESSED, AND IS
THEREFORE RETURNED TO YOU.
```

Type U.K.P.O.C.1: A boxed cachet measuring 62 m.m. by 20 m.m. with five lines of Roman Capitals 2 m.m. high and reading:

> THIS LETTER FORMED PART OF UNDELIVERED
> MAILS WHICH FELL INTO THE HANDS OF
> THE ALLIED FORCES IN GERMANY. IT IS
> UNDELIVERABLE AS ADDRESSED, AND IS
> THEREFORE RETURNED TO YOU.

The cachet is struck in purple and is recorded on mail from England posted in January 1945. The letters have been returned to sender and the address has been crossed out with blue crayon.

```
THIS LETTER HAS BEEN RETURNED BY THE
SWISS/        POST OFFICE WHO WERE
UNABLE TO REFORWARD IT TO GERMANY
BECAUSE OF THE INTERRUPTION OF
COMMUNICATIONS.
```

Type U.K.P.O.C.2: A boxed cachet measuring 59 m.m. by 16 m.m. with five lines of Roman Capitals 1.75 m.m. high and reading:

> THIS LETTER HAS BEEN RETURNED BY THE
> SWISS/   POST OFFICE WHO WERE
> UNABLE TO REFORWARD IT TO GERMANY
> BECAUSE OF THE INTERRUPTION OF
> COMMUNICATIONS

The cachet is struck in purple and is recorded on mail from England of late usage May 1945, at a time when the camps were already liberated. The cachet is of extra interest because it was produced for application to letters being delivered by the International Red Cross through either the Swedish or Swiss Post Offices. On the second line, after the word 'SWISS' there appears the remnants of a dash, followed by a space and then the remnants of the letter 'H', obviously where the word 'SWEDISH' has been removed from the cachet.

Letters bearing this cachet have been returned to sender and the address has been crossed out with blue crayon.

> THIS LETTER HAS BEEN RETURNED BY
> THE SWISS POST OFFICE WHO WERE
> UNABLE TO REFORWARD IT TO GERMANY
> BECAUSE OF THE INTERRUPTION OF
> COMMUNICATIONS.

Type U.K.P.O.C.3: A boxed cachet measuring 60 m.m. by about 21 m.m. with five lines of Roman Capitals 1.75 m.m. high and reading:

> THIS LETTER HAS BEEN RETURNED BY
> THE SWISS POST OFFICE WHO WERE
> UNABLE TO REFORWARD IT TO GERMANY
> BECAUSE OF THE INTERRUPTION OF
> COMMUNICATIONS.

The cachet is struck in purple and is recorded on mail from England, posted in April 1945, that has been returned to sender and had the address crosssed out with blue crayon.

> *This* letter/postcard *has been returned by the Swiss Post Office who were unable to re-forward it to Germany because of the interruption of communications.*

Type U.K.P.O.C.4: A boxed cachet measuring 75 m.m. by 20 m.m. with four lines of upper and lower case Italic type, reading:

> This letter/postcard has been returned by the Swiss
> Post Office who were unable to re-forward it
> to Germany because of the interruption of
> communications.

The cachet is struck in purple and is a scarce cachet recorded on mail from Guernsey (and probably Jersey) carried on the Red Cross Relief Ship 'Vega' in 1945 and forwarded through the International Red Cross. The mail has been returned to the sender in the Channel Islands and cachet Type U.K.P.O.C.6. has also been applied.

197

> This ~~letter~~/postcard has been returned by the
> International Red Cross Committee at Geneva
> who were unable to re-forward it.

Type U.K.P.O.C.5: A boxed cachet measuring 75 m.m. by 18 m.m. with four lines of upper and lower case Italic type, reading:

> This $\frac{\text{letter}}{\text{postcard}}$ has been returned by the
> International Red Cross Committee at Geneva
> who were unable to re-forward it.

The cachet is struck in purple and is probably even more scarce than Type U.K.P.O.C.4. as it is recorded on some of the very rare Interniertenpost Lettersheets that were issued in Jersey in 1945 for transportation on the Red Cross Relief Ship 'Vega'. As the letters show no obvious signs of having travelled to England it is conjectured that this cachet may even have been applied in Switzerland.

The letters have been returned to sender in Jersey and cachet Type U.K.P.O.C.6. has also been applied.

> UNDELIVERED FOR REASON STATED
>
> RETURN TO SENDER

Type U.K.P.O.C.6: A double boxed cachet measuring 63 m.m. by 19 m.m. with a line dividing it across the middle. In the top box is a line of Roman Capitals 2.5 m.m. high reading:

> UNDELIVERED FOR REASON STATED

and in the lower box is a line of Roman Capitals 3 m.m. high reading:

> RETURN TO SENDER

The cachet is struck in red and is found on letters sent from, and returned to the Channel Islands in 1945. It is recorded used on mail bearing cachets Type U.K.P.O.C.4. and U.K.P.O.C.5.

This cachet is universal in the British Post Office and is still in use today. It could have been applied in England, or in the Channel Islands where its use is also recorded. With regards to the Internee Mail Service, it has only been recorded used on letters returned to the Channel Islands and no other examples have so far been recorded, so the cachet may well have been applied in the Channel Islands rather than in England.

```
┌─────────────────────────┐
│   RETURNED FROM         │
│   CONTINENT IN          │
│   UNDELIVERED MAILS     │
└─────────────────────────┘
```

Type U.K.P.O.C.7: A boxed cachet measuring 75 m.m. by 19 m.m. with three lines of Roman Capitals 4 m.m. high and reading:

RETURNED FROM
CONTINENT IN
UNDELIVERED MAILS

The cachet is struck in purple and is recorded on Interniertenpost stationery from the camps en-route to England in April 1945. The cachet has really been misused as the mail was in transit from the Continent when it was intercepted and so could not be 'returned from Continent' as stated in the cachet. Three examples of this cachet have been recorded on Internee mail.

RECOVERED P.O.W. MAIL
FROM EUROPE
RECENTLY RECEIVED
BY BRITISH P.O.

Type U.K.P.O.C.8: An unusual cachet having the appearance of a slogan postmark and struck in the normal position on letters for machine cancels. The cachet is struck in black and as the lettering is perfect it is diffcult to determine whether in fact it is a machine cancel or a rubber or steel cachet. (Note: The cachet is more perfect than my drawing indicates.) Four lines of Roman Capitals 4 m.m. and 4.5 m.m. high read:

RECOVERED P.O.W. MAIL
FROM EUROPE
RECENTLY RECEIVED
BY BRITISH P.O.

As the wording indicates, the cachet was applied in England and is used on letters sent from the camps in March 1945 to addresses in England.

United Kingdom Postmarks

Type U.K.P.M.1: A single circle postage paid handstamp of Great Britian. The circle is 29 m.m. in diameter and across its centre in Roman Capitals 4 m.m. high is the one word 'PAID'. Inside the circle, but around the top edge appears the word 'MANCHESTER' and around the bottom edge is 'GREAT BRITAIN'. These words are in Roman Capitals 2 m.m. high. There is no date in the mark and it is struck in red.

Only two examples of this postmark have been recorded on Internee mail. One example is on an air-mail envelope that is addressed to Guernsey from an Internee in Laufen, and the other is on a letter, dated 18 April 1945, addressed to Jersey from an Internee in Biberach. Neither letter carries any other marking or cachet, and as they have not been censored, it seems probable that they both formed part of a batch of mail sent by air, to England, from the camps, immediately after the camps were liberated, and at a time when all other postal routes were defunct.

FRENCH POST OFFICE MARKINGS

One French Post Office cachet is recorded on the mail of Channel Islands Internees and the only French Postmark to be recorded is a Paris Postmark described in detail in the chapter on Compiègne and St. Denis Frontstalag Camps.

The French Post Office cachet of significance is an instructional mark that was in use on Internee mail in the summer of 1944. It is a 'Return to Sender' cachet of Paris origin, and is recorded on mail that was addressed to the Channel Islands from the Internment camps, but which could not be delivered because of the isolation of the Islands following the D-Day landings. Examples of the cachet have been recorded on mail from Laufen, Biberach and a Swiss Internment camp, as well as on civilian mail posted in France and addressed to the Channel Islands, but the life of this cachet on the Internee mail service was only a few months as once Paris had been liberated, any mails caught in transit from the camps were brought to England rather than being returned to the sender.

The cachet is scarce, but is an important part in the story of the breakdown of the Internee mail service in 1944.

```
┌─────────────────┐
│    RETOUR       │
│  À L'ENVOYEUR   │
└─────────────────┘
```

Type Fr.P.O.C.1: A small boxed cachet, with rounded corners, and measuring 34 m.m. by 12.5 m.m. Within the box are two lines of Roman Capitals 3 m.m. high and reading:

RETOUR
A L'ENVOYEUR

The cachet is struck in black and is recorded on Internee mail in June and July 1944.

SWISS POSTMARKS, CACHETS AND CENSOR LABLES

Swiss Postmarks

Some Swiss Postmarks have been recorded struck as receiving marks on Internee mail from the camps, but these are as diverse as the destinations and hold no more significance than being very rare examples of Channel Islands Internee mail addressed to destinations other than the Channel Islands or the United Kingdom. More important and worth illustrating is a Geneva postmark, since it was from Geneva that official mail of the International Red Cross and the Y.M.C.A. was despatched to the camps. It must be emphasised that very little of this mail exists to record or study, that doubtless other Geneva postmarks besides that illustrated below were used, and that official mail also went from Berne, although I have never had the opportunity to record it.

Type Sw.P.M.1: An 18 m.m. diameter, circular postmark with parts of an inner circle cut by a 'phantom bar'. Round the top of the circle appears:

GENÈVE 1

in Roman Capitals 3 m.m. high, while around the bottom appears:

(EXP.LETT.)

in Roman Capitals 2.5 m.m. high. These two legends are separated from each other by stars. Across the centre of the circle, within the bar, is the date followed by a code number, and in the part-circle above appears the Cross of Switzerland, while in the part-circle below is a figure 1. The postmark is struck in black, and while it has only been recorded on official mail of the Y.M.C.A. it probably also appears on International Red Cross mail from Geneva.

Swiss Cachets

The International Red Cross Committee in Geneva used a variety of cachets, but I have dealt with these in a following chapter: 'The Red Cross'. No official mail of the Red Cross has been recorded to the camps and so I do not know which cachets were used; those that are recorded are on the 25 word message forms of the Red Cross.

Official mail from the Y.M.C.A. in Geneva is recorded to the camps and a cachet of that organisation is recorded below.

> „War Prisoners Aid"
> World's Committee of
> Young Men's Christian Associations
> GENEVA (Switzerland)

Type Sw.C.1: A boxed cachet of the Y.M.C.A. measuring 47.5 m.m. by 19.5 m.m. with four lines of legend reading;

> ,,War Prisoners Aid"
> World's Committee of
> Young Men's Christian Associations
> GENEVA (Switzerland)

Each line is in an upper and lower case type, but each line of type differs from the others in size and style. The cachet is struck in purple.

One letter is recorded to the Channel Islands from a Channel Islander in a Swiss Internment Camp. I have illustrated and recorded this item in detail on pages 154 and 155 of ISLANDERS DEPORTED PART I, but the Swiss cachets and censor tape found on this letter are recorded below.

Type Sw.C.2: A double circle cachet, indicating free post from a Swiss Military Internment camp. The outer circle of the cachet has a diameter of 27.5 m.m. and the inner circle has a diameter of 18 m.m. In the centre of the circle is a Swiss Cross with bars 7 m.m. by 2.5 m.m., and the words:

> Franc de port

in upper and lower case type only 1 m.m. high. Between the two circles, around the edge, is a legend, also in upper and lower case type, but with letters 2 m.m. and 2.5 m.m. high reading:

> Camp militaire d'Internement
> ★ Suisse ★

The word 'Suisse' is inverted in relation to the rest of the legend and separated from it by stars. The cachet is struck in a dark violet ink.

203

EVADES

Type Sw.C.3: A straight line cachet consisting of the one word:

EVADES

Bars, 44.5 m.m. long appear above and below the word which is made from Capital letters 5.5. m.m. high. The cachet refers to the writer of the letter being an escapee and is struck in the same dark violet ink as cachet Type Sw.C.2.

Swiss Censor Label

Only one censor label from Switzerland is recorded on Channel Islands Internee mail, and that is the one found on the letter mentioned above from a Channel Island Internee in a Swiss Military Internment Camp.

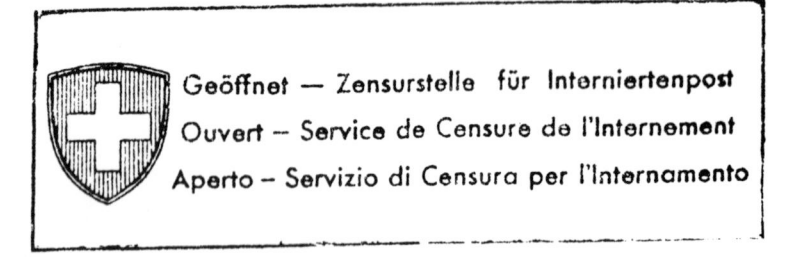

```
Geöffnet — Zensurstelle für Interniertenpost
Ouvert — Service de Censure de l'Internement
Aperto — Servizio di Censura per l'Internamento
```

Type Sw.C.T.1: A white label measuring 96 m.m. by 30 m.m. and used for sealing the letter after inspection by the Censor of the Swiss Internment Service. A Swiss Cross in shield is printed in black on the label along with the same inscription in German, French and Italian.

CACHETS AND POSTMARKS FROM THE REST OF THE WORLD

Cachets and postmarks from other countries would not normally have a reason to be applied to Internee mail except of course for the obvious exception when mail was addressed to, or sent from the foreign country.

Some Internee mail was addressed to towns in Germany or Italy and at least one family had correspondents in Switzerland, but perhaps the most likely countries that Internees might communicate with after the Channel Islands and England, were Australia and more especially Canada, where a large contingent of Channel Islands exiles lived.

Channel Islands Internee mail has been recorded both to and from Australia and Canada and in each country it has been subject to local censorship. The censorship markings of these countries is beyond the scope of this book, but Channel Islands Internee mail sent to or from there is obviously very interesting to the collector, and as it is quite scarce, it attracts a considerable premium.

The Australian Censors' Cachets that I have noted have been diamond shaped and struck in maroon ink.

Canadian Censors' Cachets are straight line cachets struck in black. (An example on Internee mail is illustrated in 'Mail from parts of the British Empire' in Section I of this book.)

Some Laufen Internee mail is known to and from countries such as Greece, Belgium and Yugoslavia. This is not Channel Islands Internee mail, but mail from the small American contingent that shared Laufen camp with the Channel Islanders. (See pages 111 and 112 'ISLANDERS DEPORTED' PART I). Again, it is beyond the scope of this book to record in detail such mail, but nevertheless it is of considerable interest to the collector and researcher who wishes to build up a complete picture of the Channel Islands Internee camps. Such mail is rare because the American contingent was small, and I have only been able to locate one letter sent from Belgrade, Yugoslavia on 24 August 1944. The postage stamp has been removed from the cover at some time and it has been censored by the Germans while in transit, but it bears no other markings or indication that it arrived in the camp.

UNIDENTIFIED CACHETS

Only one cachet found on Internee mail remains unidentified, and this is a small boxed cachet with the numbers 046 inside the box.

The cachet has been recorded on mail from Biberach to Guernsey posted in August 1944, but which has been routed to England because of the breakdown in communications with the Islands. The cachet is not unlike the individual censors' marks of the Frankfurt Transit Censors (Type Fk.C.6.) and it is my belief that it is a similar German marking, probably belonging to an individual censor of the S.S. Its use coincides with that of the 'Mysterious Four Digit Cachet' of the S.S., described earlier, and as it has not been recorded in use before August 1944, I think it is probable that it is a German Transit Censors' Cachet that came into use after the cachets of the Oberkommando der Wehrmacht were withdrawn.

As British Censorship markings tend to be confined to the octagon shapes already recorded in an earlier chapter, and the International Red Cross had not taken over the transmission of Internee mails to the Islands at the time that this mark was in use, it is unlikely that the cachet is either British or Swiss. Even if the cachet is taken to be of German origin, there it still no clue as to where or when it was actually applied to the mail. Only two examples have been recorded of the marking and each of these is struck very weakly in a thin, light grey ink.

046

Type Ud.C.1: A small boxed cachet measuring about 19 m.m. by 16 m.m. with the three digits 046 inside, each digit being 6.5 m.m. high. The cachet is struck lightly but clearly, in a pale grey ink.

THE RED CROSS

The Red Cross played a very important role in the lives of the Channel Islands Internees, although it was never solely responsible for their mail services until late 1944. I have made frequent references to the Red Cross in both PARTS I and II of this book, but in PART I especially, I have described the significance of the roles of the Red Cross Organisations, not only of Britain and Switzerland, but also in Germany, Sweden and the countries of the British Empire.

In this chapter I do not intend to repeat all that I have already written about the Red Cross, but rather, I have gathered together various items which are important to the collector, and I have described and illustrated in detail things to which I may have only referred in passing, in the preceding pages.

It should be remembered that by the outbreak of the Second World War, there was, in nearly every country in the world, a branch of the Red Cross or the Red Crescent, as well as the International Committee of the Red Cross based in Geneva, Switzerland. However, the two branches which most affected the Channel Islands Internees were of course, the International Red Cross in Switzerland and the British Red Cross Society and Order of St. John in England.

The 25 Word Red Cross Message Form

I have illustrated and recorded a Form of the Red Cross Message scheme in Section I of this part of ISLANDERS DEPORTED, but for more information, Donald McKenzie in his book 'THE RED CROSS MAIL SERVICE FOR CHANNEL ISLAND CIVILIANS 1940-45' goes into great detail about the scheme and illustrates all the known types of Red Cross Message Forms that were used to and from the Channel Islands.

The Internees had no real use for the Red Cross Message scheme because it only allowed for the transmission of a message of 25 words, whereas they, as Internees, were able to use the Internee mail service with letters and cards that permitted an unlimited number of words to be used. The very few Red Cross Messages that are recorded as being received in the Internee camps were those that were en-route to the Channel Islands at the time of the deportations and were re-addressed to deportees in the camps after being received by the local Red Cross Branches in the Channel Islands. As the Internee was already using the Internee mail service he would not need to reply to the Red Cross Message and so the scheme very quickly came to an end for the Internees.

The collector is very lucky if he is able to locate one of these Message Forms received in the camps. I have only been able to record two during my researches and these are both of English origin, although there is no reason why a Form should not be discovered from any of the other known sources in the world such as Canada, India, Rhodesia, Ceylon or the Middle East.

The International Red Cross Committee – Geneva

The International Red Cross Committee in Geneva, Switzerland maintained a careful watch over the welfare of the Internees in the camps in Germany throughout the war. Certain items of official mail passed between Geneva and the Camp Captains, as I have already described in Section I of this part of ISLANDERS DEPORTED, but very few examples of this official mail are in the hands of collectors and I am unable to record any cachet or marking used on the mail prior to 1944.

When the Red Cross took over sole responsibility for the transmission of Internee mail in late 1944, every item of mail passing through their hands in Switzerland received the double circle rubber cachet, with a Red Cross in the centre, of the International Red Cross Committee in Geneva. McKenzie describes this cachet in his book (his Type 1. 1.3.1.) and I have described and illustrated it below. It is interesting to note that of the five types of Geneva cachet that McKenzie records, only this one is recorded on Internee mail, regardless of whether it is to or from the camps, and en-route to, or from, the Channel Islands or United Kingdom. Although only this one cachet is recorded, it is still a scarce marking as it was only in use for about six months on Internee mail.

Type R.C.C.1: A double circle cachet with a 13 m.m. by 4 m.m. red cross in the centre. The concentric circles have diameters of 18 m.m. and 29 m.m. and between them are the words:

COMITÉ INTERNATIONAL DE LA CROIX ROUGE – GENÈVE

The letters are Roman Capitals, 2 m.m. high and the cachet is struck in crimson red.

The Swedish Red Cross Society

No cachet or marking of the Swedish Red Cross Society has been recorded on Channel Islands Internee mail, although some of the Internees themselves, noteably those from Kreuzburg, do talk of their mail at times being transported via Sweden or by the Swedish Red Cross.

The Swedish Red Cross was very involved in the early repatriations of Channel Islands Internees in September 1944 and March 1945, when the Internees were brought to England via the Swedish port of Gothenburg, in the Swedish Red Cross ship 'S.S. Drottningholm'. Little material from that time exists, although the Internees' landing cards from the ship are a valuable addition to any collection. An example of one of these landing cards with its cachets is illustrated on page 177 in PART I of ISLANDERS DEPORTED.

The German Red Cross Society – 'Deutsches Rotes Kreuz'

'Deutsches Rotes Kreuz' cachets have never been recorded on Channel Islands Internee mail. Even during the period in 1944-45 when the Red Cross had special responsibility for the Internee mail, the German Red Cross was involved, but none of its cachets were applied to the mail. Examples of 'Deutches Rotes Kreuz' cachets are found on Red Cross Message Forms received by the Internees in the camps, but of course these are not special to the Internees as they were normally applied when the forms were in transit to and from the Channel Islands.

During the early repatriations of 1944 and 1945 the Internees were transported across Germany to Denmark in German Red Cross trains. Some Internees are believed to have written letters on these trains and to have posted them along the route when the train stopped at various stations. An example of one of these letters is reputed to be housed in a collection, but I have not been able to inspect it myself and the reports do not mention its bearing any German Red Cross cachets.

The British Red Cross Society

The British Red Cross Society and the St. John Ambulance Association were amalgamated for war effort purposes in 1939 under the joint title of the 'War Organisation of the British Red Cross Society and the Order of St. John of Jerusalem'. This title was very unwieldy and for every day use, was often abridged to 'The Red Cross and St. John War Organisation' or more often, just 'The Red Cross'.

I have already written at length in both parts of ISLANDERS DEPORTED about the role played by the British Red Cross in the lives of the Channel Islands Internees, but for the collector and researcher it is worth drawing attention to three areas especially which give rise to tangible documents well worth preserving in a collection. The 25 word message scheme is one area, the Internee parcel post service is another and the dissemination of information within the United Kingdom about the Internees, is a third.

The Forms for the 25 word message scheme have been fully described above and are illustrated elsewhere in this book.

The parcel post for the Internees is fully described in Appendix II of Section I of this book and in those pages I have illustrated the two types of the British Red Cross Society and Order of St. John Form P/4 which are associated with the personal parcel scheme. The two types of this form are titled:

NEXT OF KIN PARCELS CENTRE

PERSONAL PARCELS CENTRE

Both types of the form served exactly the same purpose and are rare examples of a scarce postal service because the Internee could only receive four of these types of parcels in a year and so the maximum number that any Channel Islands Internee might receive during the whole of his internment was no more than twelve. Thus examples of these two types of Form P/4 are important documents to the collector since they are the only tangible evidence of a very scarce mail service.

In the first chapter of this part of ISLANDERS DEPORTED, I have described a leaflet – PW/73C/43. This is an important example of a document associated with the dissemination of information within the United Kingdom about the Internees. It was issued by the Prisoners of War Department of the War Organisation of the British Red Cross Society and Order of St. John of Jerusalem, and described how people could communicate with an Internee by letter from England. This leaflet was issued in response to an inquiry about a particular Internee and is therefore of special importance since it gave the name and correct address of the Internment camp for that Internee, and so any Channel Islands connection can easily be identified. An example of the leaflet referring to a Channel Islands Internee in Biberach is illustrated below.

PW/73C/43.

WAR ORGANISATION
of the
BRITISH RED CROSS SOCIETY and ORDER OF ST. JOHN OF JERUSALEM

PRISONERS OF WAR DEPARTMENT

Telephone No:
ABBey 5841.

St. James's Palace,
London, S.W.1.

March, 1943.

LETTERS TO CIVILIAN INTERNEES BY PRISONERS OF WAR POST

Letters should be clearly written; should deal with personal matters only, and should not exceed both sides of one sheet of notepaper.

The sender's name and address must be written on the back of the envelope; but if the writer is serving in His Majesty's Forces, the name and address of the Unit must not be given, but a private address should be substituted.

Letters should be posted in the ordinary way, and should not be sent to the Prisoners of War Department to be forwarded. They should be addressed as follows:

PRISONERS OF WAR POST

Kriegsgefangenenpost.
Mrs Irene C. Hayward,
British Civilian Internee No. 10013.
Ilag Biberach Riss,
Germany.

No stamp is required if letters are sent by ordinary mail; but if they are sent by air-mail, they must have a 5d. stamp and be marked "BY AIR MAIL".

Special Air letter-cards for use in communication with British Prisoners of War and Interned Civilians in enemy or enemy-occupied territories are now obtainable at the principal Post Offices, at a cost of 3d. each.

Enclosures:

Unmounted photographs or snapshots of a purely personal nature may be enclosed in letters to civilian internees, but no other pictures or printed matter of any kind. Any enclosure may cause the letter to be delayed for special examination. The name and address of the addressee and of the sender should be written on the back of photographs, etc.

No enclosures may be sent in Air Mail Letter Cards.

An example of the scarce leaflet PW/73C/43, giving the address of an Internee.

Another document which is an example of the 'dissemination of information role' played by the British Red Cross is a copy of one of the maps issued by The Red Cross and St. John War Organisation showing British Prisoner of War Camps in Germany and the occupied countries. These maps were published for the relatives of Prisoners of War and Internees, they cost 2d., or 3d. by post, and were periodically updated as camps changed their designation or were closed down. Although these maps were not issued with specific relevance to the Channel Islands Internees, they did show all the Internment camps in Germany, Austria and Poland, and as a contemporary record of the camps, they make an interesting addition to any collection. An example issued in September 1943 is illustrated below.

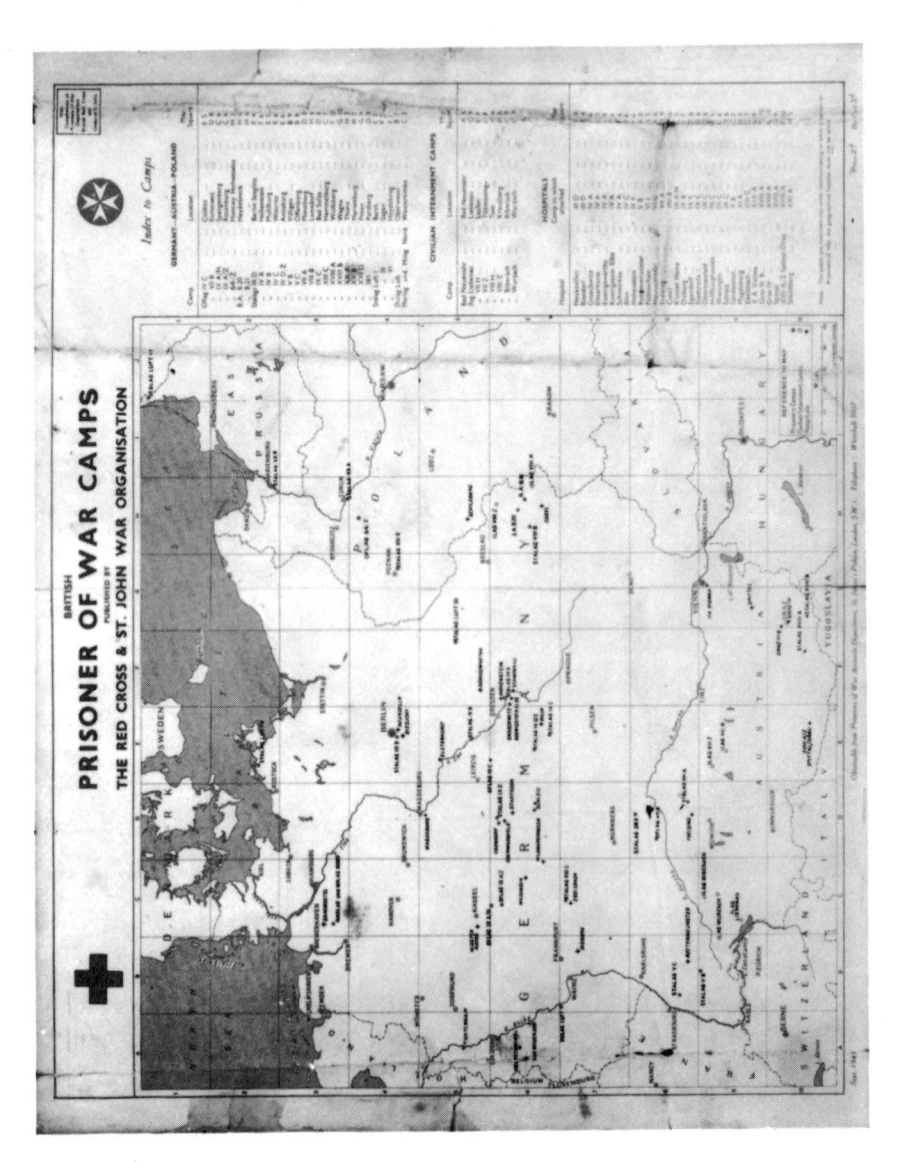

MISCELLANEOUS OBJECTS, DOCUMENTS AND EPHEMERA

Although this book is a history of the postal services associated with the Channel Islands people deported to Germany, there are various non-postal items, important to their story, which are very collectable and worth cataloguing just as much as the true postal history item. Many of these non-postal items have been described or illustrated in PART I of ISLANDERS DEPORTED while telling the story of the deportations, but in this chapter I have attempted to collate them in logical groups and to illustrate other examples which may not have been recorded before.

Official Documents

The official documents relating to the deportations are of special interest to the postal historian and can be divided into four groups:

(a) Documents issued in the Channel Islands before and during the deportations.
(b) Documents issued in England;
    (i) to relatives and friends in respect of a deported person.
    (ii) to the Internees when they were in England awaiting repatriation to the Channel Islands.
(c) Documents issued in the Camps;
    (i) by the Germans during the internment.
    (ii) by the Allies after liberation of the Camps.
(d) Documents issued, mainly in Sweden, during repatriation of the Internees to England.

(a) *Documents issued in the Channel Islands before and during the deportations.*

The documents and orders issued to the prospective deportees in the Channel Islands, fall into three main categories:

    (i) Notices published in the local newspapers.
    (ii) Notices sent through the post ordering prospective deportees to attend medical examinations or interviews.
    (iii) The Official Deportation Order, sent to the head of the family and delivered by the German troops in the first instances, but later by special delivery.

The format of these various notices and documents changed with each deportation and differed between Islands, but when the 1943 deportation took place no notices were published in the newspapers. This was an attempt by the Germans to forstall the demonstrations that had taken place with the 1942 deportations, and also to maintain an element of security since British

Commandos had learned of the earlier deportations from newspapers taken during their raid on Sark.

In the following lists the documents are catalogued by Islands.

First Deportations from Jersey 1942

J.1.Doc.1. Deportation Notice published in 'Jersey Evening Post' on 15 September 1942. Dated 15 September 1942 and signed by Feldkommandant Knackfuss. (See PART I, page 1).

J.1.Doc.2. First type of Deportation Order delivered by German troops, dated Jersey 15 September 1942 for deportation on 16 September. This is a rare document since only 280 people were mustered for this first deportation. (See PART I pages 8 & 9).

J.1.Doc.3. Second type of Deportation Order sent on 17 September for deportation on 18 September. The first two paragraphs differ from those in the first type, and four extra paragraphs are appended. 600 people were deported as a result of this order. (See PART I page 12).

J.1.Doc.4. An Official Notice to the deportees was published by the Germans on 19 September 1942 in the 'Jersey Evening Post', warning those people who had failed to leave the day before that they must hold themselves in readiness for deportation on 25 September.

J.1.Doc.5 The third type of Deportation Order was sent to various families between 19 and 28 September, initially for deportation on 25 September, but eventually for deportation on 29 September. 560 people were deported at the end of the ten days during which this order was issued.

J.1.Doc.6. 23 September 1942. An Official Notice to the deportees was published in the 'Jersey Evening Post' referring to the delay in the departure of the deportation ships.

J.1.Doc.7. 26 September 1942. An Official Notice was published in the 'Jersey Evening Post' ordering all the notified deportees to appear at the Weighbridge on 29 September.

First Deportations from Guernsey 1942

G.1.Doc.1. Deportation Notice published in the 'Guernsey Evening Press' on Wednesday 16 September 1942. The Notice was the same as that published in Jersey the day before, but appended to it was a Notice and Form with questions that had to be answered by any prospective deportee. (See PART I pages 17 & 18).

G.1.Doc.2. There was only one type of Deportation Order issued in Guernsey; it was dated 18 September 1942 and sent to the heads of families for either one of two deportation dates – 21 or 23 September. (See PART I pages 18 & 19, illustration page 19). The departure dates of these deportations were actually delayed until 26 and 27 September. This Deportation Order is more common than the Jersey ones since 825 people were affected by it.

G.1.Doc.3. Although identical to ***G.1.Doc.2.*** by far the rarest Deportation Order is one relating to a Sark family, since only eleven were issued for that Island.

Second Deportations from Jersey 1943

With the second batch of deportations from Jersey in 1943, people were summoned for medical examinations before being considered for deportation. Many more people received these summonses than were actually deported.

The orders to attend medical examinations were signed by General von Müller but the Deportation Orders still bore the name of Feldkommandant Knackfuss as the 1942 Orders had done.

J.2.Doc.1. Summonses to attend medical examinations were sent through the post to prospective deportees and dated 11, 12 or 15 January 1943.

J.2.Doc.2. Summonses to attend a medical re-examination were sent to some people on 28 January 1943.

J.2.Doc.3. Deportation Orders dated 6 February 1943 were issued to 63 people for deportation on 9 February.

J.2.Doc.4. Notifications about the postponement of the departure date of the deportation were sent to these 63 people on 8, 9 and 10 February. Eventually they left on 13 February 1943.

J.2.Doc.5. Between 14 and 24 February, more Deportation Orders were sent to families for deportation on 25 February.

J.2.Doc.6. On 18 February questionnaires were sent to past employees of the Germans, giving them the option of either working for them again or being deported.

On 25 February 1943 the last group of 37 Jersey people were deported.

Second Deportation from Guernsey 1943

G.2.Doc.1. Summonses, signed by General von Müller on 27 January 1943, were sent ordering prospective deportees to report for a medical examination on 30 January 1943.

G.2.Doc.2. On 3 February a letter was sent to all future deportees from the Bailiff of Guernsey. (See PART I page 32).

G.2.Doc.3. Between 4 and 7 February, a notice printed on yellow card was sent to families due for deportation, stating that children over the age of 18 years could choose whether or not they wished to be interned with their parents. (See PART I pages 32 and 33).

After three postponements the deportation took place on 12 February 1943.

G.2.Doc.4. On 21 February, more prospective deportees received Deportation Orders dated 20 February 1943. These orders contained a summons to appear for medical examination on 22 February, and a notice that the receiver and his family would be deported on 24 February 1943 at 8 p.m. (See PART I pages 34 and 35 and illustration, page 36). This document is very rare as only 13 people were taken from Guernsey and 25 from Sark. The deportation took place on 25 February 1943.

Official documents relating to the deportations are quite rare, but any document relating to the deportations in 1943 from either Guernsey or Jersey is obviously very scarce since only 201 people were taken in 1943. Interestingly, Orders relating to people on Sark are disproportionately high in 1943, as of those 201 deportees, 48 were from Sark.

(b) *Documents issued in England*

(i) *to relatives and friends in respect of a deported person*

During the war, the agency in England involved with the welfare of Internees abroad was the 'War Organisation of the British Red Cross Society and Order of St. John of Jerusalem'. Relatives seeking information about an Internee would write to this Organisation and receive in reply, either a duplicated letter of information, or a personal letter relative to the specific case. Examples of these two types of communication are difficult to locate today, but are described below;

U.K.Doc.1. In the preceeding pages of this Section, in the chapter entitled 'The Red Cross', I have illustrated and described in detail a leaflet – PW/73C/43. This is a scarce example of one of the duplicated letters sent to relatives of an Internee. It gives general information, as well as specific information relating to the Internee; in this case it is the proper Camp address and number for the Internee which has been typed into a space on the letter.

U.K.Doc.2. Personal letters from the 'War Organisation of the Red Cross Society and Order of St. John of Jerusalem' are perhaps even rarer than the duplicated letters, but an example of one is described in detail on pages 150 and 151 in PART I.

(ii) *to the Internees when they were in England awaiting repatriation to the Channel Islands*

Documents issued in England to the Internees on the whole related to their eventual repatriation to the Channel Islands. Although several different letters probably exist, I have only been able to locate one which is described on page 185 of PART I, it is:

U.K.Doc.3. A duplicated letter, dated by hand, from the 'Ministry of Health, Whitehall, London S.W.1', entitled '<u>Repatriation to the Channel Islands</u>'.

(c) *Documents issued in the Camps*

   (i) *by the Germans during the internment*

The German bureaucratic system issued a proliferation of forms and documents relating to the Internees, but not many of these came into the Internees' possession. Two that did were, identification 'dog' tags, and Medical Record Cards.

Cp.Doc.1. Not all camps issued the metal identification 'dog tag', but those Internees who were first sent to Dorsten were issued with tags which had their Internee number stamped onto it and the name of the camp as Stalag VIF/Z. These tags measured 60 m.m. by 40 m.m. and could be broken in two along a punched line of holes which divided the tag down the centre. The identification information was duplicated on both halves.

Cp.Doc.2. The style of Medical Card issued to the Internees varied between camps, but the face of one issued to an Internee at Laufen is illustrated below. The reverse of this card gives details of the weight of the Internee at various medical check-up times and also dates when he received any injections.

Cp.Doc.3. By far the rarest type of document issued in the Camps to an Internee was an official letter from either the German Camp Kommandant or the British Camp Captain. An example of the latter is described on page 135 of PART I.

(ii) *by the Allied Armies after liberation of the Camp*

Cp.Doc.4. Because most of the Internees had been deported from the Channel Islands without Passports and in many cases without any other official identification papers, when the camps were liberated the Intelligence Officers of SHAEF had to investigate the backgrounds of all the Internees in order to confirm that they were bonafide British subjects. When these Officers were satisfied with their investigation, they issued each Internee with an 'Identity Card for Ex-Prisoner of War' which was signed and stamped by the Officer from SHAEF. The inside of one of these cards issued to an Internee at Laufen is illustrated below. The Cachet stamped in violet reads:

PHIL T LAUNER
CAPT. QMC. SHAEF. G-I. PWX

Service No. / Serial No.		Nationality	BRITISH
Surname / Last Name			CRANCH
Initials			D.G.
Rank		PW No.	923

Regiment, Squadron, Ship or Organization

Holders Signature _Cranch_

Signature of PW Camp Contact Officer

Issued at ___Laufen___ on ___6.6.___ 1945

(d) *Documents issued, mainly in Sweden, during repatriation of the Internees to England*

Two documents are recorded issued to the Internees while passing through Sweden in 1944 and 1945.

S.Doc.1. A landing card for the Swedish Red Cross ship 'S.S. Drottningholm' with an attached photograph of the Internee, is illustrated on page 177 of PART I.

S.Doc.2. A letter from the British Ambassador in Sweden was sent to each of the Internees passing through Gothenburg on their way to England. An example is described on pages 177 and 178 of **PART I**.

Other Official Documents relating to the deportations probably exist, but these described above are the only ones that I have been able to record. Although these documents are very difficult to find, they are valuable research material and an interesting addition to any collection.

Ephemera

Pieces of ephemera relating to the Channel Islands Internees originated not only in the Camps, but also in England and the Channel Islands. Much of this ephemera is of a non-postal nature, but it is eagerly sought by researchers and collectors because it gives an immediate and graphic indication of what life and conditions were like in the Camps at the time. It is not possible to catalogue the items because in the majority of cases each piece is unique, but I have been able to group them under various titles and indicate the relative importance of individual pieces within each group.

Photographs – During the war, film for personal use was very limited and film for use by Internees in a German camp was naturally almost non-existent. Nevertheless, photographs do exist both of the Internees and their camps, but these photographs are rare and it took me many years of research to locate the photographs that illustrate this book.

Photographs taken in the Channel Islands of the deportations are particularly scarce. I have only been able to find the three illustrated on page 11 of PART I which show the deportations from Jersey, but none seem to exist for Guernsey. Although photographs were taken of the Guernsey deportations (see page 27 of PART I) the Germans ordered them to be destroyed and it seems likely that this order was totally effective.

Photographs have been discovered from nearly all the camps which housed the Channel Islands Internees, but I do not know of any that were taken in 1942 at Dorsten.

German photographic postcards exist of views of the environs of various camps and in some of these the camp itself may be featured. (See page 73 of PART I).

For a short period of time the Internees were able to send and receive photographs from friends and relatives in England and the Channel Islands. This privilege was withdrawn when it was discovered that the Internees were passing photographs from England to the Channel Islands via the Camps, at a time when the only official means of communication between England and the Channel Islands was via the twenty five word Red Cross Message Scheme. Photographs which left or entered the Camps are easily identified as they always bear, on the reverse, a cachet of the Camp censor.

Artwork – A lot of artwork exists that originated in the Camps, but for the collector three main factors govern its value:

1 The subject matter in the picture.
2 The quality of the work.
3 Whether the work is signed and if it is possible to identify the artist in the Internee lists.

Artwork that was painted on Camp Postal Stationery and then subsequently sent through the post, often as a Christmas card or Birthday card to a friend in England or the Channel Islands attracts an especially high premium.

Views of the Camp or its surroundings are always of more interest than general pictures and designs, and if these views are on Christmas cards, Birthday cards or Wedding Anniversary cards then they are eagerly sought by the collector. Many of these are illustrated in PART I.

An especially interesting and unique piece of artwork is the Repatriation card made when the Islanders were leaving their Camps. One for Wurzach is shown on page 182 of PART I and an even more unusual one in printed form from a German at Biberach is illustrated on page 72 of PART I.

Other types of artwork can be found from the Camps; Notices and Posters are recorded, and Posters for Theatre productions are often especially attractive as well as being informative as they record the names of many of the Internees.

Printed Items – Laufen was the only Internment Camp that managed to go so far as to print a book. The cover of their book 'The Bird-Cage', is illustrated on page 119 of PART I, but copies of the book are very difficult to obtain today.

More common and less expensive are Programmes printed in the Camps for Camp concerts and plays. Nearly every camp managed to produce these and, as with the posters, they hold a special significance as they list many of the Internees' names.

Camp Banknotes – The money that the Internees were able to use during their confinement is described in detail on pages 84 and 85 of PART I. The 'Lagergeld' banknotes that they used when first interned make an interesting addition to a collection, but do not hold any special value since they were in use in all the Prisoner of War Camps in Germany and cannot be identified as coming from an Internment Camp.

Although the banknotes peculiar to Wurzach camp were never used by the Internees (see page 85 of PART I) they are especially interesting and attractive and because they were 'found' by the Internees they possess a high collector value.

Camp Stamps and Lables – At the time that the Wurzach banknotes were taken from the loft of the Schloss, some 'stamps' or lables were also found and taken. These were only rediscovered in 1982 when three very crumpled examples were given to the author. They have a very similar design to the banknotes, but have no values printed on them. Instead, a pattern fills the four circles that hold the values on the banknotes and a vine design replaces the word that appears at the top of the banknotes. The 'stamps' are printed in blue on gummed paper, measure 36 m.m. by 24 m.m. and have a perforation of 11. It is difficult to comprehend their use or intention especially as they bear no values; they pre-date the war and come from a time when the Schloss was owned and used by the Catholic church. To my knowledge, no other Internment camp can claim to have had its own stamps, indeed none were necessary as the Internee post was free.

The 'stamps' found in Wurzach.

Newspaper Articles – I have already discussed earlier in this chapter the importance of the Official Notices that appeared in the Channel Islands Newspapers, but other articles were also printed about the Internees and their lives in the camps, and besides making interesting reading and research material, these articles along with the complete original newspaper are eagerly sought by collectors today. The newspapers in the Islands often printed reports of concerts or plays that had taken place in the camps and, especially in the early years, would print extracts from letters received in the Islands from the Internees. Such articles are of great interest to the researcher as the newspapers tried to include as many names of the Internees as they possibly could, but at the same time were only permitted to identify the camp by the first letter of its name. Such German censorship was especially ludicrous when on another page of the newspaper one can find an article on the correct method of addressing a letter to an Internment camp and the full address of the camp is quoted.

An article that is perhaps of more interest than most is the propaganda story related by Denis Cleary when he returned from Dorsten in November 1942. On pages 44 to 51 of PART I, I quote the story that was printed in 'The Star' in Guernsey on Thursday 19 November 1942. Other versions of his story were printed in the 'Jersey Evening Post' on 13 November 1942 and the 'Guernsey Evening Press' on 20 November 1942.

In England the main source of newspaper articles was 'The Times', but these tended to be limited to questions and statements made in Parliament. The 'Liverpool Daily Post and Echo' gave some detailed reports of the first repatriations of the Internees (see pages 178 and 179 of PART I) but the most fruitful source of information in England were copies of the Journal of the Channel Islands Refugees Committee in Great Britain entitled 'The Channel Islands Monthly Review'. These magazines are especially useful as they give the only easily obtainable lists of deported and repatriated Internees as well as a lot of information about Prisoners of War from the Channel Islands.

Sources

Official records in the Public Record Office, Kew.

Class F.O.916　War of 1939–1945
　　　　　　　　Consular (War) Department:
　　　　　　　　Prisoners of War and Internees.

   1　1940　Camps for prisoners of war and internees – reports.
   6　1941　Internees – Exchange
 81　1941　Internment of German women in Iran.
140　1941　Internment camps in France – reports.
168　1941　British subjets in the Channel Islands – assistance.
227　1942　Jan–Mar. Internees in Germany – lists.
228　1942　July–Sept. Internees in Germany – lists.
229　1942　Nov–Dec. Internees in Germany – lists.
253　1942　Civilian internment camp – Liebenau – conditions.
272　1942　Oct–Nov. Prisoners of War – placing in chains.
273　1942　Dec 1–10 Prisoners of War – placing in chains.
274　1942　Dec 11–31 Prisoners of War – placing in chains.
347　1942　Internment camps in France – report on Vittel.
348　1942　Internment camps in France – report on St. Denis.
362　1942　Imperial War Graves Commission – work in Belgium.
381　1942　British subjects in the Channel Islands – assistance.
495　1943　Internees in Germany – lists. Papers 1–13.
496　1943　Internees in Germany – lists. Papers 14–32.
497　1943　Internees in Germany – lists. Papers 33–79.
498　1943　Internees in Germany – lists. Papers 80– end.
521　1943　Civilian internment camp for women at Liebenau
555　1943　Prisoners of war and internees in enemy territory – numbers.
561　1943　Placing of prisoners of war in chains – individual letters.
622　1943　Communications with civilians in belligerent countries.
633　1943　Internment camps in France – report – St. Denis.
634　1943　Internment camps in France – report – Vittel.
659　1943　British subjects in the Channel Islands – relief.
830　1944　Prisoners of war camps in Germany – reports – Oranienburg.
831　1944　Prisoners of war camps in Germany – reports – Oflag VD.
833　1944　Prisoners of war camps in Germany – reports – Ilag Wurzach and Ilag 18.
845　1944　Ilag 13, Liebenau – civilian camp – reports.
958　1944　Transfer of internees from Italy to Germany.

963 1944 British subjects in the Channel Islands – welfare.
1133 1945 Internees in enemy territory – lists.
1145 1945 June 5–26 Civilians liberated by the Allies.
1152 1945 Prisoners of war camps in Germany – reports Oflag VD.
1155 1945 Prisoners of war camps in Germany – reports – Wurzach.
1160 1945 Ilag 13. Liebenau, reports.
1271 1945 British subjects in the Channel Islands – assistance.
1272 1945 Prisoners of war in the Channel Islands – treatment.

Class W.O.224   War of 1939–1945.
                Enemy Prisoner of War Camps.
Reports of International Red Cross and Protecting Powers.

Visits to Stalags, Oflags, Hospitals and Prisons in Germany and Italy:
1 1942 Dec–43 Mar.   Reports 746–800
2 1943 Apr–June   Reports 801–900
3 1943 June–Oct.   Reports 901–1000

71 1943 Oct–1945 Apr.   Oflag VA, Weinsberg, Stuttgart area.
72 1941 July–Sept.   Oflag VB.
75 1941 May–Aug.   Oflag VIIC
97 1944 Feb.   P.O.W. Camp Jersey C.I.

Class H.O.45   War of 1939–1945
               Home Office.

19897 1943–1945 Repatriation of Channel Islanders deported to Germany.

Class C.O.980. War of 1939–1945.
Colonial Office Prisoners of War and Civilian Internees Dept.

105 1943–45 Reports on Liebenau internment Camp in Germany.
159 1943–44 Postal arrangements for prisoners of war and civilian internees.
226 1945 Arrangements for the relief and repatriation of Colonial British subjects liberated by allied forces in Europe.

Microfilm Records in:
Picton Reference Library: Liverpool.

Photographic Libraries of:
Guernsey Evening Press and Star.
Jersey Evening Post.
Liverpool Daily Post and Echo.

Photographic Collections of:
St. Peter's Bunker War Museum Jersey.
Carel Toms, Retired Features Editor of *Guernsey Evening Press*.
The Author.

Newspapers
The Evening Post 1940–1945 and 1970's.
 Jersey Evening Post Ltd. Jersey
Guernsey Evening Press 1940–1945.
 Guernsey Press Co. Guernsey.
The Guernsey Evening Press and Star 1970's.
 Guernsey Evening Press Co. Guernsey.
Island Sun 1967.
 Jersey.
Liverpool Daily Post and Echo. 1944–1945
 Liverpool.
The Star 1940–1945.
 Star & Gazette, Guernsey.
The Times 1942–1945.
 London.

Bulletins, Journals and Publications
The Channel Islands Monthly Review
 Vol 1–Vol 9 No. 2 (no more issued)
 Journal of the Channel Islands Refugees Committee in Great Britain.
  Stockport 1941–1945.
Channel Islands Occupation Review
 Journal of the Channel Islands Occupation Society
 Guernsey and Jersey 1970–
C.I.S.S. Bulletins
 Bi-monthly Bulletins of the Channel Islands Specialists' Society.
  London 1950–
Liberation Cavalcade – Souvenir Programme
 Guernsey 1975
Prisoners of War Volumes 3 and 4.
 Official Journal of the Prisoners of War Department of the Red Cross and St. John War Organisation.
  London 1944/45
Third Reich Study Group – Bulletins
 U.S.A. 1970–

225

The Contemporary Diaries of:
L. P. Sinel
Preston John Doughty

Unpublished Research of:
Donald McKenzie

Unpublished Manuscript of:
Carel Toms

Tape Recordings of Lectures given to the Guernsey Branch of the Channel Islands Occupation Society by:
E. Coll (Biberach)
F. Priaulx (Laufen)
W. M. Ginns (Wurzach)

Detailed Correspondences with:
Frank Falla (*The Silent War*)
Michael Ginns (Wurzach internee and Secretary of the Jersey Branch of the C.I.O.S.)
A. J. Langmead (Kreuzburg internee)
Frank Stroobant (*One Man's War*)

Contemporary Correspondences and Documents in the collections of:

The Author
Brian Cropp
David Gurney
F. R. Le Goueze
Donald McKenzie
Francis Kiddle
David Laurillard
Gerald Marriner
Richard Mayne
William Newport
Gordon Russell
Ken Tait
John Thuillier
John Simpson
John Sussex
Members of the Channel Islands Specialists' Society.

Selected Bibliography

CORTVRIEND, V. V.
Isolated Island Streamline Publications, London 1945.
CRUICKSHANK, Charles.
The German Occupation of the Channel Islands Oxford University Press, London 1975, The Guernsey Press Co. Ltd., Guernsey 1975.
FALLA, Frank W.
The Silent War Leslie Frewin Ltd., London 1967.
FOOT, M. R. D. and LANGLEY, J. M.
M.I.9. Escape and Evasion 1939-1945 The Bodley Head and Book Club Associates, London 1979.
KANDAOUROFF, Prince Dimitry
Collecting Postal History Peter Lowe, Holland 1973.
MARSHALL, Michael
Hitler Invaded Sark Paramount-Lithoprint, Guernsey 1963.
MAUGHAM, R. C. F. (CBE)
Jersey Under the Jackboot W. H. Allen, London 1946.
MAYNE, Richard
Channel Islands Occupied Jarrold and Sons Ltd., Norwich 1972.
MAYNE, Richard
Forgotten Islanders - Channel Islands Occupation Review 1974 Channel Islands Occupation Society, Guernsey 1974.
McKENZIE, Donald
The Red Cross Mail Service for Channel Island Civilians 1940-1945 Picton Publishing, Chippenham 1975.
von MÖHLE, Heinz
Die Briefmarken von den Kanal-Inseln, Guernsey und Jersey, Deutsche Besetzung 1940-1945 Frankfurt am Main 1970.
MOLLET, Ralph
Jersey Under the Swastika The Hyperion Press Ltd., London 1945.
NEWPORT, William
Stamps and Postal History of the Channel Islands William Heinemann Ltd., London 1972.
REIMER, Karl Heinz
Zenurpost aus dem III Reich. Die Überwachung des Auslandbriefverkehrs während des 11. Weltkrieges durch deutsche Dienstellen Düsseldorf 1966.
Le SAUTEUR, P.
Jersey Under the Swastika Streamline Publications Ltd., London 1968.
SINEL, L. P.
The German Occupation of Jersey - A Complete Diary of Events from June 1940-June 1945 The Evening Post, Jersey, 1945.

STROOBANT, Frank
One Man's War Guernsey Press Co. Ltd., Guernsey 1967.
TOMS, Carel
Hitler's Fortress Islands The New English Library Ltd., London 1967.
WOLTER, Karl Kurt
Die Postzensure Handbuch und Katalog, Vol. II Georg Amm Nurnberg, 1966.
WOOD, Alan and Mary Seaton
Islands in Danger Evans Brothers, London 1955.

Acknowledgements

The research for this book has taken more than six years to complete and during that time I have entered into a voluminous correspondence with many people throughout the world. In 1978 a brief-case was stolen from my car in a London street and it contained, not only part of the manuscript for this book and some unique research material, but also the complete correspondence from my years of research. I have been able to re-establish contact with many people, but despite appeals in newspapers, there are some people that I have failed to locate again and so I can only thank them here and now for all the help that they gave to me and apologise for my apparent bad manners in never writing to them again.

I owe a debt of gratitude to the many people who have made every effort to assist me in my research or contribute in some way to the book, it would be impossible to name them all, but I would especially like to acknowledge the help of the following:

GUERNSEY
Mrs. G. Adams
The Bailiff's Secretary – Guernsey.
Bob Bartlett
J. M. Beaumont, Seigneur de Sark.
The Editor – *Guernsey Evening Press and Star.*
Frank W. Falla
R. R. Cooney Farnan
F. E. Hiley
A. J. Langmead
R. T. Mees
Frank Stroobant
G. A. Thomas (Mr & Mrs) for introducing me to my first internees.
Helen (daughter of Mr & Mrs Thomas) who gave me the encouragement and confidence to the start the book, but sadly died before I could complete it.
Carel Toms. Retired Features Editor of *Guernsey Evening Press and Star.*
K. H. Tough – Guernsey Branch President of the Channel Islands Occupation Society.

JERSEY
The Bailiff's Secretary – Jersey.
G. le Cappelain
Preston John Doughty

W. Michael Ginns. Jersey Branch Secretary of the Channel Islands Occupation Society.
F. R. Le Goueze
The Editor – *Jersey Evening Post*.
Richard Mayne – St. Peter's Bunker War Museum.
L. P. Sinel
Ken Tait
John Thuillier

UNITED KINGDOM
Irene Betty
Val Caren, for help in many ways, but especially for the hours spent checking the manuscripts.
T. C. Charman. Department of Printed Books, Imperial War Museum.
Helen Coleman – an early typist.
Brian Cropp
John Davey – research at Kew.
Mrs. Fawcett – Archivist – The British Red Cross Society and Order of St. John.
Paul Fodrio – photographer – for reproducing every photograph in the book.
David Gurney
Francis Kiddle
Dave Laurillard
Donald McKenzie for his help, advice, research and drawing the maps.
Barbara Morris – research at Kew.
O. W. Newport
Carolyn Palin, for many patient hours of typing.
The Readers of the Public Record Office, Kew.
Gordon Russell
O. J. Simpson
Linda Stone
John Sussex, for time spent duplicating the manuscripts.
Marjorie Tennant – another early typist.

HOLLAND
Cor van Zon

USA
Robert J. Houston
Fred Stengel

WEST GERMANY
Michael Wieneke

I would also like to thank and recommend the following Philatelic Dealers who have always gone out of their way to assist me in my researches:
Bill Bird, UK
Pauline Brooks, 'Mendip Philatelics' UK
Philip Croucher, 'Rembrandt Philatelics' UK
Tom Green, UK
Roy Moore, Jersey
Georges Robbé, Jersey
Derek Tomlin, 'Brunswick International' Guernsey

Lastly, it would be churlish of me not to admit my debt of gratitude to those 2,000 people who were taken from the Channel Islands in 1942 and 1943 and interned in Germany. Their needless suffering has enriched the field of Postal History today, has given me years of interesting research and has provided the interested layman with a fascinating aspect of World War II history.

Section IV

Catalogue of all items in SECTION I, SECTION II and SECTION III.

CATALOGUE

Notes:

(a) In the following listings, the catalogue numbers relate to those that I have used in the preceding pages, where the first letters indicate origin i.e. Lf – Laufen, Bb – Biberach and the following letters indicate what the item is i.e. P/C – Postcard, C – Cachet. The last number indicates the Type number, so Type Wz.L/S.2. would be the second type of Lettersheet printing from Wurzach.

Key to abbreviations in the order found in text and catalogue.

First Letter Group

Un.Kg.	Universal Kriegsgefangenenpost	Ps.	Paris
Un.Int.	Universal Interniertenpost	Ch.Is.	Channel Islands
Do.	Dorsten	U.K.	United Kingdom
Bb.	Biberach	Fr.	France
Wz.	Wurzach	Sw.	Swiss
Lf.	Laufen	Ud.	Unidentified
Kr.	Kreuzburg	R.C.	Red Cross
Li.	Liebenau	J.	Jersey
Cm.	Compiègne	G.	Guernsey
St.D.	St. Denis	Cp.	Camps
Fk.	Frankfurt	S.	Swedish

Second Letter Group

P/C.	Post Card	E.	Envelope
L/S.	Letter Sheet	C.T.	Censor Tape
C.	Cachet	P.O.	Post Office
P.M.	Post Mark	Doc.	Document
*	Unrecorded		

(b) If an item reasonably corresponds to an example in another published catalogue then I have also given that Catalogue number in brackets after my own. The two relevant books are:

(i) 'Stanley Gibbons – CHANNEL ISLANDS Specialised Catalogue of Stamps and Post History – First Edition' in which the catalogue numbers are either 'I P Digit' or 'I P C Digit' and which I indicate as (S.G.IP7 or S.G.IPC 23 etc.).

(ii) 'The Red Cross Mail Service for Channel Island Civilians 1940–1945' by Donald McKenzie, in which his catalogue numbers are of a totally numerical form i.e. '7.5.1. Type 1' and which I indicate as (D.McK. 7.5.1. Type 1)

(c) All the illustrations of the various cachets have been drawn by the Author and in some cases where only a portion of the cachet has been available from which to make an illustration, an 'intelligent guess' has been made as to what the complete cachet would look like. For this reason it is very important that the reader does not rely solely on the illustrations for identification of a marking, but also refers to the measurements in the text. This is especially important where the reader may feel that he has a variety of an item illustrated. It should also be remembered that the majority of these cachets were made of rubber, not steel and so some distortion is often evident from one example to another.

(d) Although both a grading and points system were considered as ways of indicating the scarcity value of each item, it was finally decided that a monetary valuation was the only one which could give an accurate relative grading for the items and also encompass the vast range of values that are indicated. The valuations are based on U.K. prices in the winter of 1983, and market prices and auction realisations have been used in conjunction with the author's knowledge of scarcity and recorded numbers.

(e) Quality is an important factor in the value of most postal history, but the very nature of the chalk surfaced Internee Postal stationery makes it almost impossible to obtain an item in perfect condition. The following catalogue values are therefore quoted for good examples, and a perfect one would naturally attract a premium, while even a poor example does have some value.

(f) In general the value of an item is not the cumulative total of all the cachets and markings on the piece, but is the value of the dearest mark. In cases where a combination of rare marks are recorded, the item may attract an added value, but it should also be remembered that many of the scarce cachets were only used in conjunction with other scarce cachets. Reference to the preceding text will identify these occasions.

(g) Mail passing between the Channel Islands and the Camps generally has a greater value than mail passing between England and the Camps, but in some instances items are only recorded from one of these routes and not both of them. Mail passing between the Camps and countries other than England or the Channel Islands is very scarce and therefore has a higher value.

SECTION I

Mail to the Internment Camps from the United Kingdom

Letters addressed to Dorsten Transit Camp	£200+,*
Letters addressed to Dorsten Transit Camp and redirected to other camps	£200+,*
Letters addressed to Biberach	£40
Letters addressed to Wurzach	*
Letters addressed to Laufen	£45
Letters addressed to Kreuzburg	*
Letters addressed to Liebenau	*
Letters addressed to Compiègne	*
Letters addressed to St. Denis	*
Letters addressed to other camps holding C.I. Internees	*
Letters addressed to Swiss Internment Camps holding Channel Islanders	*
Letters addressed to Penal Prisons and Concentration Camps holding Channel Islanders	*

Sealed letters sent post-free by surface mail		Basic value
Sealed letters sent Airmail and charged 5d.	premium	+£30
Sealed letters sent Airmail and charged 5d. – stamp and Airmail lable removed.	premium	+£25
Sealed letters sent with 2½d. Postage Stamp.	premium	+£15
Unsealed P.O.W. Post Air letter-cards	premium	+£5

Mail to the Internment Camps from the Channel Islands

Channel Islands Newspapers containing articles giving instructions for the sending of letters to the Camps	From £5
Letters addressed to Dorsten Transit Camp.	£200
Letters addressed to Dorsten Transit Camp and redirected to other camps.	£200
BRITANNIQUE Cachet used on letter to an Internment Camp	£200
Oflag VD 7 Cachet used on letter to an Internment Camp	£200
Letters addressed to Biberach	£50
Letters addressed to Wurzach	*
Letters addressed to Laufen	£60
Letters addressed to Kreuzburg	£175
Letters addressed to Liebenau	*
Letters addressed to Compiègne	£175

Letters addressed to St. Denis	£200
Letters addressed to other camps holding Internees	★
Letters addressed to Swiss Internment Camps	★
Letters addressed to Penal Prisons and Concentration Camps	£250
Letters from the Channel Islands bearing Channel Island stamps and postmarks, carry a premium of	+£20
Letters addressed to a specific part of the Camp (i.e. Theatre) premium	+£10

Mail interrupted by the D-Day landings of 1944

Letters addressed to the Channel Islands from the camps and returned to the camps	From £150
Letters from the camps to the Channel Islands addressed 'via England' in 1944	£60

Mail delivered through the International Red Cross

Letters to the U.K. bearing the Genève cachet of the International Red Cross (Type R.C.C.1.)	£60

'VEGA' Letters:
To the Channel Islands from the Camps	£125
From Guernsey to the Camps	£175
From Jersey to the Camps	£175
The special 'Interniertenpost' Letter Sheet from Jersey MINT	£100
The special 'Interniertenpost' Letter Sheet from Jersey USED	£225

Note: For letters returned by the International Red Cross after the liberation of the Camps and letters captured by the advancing Allied Armies, please see 'BRITISH POST OFFICE MARKINGS'.

Mail from Europe

Letters from Germany into the Camps bearing German stamps	£150

Inter Camp Mail

Letters sent between Internment Camps	£125
Letters sent between Internment Camps and Penal Prisons or Concentration Camps	£250

Red Cross Messages

25 word Red Cross Message Forms received in the Camps	£150

Official Mail from the International Red Cross and Y.M.C.A. in Geneva
Letters from the International Red Cross or Y.M.C.A. to the Camps £150
Letters from the Camps to the International Red Cross or Y.M.C.A. £150

Mail from parts of the British Empire
Letters from Canada £160
Letters from Australia £175

Wurzach Prisoner-of-War Reply Postcard
Reply half used back to Wurzach *

Preprinted envelopes for use to Mr. Roy N. Machon
Envelope used to Laufen *
Envelope used after the war £18

Undelivered Channel Islands Mail addressed to a deportee
Letters bearing correct cachet and endorsement £60

SECTION II

	To the C.I.	*To the U.K.*
'Universal' Stationery		
Un. Kg. P/C.1. (S.G.1P9)	£20–£45	£15–£40
Un. Kg. L/S.1. (S.G.1P16)	£20–£45	£15–£40
Un. Int. P/C.1.	£60	£55
Un. Int. L/S.1. (See Lf.L/S.4.)	★	★
Dorsten Transit Camp		
Do. P/C.1.	£200	£175
Do. C.1.	£200	£175
Do. C.2.	£200★	£175★
Do. P.M.1.	£200	£175

(N.B. As most of the Internees in Dorsten were from Guernsey, the Channel Islands mail is only recorded to that Island. An example addressed to Jersey would attract a premium of +£50).

Biberach Internment Camp		
Un. Kg. P/C.1. (Dec. 42 – Feb. 43 and Oct. 44 to April 45)	£20	£15
Un. Kg. L/S.1. (Dec. 42 – Feb. 43 and Oct. 44 to April 45)	£20	£15
Bb. L/S.1.	£20	£18
Bb. L/S.2.	£16	£14
Bb. L/S.3.	£16	£14
Bb. L/S.4.	£18	£15
Bb. L/S.5.	£25	£22
Bb. L/S.6.	£15	£12
Bb. P/C.1.	£16	£14
Bb. P/C.2.	£15	£12
Bb. P/C.3.	£14	£10
Bb. P/C.4.	£25	£22
Bb. P/C.5.	£45	£40
Bb. C.1. (S.G.IPG 16)	£75	£65
Bb. C.2. (S.G.IPC 17)	£55	£50
Bb. C.3. (S.G.IPC 18)	£18	£15
Bb. C.4. (S.G.IPC 7) (D.McK.9.1.7 Type 7)	£14	£10
Bb. C.4a.	£16	£12
Bb. C.4. (Into Camp – violet)	£55	£28
Bb. C.5. (Into Camp – blue/black)	£60	£30
Bb. C.6. (Into Camp – violet) (S.G.IPC 8)	★	£55
Bb. C.6a. (Into Camp – violet)	★	£60
Bb. C.7. (S.G.IPC 19)	£65	£60
Bb. C.8. (S.G.IPC 20)	£70	£65
Bb. C.9. To Germany £200	★	★

	To the C.I.	To the U.K.
Bb. P.M.1. (S.G.IPC 2)	£14	£10
Bb. P.M.2.	★	£40
Bb. P.M.3.	£35	£25
Bb. P.M.4.	★	£50
Bb. P.M.5. (S.G.IPC 6)	★	£180

Wurzach Internment Camp

Un.Int.P/C.1.	£60	£50
Wz.L/S.1.	£45	£35
Wz.L/S.2.	£50	£40
Wz.L/S.3.	£50	£40
Wz.P/C.1.	£50	£40
Wz.P/C.2.	£45	£35
Wz.P/C.3. (whole card)	£100	£100
Wz.P/C.3. (half card) (S.G.IP8)	£65	£60
Wz.P/C.3. (return half used)	★	★
Wz.C.1. (S.G.IPC. 21)	£120	£100
Wz.C.2. (S.G.IPC. 22)	£45	£35
Wz.C.3.	£60	£50

Laufen Internment Camp

Un.Kg.P/C.1.	£30	£25
Un.Kg.L/S.1.	£30	£25
Un.Int.P/C.1.	£60	£55
Un.Int.L/S.1. (See Lf.L/S.4.)		
Lf.L/S.1.	£25	£20
Lf.L/S.2.	£18	£14
Lf.L/S.2(a)	£50	£45
Lf.L/S.3.	£22	£17
Lf.L/S.4.	£60	£55
Lf.P/C.1.	£25	£20
Lf.P/C.2.	£22	£17
Lf.P/C.3.	£20	£16
Lf.P/C.3a.	£24	£18
Lf.P/C.4.	£18	£14
Lf.P/C.5.	£24	£18
Lf.P/C.6.	£24	£18
Lf.P/C.7. (S.G.IP 4)	£55	£50
Lf.P/C.8. (S.G.IP 5)	£55	£50
Lf.P/C.9. (S.G.IP 6)	£60	£55
Lf.P/C.10	£65	£60
Lf.P/C.11 (S.G.IP 29)	£100	£90
Lf.P/C.12	£50	£45
Lf.L/S.5.	£40	£35
Lf.L/S.6.	£40	£35
Lf.E.1. (To within Germany) £200	★	★
Lf.E.2.	£200	£180

	From Camp		Into Camp	
	To C.I.	To U.K.	From C.I.	From U.K.
Lf.G.1. (violet) (S.G.IPC 9)	£18	£14	£55	£28
Lf.C.1. (blue/black)	£20	£16	£55	£28
Lf.C.2. (violet) (S.G.IPC10)	£22	£17	£60	£30
Lf.C.2. (blue/black)	£24	£18	£60	£30
Lf.C.2. (Censor 11 crimson)	★	£80	★	★
Lf.C.3. (violet)	£25	£20	£65	£35
Lf.C.3. (blue/black)	£30	£25	£65	£35
Lf.C.4. (Censor 12 violet)	★	★	From Germany £150	
Lf.C.4. (Censor 13 violet) (S.G.IPC 11)	£40	£35	£70	£38
Lf.C.4. (Censor 13 blue/black)	★	£40	£70	£38

		To the C.I.	To the U.K.
Lf.C.5. (S.G.IPC 27)		£60	£50
Lf.C.6. (S.G.IPC 24)		£60	£50
Lf.C.6. (on Official Mail within Germany)	£200	★	★
Lf.C.7. (S.G.IPC 25)		£80	£60
Lf.C.8. (on Official Mail) (S.G.IPC 23)	£200	★	★
Lf.C.9. (on Official Mail)	£200	★	★
Lf.C.10.		£200	£180
Lf.C.11. (S.G.IPC 50)		£200	£180
Lf.P.M.1.		£18	£14
Lf.P.M.2. (S.G.IPC 4)		£150	£125
Lf.P.M.3.		£200	★

Kreuzburg Internment Camp

Kr.L/S.1. (S.G.IP 15)		£150	£125
Kr.P/C.1.		£150	£125
Kr.C.1. (S.G.IPC 12)		£150	£125
Kr.C.2. (S.G.IPC 13)		£150	£125
Kr.C.3. (S.G.IPC 14)		£150	£125
Kr.C.4. (S.G.IPC 26)		£160	£130
Kr.C.5. (To the Camp) (S.G.IPC 28)	£180	★	★
Kr. P.M.1.		£150	£125

Liebenau Internment Camp

Li.P/C.1. (S.G.IP 7)	£200	£180
Li.L/S.1.	£200	£180

Compiègne and St. Denis Frontstalag Camps

Cm.C.1. (S.G.IPC 32)	£150	£125
Cm.C.2. (S.G.IPC 30)	£150	£125
Cm.C.3. (S.G.IPC 29)	£150	£125
Cm.C.4. (S.G.IPC 31)	£160	£130

	To the C.I.	To the U.K.
St.D.C.1. (S.G.IPC 33)	£160	£130
St.D.C.2. (S.G.IPC 34)	£160	£130
St.D.C.3.	£160	£130
St.D.C.4. (S.G.IPC 35)	£165	£135
St.D.P.M.1. (S.G.IPC 5)	£170	£140

Tittmoning Camp
See Lf. P.M.2.

Other Camps	To the C.I.	To the U.K.
Ilag XVIII Spittal Drau Austria (pages 139–142 PART I)	*	*
Marlag und Milag Nord Ilag Westertimke (pages 143 PART I)	*	*
Stalag VIII B Teschen (page 144 PART I)	*	*
Oranienburg (page 145 PART I)	*	*
Ilag XIII Wulzburg: Weisenburg/By. (pages 146–148 PART I) (S.G.IP 18)	*	*
Swiss Internment Camps (pages 154–155 PART I)	From £250	
Penal Prisons and Concentration Camps	To or From C.I. £250	

243

SECTION III

	To the C.I.	To the U.K.
German Censorship		
Fk.C.1. (S.G.IPC 38)	£35	£30
Fk.C.2.	£35	£30
Fk.C.3. (S.G.IPC 45)	£90	£80
Fk.C.4. (S.G.IPC 47)	£70	£65
Fk.C.5.	£65	£60
Fk.C.6.	£35	£30
Fk.C.7.	£45	£40
Fk.C.T.1. (used on letter to the Camp) (S.G.IPC 44)	*	£75
Ps.C.1. (S.G.IPC 48)	£70	£65
Channel Islands Censor		
Ch.Is.C.1. (to the Camps from the C.I.) (As D.McK.9.2. but without number)	£200	
'Mysterious' Four Digit Cachet		
In red	£40	£35
In purple	£80	£70
German Prisoner of War Camps		
Mail to the C.I. from P.O.W. in a Stalag (S.G.PW 1)		£20
Mail to the C.I. from P.O.W. in a Oflag (S.G.PW 2)		£25
Mail to the C.I. from P.O.W. in a Marlag (S.G.PW 3)		£30
Mail to the C.I. from P.O.W. in a Luftlager (S.G.PW 4)		£30
Mail to the C.I. from P.O.W. in a Dulag (S.G.PW 5)		£35
Mail to the C.I. from P.O.W. in a Stralag (S.G.PW 6)		£45
Mail to the C.I. with German town postmark on P.O.W. card or lettersheet (S.G.PW 8)		£50
Mail to the C.I. from P.O.W. in an Italian Camp (S.G.PW 13)		£75
Mail from the C.I. to a German P.O.W. Camp (S.G.PW 7)		£75
British Censorship		
U.K.C.1. in crimson (D.McK.7.2.)		£15
U.K.C.1. in blue		£45
U.K.C.1. in maroon		£45
U.K.C.2. in crimson (D.McK.7.1.1. Type 1)		£50
U.K.C.2. in purple		£100
U.K.C.3.		£150
U.K.C.T.1. (D.McK. 7.1.3. Type 3)		£30
U.K.C.T.2.		£50
United Kingdom Censorship Leaflets		
Leaflet 'P.C. 199'		£15
Leaflet 'P.C. 223' (D.McK.10.3.3. Type 2)		£15

British Post Office Markings
U.K.P.O.C.1.	£50
U.K.P.O.C.2.	£50
U.K.P.O.C.3.	£50
U.K.P.O.C.4.	£180
U.K.P.O.C.5. (S.G.IPC 52)	£200
U.K.P.O.C.6. (S.G.IPC 51)	£100
U.K.P.O.C.7. (S.G.IPC 53)	£75
U.K.P.O.C.8.	£75
U.K.P.M.1.	£100

French Post Office Markings
Fr.P.O.C.1. (S.G.IPC 54)	£75

Swiss Postmarks, Cachets and Censor Labels
Sw.P.M.1.	£150
Sw.C.1.	£150
Sw.C.2.	£250
Sw.C.3.	£250
Sw.C.T.1.	£250

Cachets and Postmarks from the Rest of the World
Cachets or Postmarks of Italy, Switzerland, Austria and Canada on mail from the Internee Camps.	From £100
American Cachets or Postmarks on mail to or from the American contingent in Laufen	From £100
Cachets or Postmarks of Greece, Belgium or Yugoslavia on mail to or from the American contingent in Laufen	From £120

Unidentified Cachets
Ud.C.1.	£60

The Red Cross
25 Word Red Cross Message Form received in a Camp	£150
R.C.C.1. (D.McK. 1.3.1. Type 1)	£60
Form P/4 Next of kin parcels	£50
Leaflet PW/73C/43 (see U.K.Doc.1.)	
British Prisoner of War Camps Maps.	£20

Official Documents
J.1.Doc.1.	£25	G.1.Doc.1.	£25
J.1.Doc.2.	£70	G.1.Doc.2.	£35
J.1.Doc.3.	£40	G.1.Doc.3.	£100
J.1.Doc.4.	£10		
J.1.Doc.5.	£50		
J.1.Doc.6.	£10		
J.1.Doc.7	£10		

Official Documents—*continued*

J.2.Doc.1.	£25	G.2.Doc.1.	£25
J.2.Doc.2.	£30	G.2.Doc.2.	£50
J.2.Doc.3.	£75	G.2.Doc.3.	£35
J.2.Doc.4.	£25	G.2.Doc.4.	£100
J.2.Doc.5.	£75		
J.2.Doc.6.	£30		
U.K.Doc.1	£40	Cp.Doc.1.	£20
U.K.Doc.2.	£45	Cp.Doc.2.	£15
U.K.Doc.3.	£35	Cp.Doc.3.	From £25
		Cp.Doc.4.	£20
S.Doc.1.	£50		
S.Doc.2.	£30		

Ephemera

Photographs of deportations		RARE
Photographs of the Camps	From	£10
German Photographic Postcards		£10
Photographs carrying Censor Cachet		£20
Artwork on Camp Postal Stationery		£30
Views of the Camp	From	£15
Repatriation cards		£35
Posters	From	£10
Printed Items – 'The Bird Cage'		£30
– Programmes		£10
Camp Banknotes. Wurzach		£25 each
Camp 'Stamps'. Wurzach		£30 each
Newspaper Articles	From	£5
Denis Cleary Newspaper Article		£20
'The Channel Islands Monthly Review'	From	£5 each

The Publisher of **Islanders Deported** is C.I.S.S. Publishing, a part of the

CHANNEL ISLANDS SPECIALISTS' SOCIETY

Founded 1950. For the study of stamps and Postal History of the Channel Islands.

Membership is open to all interested in Channel Islands stamps and postal history.

Benefits include:

- Regular Bulletins of news and events.
- A Research Journal "Iles Normandes".
- Exchange packets.
- Auctions.
- Meetings three or four times a year in London and the provinces.
- Weekend meetings in England or the Channel Islands.
- Members' discount on all books published by C.I.S.S. Publishing.

If you would like further information, then please, write to the Membership Secretary

---

Brian Cropp 17 Westlands Avenue, Huntercombe, Burnham, Slough, BERKS SL1 6AG

CHANNEL ISLANDS POSTAL HISTORY

I am pleased to be able to offer to all members of the CISS the following services:

Special offer list issued 6–8 times a year containing good material from Channel Islands Postal History from the 18th to 20th Century. Including pre-stamp material, postal markings, Ship Letters, Parish marks, Small islands, German Occupation.

Want-list Service. Most of the better material I sell is placed to customers who tell me of their special requirements, and therefore does not appear on my special offer lists. Please send me your want-list. All items are sent strictly on FULL APPROVAL, with no obligation to purchase.

NEW. Approval Service. If you would like an approval selection sent to you of any particular field, please let me know. You can then examine the material in the comfort of your home.

BUYING. If you wish to sell or exchange any part of your Channel Islands collection I shall be pleased to deal with this with the utmost discretion and speed. I have bought in the past many fine collections from CISS members, and I am sure they have found a satisfactory deal with little or no argument regarding price!

Please write or phone any time to take advantage of these services.

I look forward to hearing from you!

T.D. GREEN
Fairfield, Low Ham, Langport, Somerset, England
Telephone (0458) 250832

Channel Islands Specialist Material

We stock all specialised material of the Channel Islands, including—

Pre-stamp E.L.
Ship letters
19th century covers and entires
Specialised postmarks and Sub-Post Offices
Postage due and instructional marks
German Occupation Stamps, Feldpost and
 Internee Mails
Bisects, France – Channel Islands letters
German, Swiss and English Red Cross letters
Flight covers, slogan postmarks
Special Commemorative covers
Herm, Alderney and Sark
Local issues and independent issues
We also stock Tristan da Cunha, Gibraltar and
 Faroe Islands

Auctions are held approximately every two months with over 1,000 lots. Auction catalogues are free. Send for one now!

BUYING I am always interested in buying Channel Islands material from Kiloware to specialised collections. I will also purchase collections or sets from the South Atlantic area, local issues and good British Commonwealth.

TERMS are C.W.O. subject unsold, postage extra. Bankers are Midland Bank, High Street, Guernsey, Account number 51154273. Our telephone number is (0481) 20616.

Brunswick International Stamps and Auctions Ltd
Post Office Box 224
5 Place du Commerce,
Bouet, St. Peter Port
Guernsey, Channel Islands

The Publisher of *Islanders Deported*
is **CISS PUBLISHING** a part of

CHANNEL ISLANDS SPECIALISTS' SOCIETY

CISS PUBLISHING Have also Published

The Postage Stamps of the Smaller Channel Islands
By Anders Backman and Robert Forrestor   Price £4.50

The Booklet Stamps of Guernsey First Sterling Issues
By Lt. Col. G. N. A. Curtis MA   Price £3.50

The 1942 Jersey ½d Arms a Plating Study
By Ian Griggs   Price £3.50

Islanders Deported Part I
By Roger Harris   Price £4.50

Channel Islands Revenues
By John Simpson   Price £4.00

All Prices Include Postage
To obtain any of the above books please write to:
CISS PUBLISHING
63 Ravensbourne Gardens, Clayhall, Ilford IG5 0XH

The **CHANNEL ISLANDS SPECIALIST'S SOCIETY** was formed in 1950 for the Study of Stamps and Postal History of the Channel Islands. For further information please write to the Membership Secretary.
Brian Cropp, 17 Westlands Avenue, Huntercombe, Slough SL1 6AG